NEGLIGENT HEALTHCARE RISK MANAGEMENT IN THE UNITED STATES AND GERMANY

This book proposes a theory of liability for negligent clinical risk management that responds to the complexities of modern healthcare delivery. It uses a comparative and interdisciplinary approach to explore the interaction between law, economics and organisational science, risk and medicine. In doing so, it highlights the healthcare organisation as a critical source of medical harm and provides a pathway for corresponding liability.

Negligent Healthcare Risk Management in the United States and Germany

Mindy Duffourc

•HART•
OXFORD • LONDON • NEW YORK • NEW DELHI • SYDNEY

HART PUBLISHING
Bloomsbury Publishing Plc
Kemp House, Chawley Park, Cumnor Hill, Oxford, OX2 9PH, UK
1385 Broadway, New York, NY 10018, USA
Bloomsbury Publishing Ireland Limited, 29 Earlsfort Terrace, Dublin 2, D02 AY28, Ireland

HART PUBLISHING, the Hart/Stag logo, BLOOMSBURY and the Diana logo are trademarks of Bloomsbury Publishing Plc

First published in Great Britain 2026

1

A catalogue record for this book is available from the British Library.

A catalogue record for this book is available from the Library of Congress.

ISBN: HB: 978-1-50999-327-7
ePDF: 978-1-50999-328-4
ePub: 978-1-50999-329-1

Typeset by Amnet, Chennai, India

For product safety related questions contact productsafety@bloomsbury.com

To find out more about our authors and books visit www.hartpublishing.co.uk. Here you will find extracts, author information, details of forthcoming events and the option to sign up for our newsletters.

For my Maw Maw Barbara,

and all the other resilient women who carry the world on their shoulders.

Acknowledgements

MY COMPLETION OF this book was only possible because a great many people provided guidance, support and encouragement throughout my decade-long journey from legal practice to academia, which included mothering a toddler, a global pandemic and two transatlantic moves. To them, I am forever grateful. I owe an especially huge debt of gratitude to my husband René and son Rainier, both of whom not only endured being dragged around the world, but did so with great élan!

Table of Contents

List of Abbreviations

AHRQ	Agency for Healthcare Research and Quality (US)
AI	artificial intelligence
AI Act	Artificial Intelligence Act (Regulation (EU) 2024/1689)
AMA	American Medical Association
AOK	Allgemeine Ortskrankenkasse (public health insurer, Germany)
APS	Aktionsbündnis Patientensicherheit (German Coalition for Patient Safety)
ÄZQ	Ärztliches Zentrum für Qualität in der Medizin (German Medical Centre for Quality in Medicine)
BGB	Bürgerliches Gesetzbuch (German Civil Code)
BGBI	Bundesgesetzblatt (Federal Law Gazette, Germany)
BGH	Bundesgerichtshof (German Federal Court of Justice)
BOÄ	Berufsordnung für Ärzte (Professional Code for Physicians, Germany)
CFR	Code of Federal Regulations (US)
CIRS	Critical Incident Reporting System
CMS	Centers for Medicare and Medicaid Services (US)
DHHS	Department of Health and Human Services (US)
EAHC	European Agency for Health and Consumers
EHR	Electronic Health Record
EU	European Union
EU AI Act	Artificial Intelligence Act (Regulation (EU) 2024/1689)
EUNetPaS	European Union Network for Patient Safety
FDA	Food and Drug Administration (US)
FMEA	Failure Modes and Effect Analysis
FTA	Fault Tree Analysis
G-BA	Gemeinsamer Bundesausschuss (Federal Joint Committee, Germany)
HAS	Haute Autorité de Santé (French National Authority for Health)
HHS	Department of Health and Human Services (US)
HIPAA	Health Insurance Portability and Accountability Act of 1996 (US)
HRQA	Healthcare Research and Quality Act (US)
ICU	intensive care unit
IfPS	Institut für Patientensicherheit (Institute for Patient Safety, Germany)
IMDRF	International Medical Device Regulators Forum
IOM	Institute of Medicine (US)
ISO	International Organization for Standardization
IT	information technology
LG	Landgericht (Regional Court, Germany)
MDR	Medical Device Regulation (Regulation (EU) 2017/745)

MDS	Medizinischer Dienst des Spitzenverbandes Bund der Krankenkassen (Medical Service of the National Association of Health Insurance Funds, Germany)
ML	machine learning
NQF	National Quality Forum (US)
OECD	Organisation for Economic Co-operation and Development
OLG	Oberlandesgericht (Higher Regional Court, Germany)
PaSQ	European Network on Patient Safety and Quality of Care
PLD	Product Liability Directive (Directive (EU) 2024/2853)
PPACA	Patient Protection and Affordable Care Act (US)
PRA	probabilistic risk assessment
PRG	Patientenrechtegesetz (Patients' Rights Act, Germany)
PSMLI	Patient Safety and Medical Liability Initiative (US)
PSO	patient safety organization
PSQCWG	Patient Safety and Quality of Care Working Group
PSQIA	Patient Safety and Quality Improvement Act (US)
PSWP	Patient Safety Work Product
QM	quality management
QuIC	Quality Interagency Coordination Task Force (US)
RAISE Act	Responsible AI Safety and Education Act (New York)
RCA	root cause analysis
RM	risk management
RMS	Risk Management System
SGB V	Sozialgesetzbuch V (German Social Code, Book V)
ST-PRA	Sociotechnical Probabilistic Risk Assessment
US	United States
USC	United States Code
VA	Department of Veterans Affairs (US)
WAPS	World Alliance for Patient Safety
WebM&M	Web Morbidity and Mortality (AHRQ Patient Safety Network programme)
WHO	World Health Organization
ZPO	Zivilprozessordnung (German Code of Civil Procedure)

Table of Cases

United States

Germany

England

Table of Statutes

United States

Federal Law and Regulations

State Laws and Regulations

Germany

Introduction

Two long-recognised principles lie at the heart of this book. The first is the *maxim primum non nocere*, which articulates the fundamental bioethical principle that doctors are obliged, first, to do no harm. The second is the proverb *errare humanum est*, meaning 'to err is human', a sentiment popularised by Alexander Pope in 'An Essay on Criticism' and later adopted by the Institute of Medicine (IOM) to express that all humans, even doctors, make mistakes. In the context of medical liability, these two principles raise a fundamental question: who should be responsible when medical errors cause a patient to suffer harm? The answer historically adopted by the medical liability system in both the United States (US) and Germany is a seemingly straightforward one: doctors and nurses are primarily responsible. This answer, however, ignores the complexities of modern healthcare delivery. It ignores the fact that behind the faces of doctors and nurses is an intricate and complex organisation, one that has both the *ability to induce* and the *power to reduce* medical errors by designing a safe system.

Modern error prevention research proves that design defects in a healthcare organisation's systemic processes play a prominent role in medical errors. Building on error prevention approaches in other high-risk industries, like aviation and nuclear power, the IOM challenged the healthcare industry in 1999 to abandon the then-prevailing culture of individual blame and shame, and adopt a systems-based approach to medical error prevention. Over a quarter of a century later, despite ongoing industry efforts – led by medical professional organisations, patient safety advocates, national and international policymakers, legislators, regulatory and credentialing bodies, insurance companies, industry standards organisations, and medical schools – the amount of harm caused by medical errors is still shocking.

In early 2018, I arrived at the headquarters of the Berlin Chamber of Physicians (*Ärztekammer Berlin*) to meet with its president, Dr Günther Jonitz. He had responded to a cold email and graciously invited me, a completely unknown young American litigator-turned-academic, for a meeting to discuss medical error-reporting systems. Fairly early in the meeting, I asked him whether there were any statistics reflecting how many people die from medical errors each year in Germany (I had recently read about such statistics in the US). His response was that we shouldn't focus on statistics; we already know that patient safety is a problem, and it is better to focus on fixing that problem. He was disappointed by the media's tendency to focus on the undisputed problem of medical errors, to prioritise fear and search for blame. In keeping with Dr Jonitz's focus on solutions, I will not cite statistics that attempt to quantify the number of deaths caused by medical errors. It suffices to say that it is a problem, and a big one. What I will do in this book is examine how the medical liability system impacts patient safety and how a theory of negligent clinical risk management might become part, however small, of the larger solution to the problem of medical errors.

This book is organised into three parts. Part one examines the modern healthcare system and the healthcare industry's approach to medical error prevention. Part two introduces the medical liability frameworks in the US and Germany. Part three proposes a theory of liability for negligent clinical risk management and establishes a framework for its operation within the existing medical liability system of both jurisdictions.

Part I consists of chapters one and two. Chapter one traces the historical development of the modern healthcare system and the modern hospital, charting medicine's transformation from an endeavour with little reliable therapeutic benefit into today's complex, technology-driven system of healthcare delivery. It examines how modern medical technology and, more recently, artificial intelligence (AI)-driven technology, adds new dimensions of complexity and risk to healthcare delivery. The chapter also provides a high-level doctrinal overview of medical liability to identify the existing system's limitations in addressing liability for medical errors within modern healthcare organisations.

Chapter two discusses the paradigm shift in thinking about medical error prevention initiated in 1999 by the IOM's 'To Err Is Human' report, which ignited an international shift away from individual blame and towards a systems-based approach to error prevention in healthcare. The chapter then examines the role of clinical risk management in medical error prevention and discusses how the rapid integration of digital technologies into healthcare delivery impacts patient safety risks. It highlights the role of the medical liability system as an external factor that influences patient safety culture and error prevention efforts within the healthcare system. It concludes that the medical liability system can strengthen industry error prevention efforts by holding healthcare organisations responsible for preventing errors through clinical risk management.

Part two consists of chapters three and four. Chapter three introduces the general legal framework for medical liability in the US and Germany. It examines distinctions between common law and civil law systems, and between contract versus tort law as the main legal basis for medical liability in private law. The chapter demonstrates that despite these differences, the medical liability system in both jurisdictions is centred around the concept of negligence, which as interpreted by the courts in medical liability cases, results in similar doctrinal rules. Following this, the chapter identifies the goals of negligence-based liability in the two jurisdictions as compensation, deterrence and, more broadly, fairness. It focuses on deterrence as a goal because, like clinical risk management, it has a preventive end goal. The chapter also discusses how a perceived increase in medical malpractice claims influenced the medical liability landscape and triggered debates about reform in both countries, both of which ultimately chose to retain a negligence-based system. The chapter concludes that liability for negligent clinical risk management, would complement rather than inhibit the healthcare industry's error prevention efforts, because the liability systems' deterrence goals would better align with the industry's approach to medical error prevention.

Chapter four examines how medical negligence claims operate in both the US and German medical liability systems. It first outlines the legal elements for establishing medical negligence in both jurisdictions, including claims based on treatment errors and organisational errors. It then discusses the rules of proof applicable to these claims, comparing how the jurisdictions govern the standard of proof (how much evidence is needed to prove each element) and burden of proof (which party must prove each element). In particular, this chapter highlights burden of proof shifting mechanisms in both jurisdictions: the US through the doctrine of *res ipsa loquitur* and Germany through burden of proof rules codified in the Patients' Rights Act.

It also addresses practical matters surrounding obtaining evidence needed to prove or disprove different elements of a medical negligence claim, noting that the primary source of evidence is the patient's medical treatment record. While the patient generally has clear legal pathways to access their medical records, both jurisdictions apply some evidentiary protections that prevent access to certain documents in medical liability cases. It explains how information that relates to hospital activities outside of the individual patient's medical treatment might be subject to these legal protections. The chapter concludes by observing that, although neither country has recognised or established a framework for liability based on a healthcare organisation's negligent clinical risk management, incorporating such liability under the existing rules for proving medical negligence is both possible and crucial for effectively preventing medical errors.

Part three consists of chapters five and six. Chapter five proposes a legal framework for liability based on negligent clinical risk management under the current medical liability system in both countries. The framework builds on German legal academic discussions that have identified a legal obligation to conduct clinical risk management under German law. The chapter examines how German legal scholars support liability for negligent clinical risk management as an extension of existing organisational liability under Germany's general negligence laws, and by drawing an analogy between the legal obligations of manufacturers in product liability law and the legal obligations of healthcare organisations in medical negligence law. It applies this analytical framework to the US to argue that liability for negligent clinical risk management is similarly supported under general tort law, organisational negligence law, and product liability law. It examines how existing legal and regulatory obligations in both jurisdictions – including those arising from the Patients' Rights Act in Germany and from federal, state, and industry standards in the US – further support finding a duty to conduct clinical risk management in the medical liability system.

The chapter also examines how the EU Artificial Intelligence Act and related regulatory developments governing the development and deployment of AI-driven medical technologies in both jurisdictions reinforce the importance of clinical risk management and its increasing role in law. In concludes by finding that the legal framework in both jurisdictions supports an extension of organisational liability to encompass a duty to conduct clinical risk management.

Chapter six establishes the operational framework for a cause of action for negligent clinical risk management. It first sets forth legal standards of care for clinical risk management that flow from the internationally accepted clinical risk management process, which occurs in four iterative phases: risk identification; risk analysis; risk assessment; and risk control. These standards are grounded in recognised methodologies drawn from medical and error prevention science, and illustrated with examples from the healthcare literature demonstrating how properly conducted clinical risk management can measurably improve patient safety in modern healthcare organisations.

The chapter then proposes legal proof rules that balance the confidentiality required to carry out clinical risk management activities with the transparency required to hold healthcare organisations accountable for negligence in the clinical risk management process. These rules take two forms: first, discovery and evidentiary protections for clinical risk management activities that require confidentiality to sustain safety culture in healthcare organisations; and second, burden-shifting rules informed by Germany's Patients' Rights Act that ensure injured patients have a viable cause of action against organisations for negligent clinical risk management. The chapter concludes by situating a theory of negligent clinical risk management within the larger medical liability system, demonstrating how it operates alongside existing individual and organisational liability theories to advance the patient safety goals identified throughout the book.

Part I

Medical Errors in the Modern Healthcare System

1

Medical Errors and Liability in the Modern Healthcare System

THE PROBLEM OF medical errors in today's healthcare system is shaped by modern medicine's success in treating and curing medical conditions and the emergence of the modern hospital as a complex system that organises the medical treatment process. Within the modern healthcare system, the integration of modern technologies, and more recently, those driven by artificial intelligence (AI) add new dimensions to the already complex processes driving healthcare. Before understanding the cause of medical errors and examining liability approaches that can help prevent medical errors, one must first understand the development and organisation of the modern healthcare system in which those errors occur. This chapter outlines the historical development of the modern healthcare system and the medical liability system's existing framework (and limitations) for addressing medical injury claims that occur within the modern healthcare system.

I.I THE MODERN HEALTHCARE SYSTEM

For most of medicine's 3,500-plus-year history, it did not provide a reliable or effective response to human illness.[1] Medical historian Roy Porter noted that the Greek word *pharmakos* referred to remedies and poisons alike and observed, 'That double idea – death and the doctors riding together – has loomed large in history'.[2] As late as the eighteenth century, therapeutic medicine was highly unsuccessful and, in many cases, positively harmful.[3] In 1714, English poet, Matthew Prior wrote 'The Remedy Worse than the Disease':

> I SENT for Eatcliffe; was so ill,
> That other doctors gave me over:
> He felt my pulse, prescrib'd his pill.

[1] FG Kilgour, 'Modern Medicine in Historical Perspective' (1962) 50 *Bulletin of the Medical Library Association* 42.

[2] R Porter, *The Greatest Benefit to Mankind: A Medical History of Humanity* (London, HarperCollins, 1997).

[3] ibid.

And I was likely to recover.
But, when the wit began to wheeze,
And wine had warm'd the politician,
Cur'd yesterday of my disease,
I died last night of my physician.[4]

Even when it was not positively harmful, the physician's work focused primarily on providing patients with comfort, not cures.[5] And even when eighteenth-century advancements in biomedical science began to show promise for improving public health, medical treatment itself was still extremely risky.[6] In the early nineteenth century, patients had less than a 50 per cent chance of benefiting from medical treatment.[7]

The rapid advances in preventive medicine, surgery, and treatments for endocrine, metabolic, and infectious diseases in the nineteenth and twentieth centuries birthed modern medicine.[8] Riotte notes the rapid increase in survival rates for babies born by caesarean section – from 30 per cent in the period of 1865–74 to almost 90 per cent in the 1890s – in Germany's Baden region.[9] Medical treatment for thyroid disease is another example of how advancement in medical science began to translate to success in medical therapy. In 1875, doctors believed that the thyroid was useless and removed the gland from diseased patients. By 1940, however, thyroid function was well understood, and treatment was primarily non-surgical.[10] According to Eliot Freidson, the scientific developments of the late nineteenth century established a foundation for medicine as a 'true consulting profession' that, for the first time, offered its users an advantage over services provided by other healing professions.[11]

With the increased success rate of modern medicine, public expectations for medicine began to change. Porter observed:

> The more medicine seemed scientific and effective, the more the public became beguiled by the allure of medical beneficence, regarding the healing arts as a therapeutic cornucopia showering benefits on all, or, like a fairy godmother, potentially granting everybody's wishes.[12]

[4] M Prior, 'The Remedy Worse Than the Disease' (first published 1714) in A Dobson (ed), *Selected Poems of Matthew Prior* (London, Kegan Paul, Trench & Co, 1889).

[5] M Stauch, *The Law of Medical Negligence in England and Germany: A Comparative Analysis* (Oxford, Hart Publishing, 2008).

[6] ibid.

[7] ibid.

[8] Kilgour (n 1).

[9] T Riotte, 'Medical negligence in nineteenth-century Germany' in M Dickson, E Taylor-Brown and S Shuttleworth (eds), *Progress and Pathology: Medicine and Culture in the Nineteenth Century* (Manchester, Manchester University Press, 2020).

[10] ibid.

[11] E Freidson, *Profession of Medicine: A Study of the Sociology of Applied Knowledge* (New York, Harper & Row, 1970).

[12] Porter (n 2).

Twentieth-century medicine made the provision of healthcare an economic and political endeavour, prompting Porter to compare modern medicine to 'the military machine or the civil service'.[13] Medicine expanded its objectives from providing reactionary healing to becoming a central figure in society, bringing with it the promise of a holistic approach to societal health.[14] According to Porter, 'Medicine in mass society inexorably became inseparable from economics, central and local administration, the law, the social services and the media.'[15] It is from this place in society that medicine is judged today, against its twentieth-century promises to prevent the unpreventable, treat the untreatable, and cure the incurable. Nevertheless, medicine has chosen to assume this heroic role in modern society, and with that choice comes great responsibility and the corresponding potential for great liability.

The development of the modern hospital is, of course, entwined with that of modern medicine. Just as doctors historically had little success as healers, hospitals had little success as healing institutions. Until the middle of the nineteenth century, hospitals housed mentally ill, poor, diseased, dying, and homeless populations and served as learning institutions for medical students, but they rarely improved patients' medical conditions.[16] To the contrary, in many instances, hospital conditions were responsible for patient deaths. Porter provides a glimpse of eighteenth-century hospitals:

> Pivotal to the public provision of health-care facilities was the hospital, but it was also perhaps the nub of the problem. Nominally a site of recuperation, it became a spreader of disease. Hospitals took many forms and served many functions. In France, the hôpital général, an institution similar to the English poorhouse, sheltered beggars, orphans, vagabonds and prostitutes, together with the sick and mad. The Paris Hôtel Dieu was a healing institution, but had an atrocious reputation as a hotbed of infection . . . Similar developments occurred in North America . . . Hospitals provided treatment, food, rest and convalescence, but they restricted themselves to complaints that would respond to treatment, excluded infectious cases and, in any case, could treat only a fraction of the sick. Their effects were consequently somewhat slight.[17]

Medical camps for injured soldiers had a similar reputation, and their unhygienic conditions were responsible for more soldier deaths than battle injuries.[18] In 1854, during the Crimean War, Florence Nightingale linked poor sanitation practices at a British medical camp in Turkey to poor recovery rates.[19] Following Nightingale's insistence on better hygiene, lighting, diet, and activity, the death

[13] ibid.
[14] ibid.
[15] ibid.
[16] See ME Valentinuzzi and R Leder, 'The Modern Hospital in Historical Context' (2009) 2009 Annual International Conference of the IEEE Engineering in Medicine and Biology Society 1089.
[17] Porter (n 2).
[18] Valentinuzzi and Leder (n 16).
[19] ibid.

rate for injured soldiers in the camp decreased from 42 per cent to less than three per cent.[20] After the war, Nightingale continued to advocate for better hospital conditions in both civilian and military hospitals.[21] Nightingale's work exposed the risks associated with institutional conditions, separate from the inherent risk of medical treatment itself or the poorly skilled healthcare provider.

As medical practice gained success and acceptance as a central societal institution, hospitals also transformed from houses for the sick and dying to institutions for teaching, research, and healing. The medical achievements of the nineteenth and twentieth centuries transformed the purpose and organisation of hospitals. Advances in surgery, made possible by anaesthetics and antiseptics, required operating rooms and post-surgical care in hospitals.[22] American hospitals grew exponentially in the nineteenth century – from two in 1800 to 5,000 by 1914.[23] Porter noted that hospitals were 'fast becoming the headquarters of medicine'.[24] For a physician practicing during this time, the transformation of hospitals was readily observable over the course of a medical career:

> All over the world the very name 'hospital' suggested pestilence or insanity; few people would go voluntarily to such a place, no matter how well equipped it was for doing routine work efficiently. Today, almost everybody with any illness at all serious wishes to go there.[25]

Modern hospitals are complex organisations with elaborate infrastructures, bureaucracies, policies, procedures, and budgets.[26] They control the organisation of the treatment process within the hospital and thus have considerable influence over how and where patients receive medical treatment. They maintain identities separate from those of the providers they house, and they play a direct role in the delivery of healthcare. The US News & World Report's 2018 hospital rankings by specialty features, among others, Mayo Clinic, Johns Hopkins, Cleveland Clinic, and University of Texas MD Anderson Cancer Center – hospitals that have become household names.[27] Hospitals also recognise their influence on patients and actively develop and maintain their identities through the practice of reputation management. It works. Patients in both the US and Germany confirm that reputation is an important consideration when choosing a hospital.[28] In addition to influencing patients' provider choices, systems design and operation in the hospitals affect patient care.

[20] ibid.
[21] ibid.
[22] Kilgour (n 1).
[23] Porter (n 2).
[24] ibid.
[25] ibid.
[26] ibid.
[27] US News & World Report, 'Best Hospitals by Specialty National Rankings', health.usnews.com/best-hospitals/rankings.
[28] See W de Cruppé and M Geraedts, 'Hospital Choice in Germany from the Patient's Perspective: A Cross-Sectional Study' (2017) 17 *BMC health services research* 720.

1.2 MODERN MEDICAL TECHNOLOGY

The rapid introduction of new health technologies adds a layer of technological complexity to healthcare organisations. Mello and Studdert point out that 'To err is human, but to really screw up you need a computer.'[29] In 1918 a Dutch radiologist, remarked as follows on new x-ray technology: 'An image may appear which gives the diagnosis another direction, a direction that was clinically supposed, but of which the correctness until now could in no other way be confirmed.'[30] By 2020, AI-enabled diagnostic tools were capable of autonomously interpreting chest X-rays and producing radiology reports.[31] Today, technology is embedded in both the administrative tools used by healthcare organisations in the healthcare delivery process and in clinical tools used by providers to deliver patient care.

Advanced health technologies can increase healthcare quality by promoting administrative efficiency, enabling new avenues for patient communication and access to care, and improving clinical outcomes.[32] New technologies can also enhance clinical risk management activities. For example, AI-driven tools can help predict and detect adverse events, reduce medication errors, and support patient monitoring.[33] But integration of these recent technologies across various aspects of an already complex system of healthcare delivery also introduces new opportunities for organisational errors that can directly impact patient care. Organisational decisions about which technologies to adopt, how to configure and implement them, how to train staff, and how to monitor their performance can have a significant impact on patient safety.

Electronic health records (EHRs) provide an early example of the benefits and risks of health technologies. EHRs can provide clinicians with current and comprehensive patient information to support clinical decision-making,[34] but they can also be difficult to use,[35] introduce distractions, and propagate data entry errors in clinical records.[36] When incomplete or incorrect information in

[29] MM Mello and DM Studdert, 'Deconstructing Negligence: The Role of Individual and System Factors in Causing Medical Injuries' (2008) 96 *Georgetown Law Journal* 599.

[30] JJP Dietz, 'Roentgendiagnosis in Miliary Tuberculosis' (1918) 1 *Nederlands Tijdschrift voor Geneeskunde* 50.

[31] LL Plesner et al, 'Autonomous Chest Radiograph Reporting Using AI: Estimation of Clinical Impact' (2023) 307 *Radiology* e222268.

[32] Hausärztinnen- und Hausärzteverband, 'Positionspapier KI in der Hausarztpraxis' (5 July 2024), www.haev.de/fileadmin/user_upload/2024_07_05_PM_KI_Papier_final.pdf.

[33] See M Ferrara et al, 'Risk Management and Patient Safety in the Artificial Intelligence Era: A Systematic Review' (2024) 12 *Healthcare* 549; WD Bates et al, 'The Potential of Artificial Intelligence to Improve Patient Safety: A Scoping Review' (2021) 4 *NPJ Digital Medicine* 54.

[34] Assistant Secretary for Technology Policy (ASTP), 'Improved Diagnostics & Patient Outcomes' (Office of the Secretary for the US Department of Health and Human Services, last updated 1 December 2025), healthit.gov/health-it-basics/improved-diagnostics-patient-outcomes/.

[35] DC Classen et al, 'Inpatient EHR User Experience and Hospital EHR Safety Performance' (2023) 6 *JAMA Network Open* e2333152.

[36] See B Jochimsen 'Elektronische Patientenakte: Meilenstein der Digitalisierung' (2025) 105 *Wirtschaftsdienst* 318.

an EHR system leads to a medical error, it does not take much logical effort to conclude that those errors have more to do with the system than with a provider's clinical judgement. In a study including results from 112 US hospitals, Classen et al found a significant correlation between EHR usability and patient safety in the context of medication errors, and they 'speculate that this link may represent an association between how well a hospital implements and optimizes their EHR for both user satisfaction and safety performance'.[37] The authors note that coordinated efforts to improve software by manufacturers, airlines, and regulators in the aviation industry resulted in safer software systems as well as higher rates of pilot satisfaction.[38] A study exploring EHR limitations in a large German university medical centre revealed similar usability challenges.[39] Hoop and Neumuth describe physician frustrations caused by fragmentation of information across the hospital's EHR system, which made it difficult to record and locate important clinical information. Relatedly, the EHR system design led to administrative overload for physicians, who already carry heavy cognitive loads, by requiring numerous and duplicate EHR entries, which also increases the risk for documentation errors. The authors point out that poor usability design 'not only affects task load but also may impact patient safety'.[40]

More recently, AI-driven medical technologies provide a telling example of how rapid development can outpace organisational and clinician readiness for adoption and use. In 2015, the Food and Drug Administration cleared six AI/machine learning (ML) medical devices compared to 221 in 2023.[41] In December 2025, there were more than 1,300 AI/ML medical devices on the US market.[42] In the US, the American Medical Association (AMA) described physician adoption of AI as 'unusually fast for healthcare technology adoption', noting that its 2024 survey results showed that nearly 70 per cent of physicians reported using AI compared to only 38 per cent in 2023.[43] Despite this increase, clinicians still highlight the importance of safe integration, adequate training, and regulatory oversight.[44] The AMA's chief medical information officer stresses that 'Effective organisational governance is essential to ensure that AI systems support rather than disrupt clinical workflows, embed ongoing clinical oversight, uphold care

[37] Classen et al (n 35).

[38] ibid.

[39] See T de Hoop and T Neumuth, 'Evaluating Electronic Health Record Limitations and Time Expenditure in a German Medical Center' (2021) 12 *Applied Clinical Informatics* 1082.

[40] ibid.

[41] E Reuter and JY Han, 'The Number of AI Medical Devices Has Spiked in the Past Decade' (MedTech Dive, 9 October 2024), www.medtechdive.com/news/fda-ai-medical-devices-growth/728975.

[42] E Reuter and JY Han, 'AI in Medtech Is Booming. Track New Devices Here' (MedTech Dive, 9 February 2026), www.medtechdive.com/news/ai-medtech-track-new-devices-fda/748397.

[43] A Fox, 'AMA Recommends a Risk-Based Approach in Its New AI Governance Framework' (HealthcareIT News, 19 August 2025), www.healthcareitnews.com/news/ama-recommends-risk-based-approach-its-new-ai-governance-framework.

[44] See TA Henry, '2 in 3 Physicians Are Using Health AI—Up 78% from 2023' (American Medical Association, 26 February 2025), www.ama-assn.org/practice-management/digital-health/2-3-physicians-are-using-health-ai-78-2023.

quality and provide clear mechanisms for accountability.' German physicians also report an overall positive outlook towards potential benefits for integration of AI in clinical practice, but currently experience significantly lower adoption rates than their US counterparts. Still, similar obstacles to physician trust in AI-driven technologies exist in both countries; Heinrichs et al identified fragmented IT systems, lack of interoperable infrastructure, and insufficient training as obstacles to AI adoption in Germany, noting that 'The adoption of AI is perceived as outpacing system readiness, leaving physicians frustrated with inefficient workflows and misaligned tools.'[45]

Overall, while clinicians recognise the potential for AI-driven medical technologies to improve clinical workflows and patient outcomes, they still highlight design, integration, oversight, and liability concerns.[46] As the pace and sophistication of digital health technologies continue to accelerate, healthcare organisations must adapt processes for both care delivery and risk management. This is especially important during transition periods when clinical experience and evidence are still being developed, clear legal frameworks for regulation and liability are lacking, and the risks of modern technologies are not fully identified or understood.

1.3 MEDICAL LIABILITY AND ITS LIMITATIONS

The medical liability system is designed to resolve disputes between individuals and healthcare providers involving injuries caused by the provision of healthcare. In both the US and Germany, medical liability operates within a negligence-based system that imposes liability on actors who exhibit substandard conduct. Through this model, the medical liability system seeks to both provide compensation for injuries caused by negligent conduct and deter actors from engaging in such conduct. The legal doctrines that underlie medical liability claims in the US and Germany and the rules that govern whether these claims are ultimately successful are discussed in depth in chapters three and four. For now, it is helpful to provide a general overview of the different potentially liable parties and the legal basis for asserting claims against them in the event of a medical injury.

When patients experience harm in connection with their medical treatment, they (or their representatives) can initiate medical liability claims. Depending on the causes of the alleged harm, patients might file claims against individual providers, healthcare organisations, or medical device manufacturers. Many medical liability cases can involve claims against several of these parties

[45] H Heinrichs et al, 'Physicians' Attitudes Toward Artificial Intelligence in Medicine: Mixed Methods Survey and Interview Study' (2025) 27 *Journal of Medical Internet Research* e74187.

[46] See American Medical Association, 'AMA Augmented Intelligence Research, Physician Sentiments Around the Use of AI in Health Care: Motivations, Opportunities, Risks, and Use Cases' (February 2025), www.ama-assn.org/system/files/physician-ai-sentiment-report.pdf. See also Heinrichs (n 45).

simultaneously; however, despite the organisation of modern healthcare, which relies on complex 'interrelationships among health care providers, the tools they use, and the environment in which they carry out their work, claims based on the actions of individual providers occupy center stage in medical liability law'.[47]

In medical liability claims against individual healthcare providers, like doctors and nurses, a breach of the standards of care applicable to their practice will constitute negligent behaviour.[48] Patients may allege multiple instances of negligence by various individuals involved in their care. Allegations of negligence against individual providers can also anchor a new claim against the healthcare organisation that employs or oversees the individual providers through the doctrine of vicarious liability.[49] Under this doctrine, healthcare organisations in both jurisdictions can be vicariously liable for patient harm caused by the negligence of individuals doctors or nurses.[50] In the US, hospitals were traditionally immune from vicarious liability for injuries caused by medical treatment based on the view that they lacked control over employee doctors and nurses who possessed special skills.[51] This view began to change in 1957 after the court in *Bing v Thunig* found that a hospital could be vicariously liable for the medical actions of its employees.[52] The *Bing* court rejected the argument that modern hospitals merely provide facilities for healthcare providers to treat patients, noting that 'the person who avails himself of 'hospital facilities' expects that the hospital will attempt to cure him, not that its nurses or other employees will act on their own responsibility'.[53]

Claims based on individual negligence, whether they are made against the individual provider or against the healthcare organisation under vicarious liability, focus on the behaviour of the individual provider. For the reasons more thoroughly discussed in chapter two, Mello and Studdert point out that focusing solely on the behaviour of individuals in a complex system is 'dead wrong'.[54] They criticise the medical liability system's 'atomistic view of the individual provider's role in causing injury' as outdated and out of sync with both modern healthcare delivery systems and error prevention science.[55]

Healthcare organisations, like hospitals, can also be liable for patient harm independent of individual providers' behaviour. This type of direct liability claim against a healthcare organisation is not based on vicarious liability, but rather on the negligent behaviour of the organisation itself. Organisational behaviour

[47] Mello and Studdert (n 29).
[48] See ch 4, s 4.1.2.
[49] See ch 4, s 4.3.1.
[50] ibid.
[51] F Seroog, 'Torts: Bing v. Thunig: The End of Hospital Immunity in New York' (1958) 41 *Marquette Law Review* 311.
[52] *Bing v Thunig* 143 NE 2d 3 (NY 1957).
[53] ibid.
[54] ibid.
[55] ibid.

can include, for example, hiring and training employees and maintaining hospital equipment and facilities. Eight years after the *Bing* court recognised vicarious liability for hospitals, the Illinois Supreme Court, in *Darling v Charleston Community Memorial Hospital*, established the legal concept of direct organisational liability for hospitals.[56] In Germany, more than 10 years before the *Darling* court articulated the concept of direct organisational negligence in the US, the German Federal Court explained that the treatment contract between the hospital and a patient extends beyond the 'provision of accommodation and meals' to include the provision of care provided to the patient within the hospital.[57] In addition to vicarious liability for the negligence of the providers who treated the patient, the court found that the hospital itself could be directly liable when it failed to inform the treating doctors about safety measures which led to the patient's alleged injury.[58] Giesen notes the trend of 'increasing the accountability of hospitals to their patients', both the US and Germany have been expanding this type of direct liability for healthcare organisations.[59] By 1985, the German Federal Court articulated the broad scope of direct hospital liability noting that a hospital is 'obligated not only in contract, but also in tort, to do everything reasonable within its power to avert possible dangers to patients'.[60] Still, despite the expanding legal framework for organisational negligence in both jurisdictions, Quick notes an unyielding psychological predisposition to focus on individual responsibility based on humans' ability to connect with individual providers and the individualistic culture that dominates medical practice and professional responsibility.[61] This ignores evidence that organisational behaviour related to the design of healthcare delivery systems plays a prominent role in causing medical injuries.[62]

Beyond fault-based claims, medical injuries can also lead to claims against manufacturers of medical devices used in a patient's care. These claims are primarily based on product liability law and are often characterised as strict liability claims because they do not require the claimant to prove negligent behaviour. Instead, product liability claims against manufacturers require only that the alleged injury be caused by a defective medical device.[63] Medical devices can be defective as a result of design flaws, manufacturing errors, or inadequate

[56] *Darling v Charleston Community Memorial Hospital* 211 NE2d 253 (Ill 1965).

[57] Bundesgerichtshof (BGH) 27 February 1952, BGHZ 5, 321.

[58] ibid.

[59] See D Giesen, *International Medical Malpractice Law: A Comparative Law Study of Civil Liability Arising from Medical Care* (Tübingen, JCB Mohr (Paul Siebeck), 1988).

[60] BGH 18 June 1985, NJW 1985, 2189.

[61] See O Quick, *Regulating Patient Safety: The End of Professional Dominance?* (Cambridge, Cambridge University Press, 2017).

[62] See Mello and Studdert (n 29).

[63] See Giesen (n 59); MN Duffourc and S Gerke, 'Decoding U.S. Tort Liability in Healthcare's Black-Box AI Era: Lessons from the European Union Black Box Era' (2024) 27 *Stanford Technology Law Review* 1.

instructions or warnings.[64] Notably, product liability claims would focus on the condition of a medical device by asking whether it was defective rather than the quality of behaviour surrounding its use in patient care. This distinction is important because the law of negligence only recognises natural and legal persons as capable of exhibiting behaviour; in other words, products cannot be negligent.[65] Some new AI-driven medical technologies can mimic human behaviour by using complex algorithmic reasoning to independently complete tasks that would ordinarily be performed by humans.[66] In addition to introducing new risks in the treatment process, complex AI-driven medical tools also stress the current medical liability framework in both jurisdictions by challenging its fundamental assumption that products cannot behave.[67]

While recognising some political, practical, and doctrinal challenges for spotlighting organisational behaviour in medical liability claims, Mello and Studdert call for 'Doctrinal realignment to reflect the realities of medical injury causation and prevention' by strengthening the role of organisational liability.[68] A theory of negligent clinical risk management would result in an actionable organisational duty to design systems capable of identifying and eliminating conditions that induce human error in a modern, and increasingly digitalised, healthcare system. This does not mean that individual providers are excused from their duties to provide non-negligent healthcare or that manufacturers of medical technologies escape liability for putting defective products into the healthcare market. A theory of negligent clinical risk management would run parallel to claims against individual providers, recognising the reality that organisational behaviour contributes to medical errors. While the medical liability system cannot, and is not expected to, be the driving force for medical error prevention, it should ideally reinforce accepted norms governing error prevention in modern healthcare and, at least, not hinder error prevention efforts of the healthcare industry.

[64] See sources cited in n 63.

[65] See MN Duffourc, 'Malpractice by the Autonomous AI Physician' (2023) 2023 *Illinois Journal of Law, Technology & Policy* 1.

[66] ibid.

[67] See generally Duffourc (n 65).

[68] Duffourc (n 65).

2

A Modern Approach to Medical Error Prevention

IN 1859, FLORENCE Nightingale had already identified the organisation of healthcare as a central component of patient safety: 'Let whoever is in charge keep this simple question in her head (not, how can I always do this right thing myself, but) how can I provide for this right thing to be always done?'[1] Over a century later, the problem of medical errors still loomed large: in 1994, Leape quantified the rate of medical errors in the average intensive care unit (ICU) to conclude that ICUs have a 99 per cent proficiency level.[2] He then explained the effects of a much higher 99.9 per cent proficiency level in the banking and aviation industries, noting that such performance would result in two dangerous landings every day at O'Hare International Airport and 32,000 checks being withdrawn from the wrong bank account every hour.[3] While errors generally describe unintentional failures in achieving a planned aim,[4] individual medical errors are predictable features of a complex, high-risk healthcare system. Patient safety in this context is not merely the absence of individual errors, but the presence of an organisational system that reduces defects in the healthcare process to eliminate 'accidental injury'.[5] This chapter discusses the shift from thinking about medical error prevention as an individual responsibility to understanding it as a systemic and organisational endeavour, examines the role of clinical risk management in the healthcare industry's systems-focused error prevention efforts, and examines how the rapid integration of digital technologies into healthcare delivery adds a new dimension to the role of healthcare organisations in driving patient safety.

[1] F Nightingale, *Notes on Nursing: What It Is, and What It Is Not* (Philadelphia, JB Lippincott Company, 1946).

[2] LL Leape, 'Error in Medicine' (1994) 272 *Journal of the American Medical Association* 1581.

[3] ibid.

[4] O Quick, *Regulating Patient Safety: The End of Professional Dominance?* (Cambridge, Cambridge University Press, 2017).

[5] Institute of Medicine (IOM) Committee on Quality of Health Care in America, *To Err is Human: Building a Safer Health System* (LT Kohn, JM Corrigan and MS Donaldson eds, Washington DC, National Academies Press, 2000).

2.1 ERROR PREVENTION IN THE HEALTHCARE INDUSTRY: A PARADIGM SHIFT

In 1999, the Institute of Medicine (IOM)'s *To Err is Human: Building a Safer Health System* report became the seminal work for modern medical error prevention.[6] It debunked the myth that medical errors were caused solely by individual healthcare providers by recognising what other high-risk industries did a decade before: 'The problem is not bad people; the problem is that the system needs to be made safer.'[7] When the IOM issued its report, the idea that medical errors could be prevented by better trained, more skilled, and less stressed healthcare practitioners permeated public opinion.[8] While organisational influences lingered in the background of this individual-focused perception, 'Most people view[ed] medical mistakes as an "individual provider issue" rather than a failure in the process of delivering care in a complex delivery system.'[9] Healthcare providers themselves, immersed in a culture that demands perfection, also associated medical errors with the actions and qualifications of individual healthcare providers.[10] The IOM attempted to shift the focus from individual failures to organisational failures, not to excuse negligent provider actions, but rather to highlight and advocate for a new approach to preventing medical errors, one that had proven successful in other high-risk industries.[11]

The IOM heavily relied upon the research of sociologist Charles Perrow, and psychologist James Reason to explain why errors occur in the modern healthcare system.[12] Perrow's normal accident theory accepted that high-risk systems were accident-prone.[13] According to Perrow, the level of risk inherent in a system depends upon whether it is: (1) complex or linear; and (2) tightly or loosely coupled.[14] Complex, tightly coupled systems present the highest risk.[15] Complexity is measured by the dependency of the system's interrelated processes on one another.[16] In a complex system, when a single process fails, it causes the subsequent failure of several other dependent processes.[17] In addition, the more specialised those processes are, the more complex the system becomes.[18] 'Coupling' refers to the amount of time the system can tolerate

[6] ibid.
[7] ibid.
[8] ibid.
[9] ibid.
[10] ibid.
[11] ibid.
[12] See IOM (n 5).
[13] ibid.
[14] ibid.
[15] ibid.
[16] ibid.
[17] ibid.
[18] ibid.

between processes and the flexibility of the system's process order.[19] Tightly coupled systems have fixed-order processes that occur in rapid succession.[20]

The IOM defines a 'system' as 'a set of interdependent elements interacting to achieve a common aim'.[21] Healthcare systems encompass everything from a large regional multispecialty healthcare delivery system, to a hospital specialty unit, to a single operating room, all of which are interdependent.[22] This interdependence combined with the specialisation of healthcare delivery makes healthcare systems complex.[23] In addition, because there is little buffer between the 'dependent processes and sequences' in healthcare systems, they can be classified as tightly coupled.[24] The IOM concluded that like other complex tightly coupled systems, including aviation and nuclear power plants, healthcare systems are error-prone.[25]

James Reason's Swiss Cheese Model describes how active failures and latent conditions, represented as holes in Swiss cheese, can align to cause an accident and result in damage.[26] Active failures include the easily recognisable individual actions that are usually temporally connected to the resulting damage.[27] Latent conditions include system design, structure, oversight, and maintenance problems that can unexpectedly combine to cause or induce a subsequent active error.[28] Because latent conditions occur earlier in the process chain, they are more difficult to identify than damage-causing active failures.[29] In addition, hindsight bias can also conceal latent errors.

> Hindsight bias means that things that were not seen or understood at the time of the accident seem obvious in retrospect. Hindsight bias also misleads a reviewer into simplifying the causes of an accident, highlighting a single element as the cause and overlooking multiple contributing factors. Given that the information about an accident is spread over many participants, none of whom may have complete information, hindsight bias makes it easy to arrive at a simple solution or to blame an individual, but difficult to determine what really went wrong.[30]

Recognising that active errors do not occur in a vacuum, but rather within a complex system, is critical not only for understanding why an error occurred, but also for developing successful error-prevention strategies.

[19] ibid.
[20] ibid.
[21] ibid.
[22] ibid.
[23] ibid.
[24] ibid.
[25] ibid.
[26] J Reason, 'Human Error: Models and Management' (2000) 320 *British Medical Journal* 768.
[27] ibid.
[28] ibid.
[29] See Reason (n 26); IOM (n 5).
[30] IOM (n 5).

Although human error is admittedly the cause of most accidents, these errors can often be prevented by better system design.[31] Reason explains that, 'We cannot change the human condition, but we can change the conditions under which humans work.'[32] He further provides the following analogy to illustrate the systems approach to preventing errors:

> [A]ctive failures are like mosquitoes. They can be swatted one by one, but they still keep coming. The best remedies are to create more effective defences and to drain the swamps in which they breed. The swamps, in this case, are the ever present latent conditions.[33]

The IOM, adopting Reason's theory of accident causation, concluded that latent errors pose the greatest threat to patient safety.[34] As a result, punishing individuals who commit active errors is not an effective way to prevent future errors, because: (1) the active error can be caused or induced by a specific combination of latent errors that is unlikely to repeat; and (2) failing to address the latent errors allows them to accumulate making the system more error-prone.[35]

Central to the success of a systems approach to medical error prevention is the development of a culture of safety within the healthcare organisation itself.[36] The IOM found that, 'Health care organizations must develop a culture of safety such that an organization's care processes and workforce are focused on improving the reliability and safety of care for patients.'[37] This culture of safety stands in stark contrast to the culture of blame that historically prevailed in healthcare.[38] Replacing a culture of blame with a culture of safety enables healthcare systems to become highly reliable.[39] According to high reliability theory, high-risk organisations can overcome their proclivity for accidents by maintaining an organisational culture that enables identification and elimination of organisational defects through the process of clinical risk management.[40]

To Err is Human forced the healthcare industry worldwide to prioritise patient safety. Stelfox et al observed that the IOM's report 'stimulated research and discussion about patient safety issues'.[41] It also ignited a paradigm shift in the way healthcare researchers approached patient safety.[42] According to a study that evaluated the effects of the IOM report on patient safety publications,

[31] ibid.
[32] Reason (n 26).
[33] ibid.
[34] IOM (n 5).
[35] ibid.
[36] ibid.
[37] ibid.
[38] ibid.
[39] ibid.
[40] ibid.
[41] See HT Stelfox et al, 'The "To Err Is Human" Report and the Patient Safety Literature' (2006) 15 *BMJ Quality & Safety* 174.
[42] See ibid.

pre-report publications focused on medical malpractice, while post-report publications focused on organisational culture.[43] The study's authors noted that, 'the IOM report has changed the very nature of the patient safety conversation from focusing on dispensing blame to improving systems'.[44]

Days after the IOM published *To Err is Human*, United States (US) President Bill Clinton signed the Healthcare Research and Quality Act of 1999 into law.[45] The Act reauthorised the Agency for Healthcare Research and Quality (AHRQ), which received a congressional mandate to:

> [C]onduct and support research and build private-public partnerships to: (1) identify the causes of preventable health care errors and patient injury in health care delivery; (2) develop, demonstrate, and evaluate strategies for reducing errors and improving patient safety; and (3) disseminate such effective strategies throughout the health care industry.[46]

Weeks later, AHRQ called for research to identify 'systems-related best practices'.[47] That same year, the National Center for Patient Safety was established within the US Department of Veterans Affairs (VA).[48] The VA National Center for Patient Safety seeks to establish patient safety culture in the VA Health System, which is the country's largest integrated healthcare delivery system.[49] In September 2000, the AHRQ-led Quality Interagency Coordination Task Force (QuIC) began efforts to develop a national strategy for identifying and preventing threats to patient safety in the US.[50] This strategy included $50 million of patient safety project funding, which ultimately led to the development of tools designed to help healthcare organisations create a culture of safety, reduce hospital-acquired infections, eliminate medication errors, and promote error-reporting, among others.[51]

The Joint Commission, a private non-profit regulatory body, also took swift action to improve patient safety following the IOM's report. Although Joint Commission accreditation is not mandatory, it is required for hospitals that receive federal support through Medicare and Medicaid as well as for those who maintain internship and residency programmes.[52] In 1999, the

[43] ibid.
[44] ibid.
[45] CM Clancy, 'AHRQ: One Decade after To Err Is Human' (Patient Safety & Quality Healthcare Analyses, 8 September 2009), www.psqh.com/analysis/september-october-2009-ahrq.
[46] Healthcare Research and Quality Act (HRQA) of 1999, 42 USC § 299 et seq.
[47] Agency for Healthcare Research and Quality (AHRQ), 'Advancing Patient Safety: A Decade of Evidence, Design, and Implementation' (Publication No 09(10)-0084, 2009) www.ahrq.gov/sites/default/files/publications/files/advancing-patient-safety.pdf.
[48] US Department of Veterans Affairs, 'VHA National Center for Patient Safety', www.patientsafety.va.gov.
[49] S Upadhyay, 'Keeping Patients Safe: How Has the Patient Safety Movement Evolved in the U.S.?' (Patient Safety & Quality Healthcare Analyses, 23 June 2020), www.psqh.com/analysis/keeping-patients-safe-how-has-the-patient-safety-movement-evolved-in-the-u-s.
[50] Clancy (n 45).
[51] ibid.
[52] KA Kearney and EL McCord, 'Hospital Management Faces New Liabilities' (1992) 6 *Health Law* 1.

Joint Commission amended its mission statement to include patient safety as an explicit goal.[53] In 2002, the Joint Commission began its annual publication of National Patient Safety Goals, which uses information gathered from industry experts to articulate goals and recommendations for improving patient safety in various care and practice settings, including ambulatory, laboratory, home health, hospital, and nursing homes.[54] That same year, in conjunction with the National Quality Forum (NQF), the Joint Commission established the John M Eisenberg Patient Safety and Quality Awards to recognise individuals and projects that advance healthcare quality and patient safety.[55] In 2004, the Joint Commission launched Shared Visions-New Pathways, an initiative that redesigned the Commission's accreditation process to focus on patient safety and organisational performance.[56] In 2008, the Joint Commission created the Center for Transforming Healthcare 'to address obstacles that prevent patient safety measures from being carried out'.[57] The Center uses high-reliability science and the systems approach to error prevention to help organisations improve quality of care.[58]

In 2005, Congress passed the Patient Safety and Quality Improvement Act (PSQIA) to improve patient safety and the quality of healthcare.[59] Through the PSQIA, Congress attempted to promote patient safety culture by protecting the confidentiality of certain information gathered by healthcare providers following adverse events. The Senate recognised that 'patient safety can best be improved by fostering efforts to identify and fix errors while ensuring that providers remain accountable for malpractice'.[60] To further this goal, the Act provides a sphere of legal protection for three categories of data defined as Patient Safety Work Product (PSWP).[61] PSWP means:

> [A]ny data, reports, records, memoranda, analyses (such as root cause analyses), or written or oral statements–
>
> (i) which–
>
> (I) are assembled or developed by a provider for reporting to a patient safety organization and are reported to a patient safety organization; or

[53] Joint Commission, 'The Joint Commission History Timeline' (2024), digitalassets.jointcommission.org/api/public/content/fa21761405c44eac8bf95637fc450598?v=441260d1.

[54] ibid; Joint Commission, 'International Patient Safety Goals' www.jointcommission.org/standards/national-patient-safety-goals.

[55] Joint Commission (n 54). See also Joint Commission, 'John M. Eisenberg Patient Safety and Quality Awards', www.jointcommission.org/en-us/about-us/recognizing-excellence/awards/john-m-eisenberg-award.

[56] See RP Katzfey, 'JCAHO's Shared Visions–New Pathways: The New Hospital Survey and Accreditation Process for 2004' (2004) 61 *American Journal of Health-System Pharmacy* 1358.

[57] MR Chassin and JM Loeb, 'High-Reliability Health Care: Getting There from Here' (2013) 91 *The Milbank Quarterly* 459.

[58] ibid.

[59] Patient Safety and Quality Improvement Act of 2005, 42 USC § 299b-21–b-26.

[60] See Senate Report Number 108-196 (2003).

[61] See Patient Safety and Quality Improvement Act of 2005, 42 USC § 299b-21.

(II) are developed by a patient safety organization for the conduct of patient safety activities;

and which could result in improved patient safety, health care quality, or health care outcomes; or

(ii) which identify or constitute the deliberations or analysis of, or identify the fact of reporting pursuant to, a patient safety evaluation system.[62]

Patient safety organizations (PSOs) are privately or publicly formed and funded associations that focus on decreasing healthcare risks.[63]

In 2009, in response to President Barack Obama's directive to support projects focused on improving patient safety and reducing medical malpractice, the Department of Health and Human Services (DHHS) in conjunction with the AHRQ established the Patient Safety and Medical Liability Initiative (PSMLI).[64] The PSMLI funded seven demonstration projects focused on: '(1) improving communication, (2) preventing harm through the use of "best practices," and (3) exploring alternative methods of settling claims.'[65] Although a five-year evaluation of their impacts was limited, the projects generated a plethora of useful resources for improving patient care and patient safety culture.[66]

In 2010, the US Congress passed and President Obama signed into law, the Patient Protection and Affordable Care Act (PPACA).[67] Although the most championed goal of the PPACA was to improve healthcare access, it also promised to improve healthcare quality.[68] The law's payment reforms included systems designed to reward or penalise providers based upon quality-of-care metrics.[69] The PPACA also created the Center for Medicare and Medicaid Innovation charged with improving the quality of healthcare funded by Medicare and Medicaid.[70] Although data show improvements in healthcare quality following the enactment of the PPACA, David Blumenthal and Melinda Abrams note that quality improvements were trending upward prior to the law's enactment, shedding doubt on whether the PPACA had a direct impact on healthcare quality.[71]

[62] ibid § 299b-21(7).

[63] ibid § 299b-21(4); AHRQ, 'Frequently Asked Questions', www.pso.ahrq.gov/faq. ('What is a PSO?' and 'Do PSOs receive federal funding?').

[64] TL Hafemeister and JH Porter, 'The Health Care Reform Act of 2010 and Medical Malpractice Liability: Worlds in Collision or Ships Passing in the Night' (2011) 64 *Southern Methodist University Law Review* 735.

[65] AHRQ, 'Longitudinal Evaluation of the Patient Safety and Medical Liability Reform Demonstration Program: Demonstration Grants Final Evaluation Report' (prepared by James Bell Associates and RAND Corporation, AHRQ Publication No 16-0038-2-EF, May 2016), www.ahrq.gov/sites/default/files/wysiwyg/professionals/quality-patient-safety/patient-safety-resources/resources/candor/psml-demo-grants-final-report.pdf.

[66] ibid.

[67] Patient Protection and Affordable Care Act, Pub L No 111-148, 124 Stat 119 (2010) (codified as amended in scattered sections of the USC).

[68] D Blumenthal and M Abrams, 'The Affordable Care Act at 10 Years – Payment and Delivery System Reforms' (2020) 382 *New England Journal of Medicine* 1057.

[69] ibid.

[70] ibid.

[71] ibid.

In 2015, the Joint Commission added a 'Patient Safety Systems' chapter to its accreditation manual for hospitals.[72] The chapter recognised that patient safety was central to the high-quality healthcare expected of its accredited organisations.[73] It also acknowledged that creating 'a fair and just safety culture' in which individual providers are not punished for systemic deficiencies, was central to the ultimate goal of zero harm.[74] The Joint Commission subsequently included the same chapter in accreditation manuals for ambulatory care, critical access, laboratory, nursing care, and behavioural health organisations.[75] In all settings, the chapter's intent is, 'to provide organizations [and their leaders] with a proactive approach to designing or redesigning a patient-centered system that aims to improve quality of care and patient safety'.[76]

In Europe, the European Commission Directorate-General for Health & Consumers has undertaken initiatives to promote patient safety and healthcare quality in the European Union (EU). In 2005, the Commission published the Luxembourg Declaration on Patient Safety recognising the human and financial costs of patient injuries and placing patient safety high on the EU's political agenda.[77] At the international level, the declaration recommended international collaboration to help policymakers understand and propose solutions for patient safety issues and the development of patient safety-focused regulations and standards that govern the provision of medical goods and services.[78] At the national level, the declaration recommended patient empowerment, including: giving patients access to records and information concerning their medical treatment; improving training and working conditions for healthcare professionals; promoting patient safety culture through risk management, quality assurance, and error reporting and learning; providing collaborative space for all stakeholders in the healthcare industry to discuss patient safety; and using technology to solve patient safety problems.[79] At the industry level, the declaration recommended collaboration to increase patient safety, promotion of patient safety culture in healthcare organisations, and improved communications with patients and families about medical errors.[80]

From 2008 through 2010, the European Commission and the European Agency for Health and Consumers (EAHC) funded the European Union Network for

[72] Joint Commission, 'Patient Safety Systems (PS)' in *Comprehensive Accreditation Manual for Hospitals* (Joint Commission, 2026), digitalassets.jointcommission.org/api/public/content/40ee770460f44e58acb6e27f6658fb9e?v=f86c3d79.

[73] ibid.

[74] ibid.

[75] Joint Commission, 'Patient Safety Systems' (PS) Chapter', www.jointcommission.org/en-us/knowledge-library/support-center/standards-interpretation/patient-safety-systems-chapter.

[76] Joint Commission (n 72).

[77] European Commission, DG Health and Consumer Protection, 'Patient Safety – Making it Happen! Luxembourg Declaration on Patient Safety' (2005), ec.europa.eu/health/ph_overview/Documents/ev_20050405_rd01_en.pdf.

[78] ibid.

[79] ibid.

[80] ibid.

Patient Safety (EUNetPaS), a project initiated by the Patient Safety and Quality of Care Working Group (PSQCWG) and coordinated by the French National Authority for Health (HAS).[81] As the first patient safety project to include all 27 EU Member States, EUNetPaS's objectives were two-fold.[82] They included both collaborative international research and development of uniform systems and standards to improve patient safety as well as national networks focused on sharing patient safety information with all relevant stakeholders.[83] One main focus of EUNetPaS's collaborative efforts was to improve patient safety culture. It defined a 'culture of safety' as 'An integrated pattern of individual and organisational behaviour, based upon shared beliefs and values that continuously seeks to minimise patient harm, which may result from the processes of care delivery.'[84] Drawing from the IOM's finding that systemic deficiencies could only be improved by creating a safety culture in healthcare organisations, EUNetPaS sought to identify patient safety indicators that led to an improvement in patient safety culture.[85]

In 2009, the Council of the European Union issued a recommendation on patient safety, including the prevention and control of healthcare associated infections.[86] According to the recommendation, 'A large proportion of adverse events, both in the hospital sector and in primary care, are preventable with systemic factors appearing to account for a majority of them.'[87] The Council's recommendations on general patient safety issues mimicked those articulated in the Luxembourg Declaration and included: the development of national patient safety policies and programmes; empowerment of citizens; establishment of error reporting and learning systems; patient safety; education and training of healthcare professionals; implementation of a system for classifying and measuring patient safety; initiation of national and international collaboration and information sharing; and promotion of patient safety research.[88]

In 2012, the European Network on Patient Safety and Quality of Care (PaSQ) launched with funding and support from the European Commission's Public Health Programme.[89] PaSQ seeks to support implementation of the Council's

[81] A Pauli, *Risikomanagement und CIRS als Gegenstand der Krankenhaushaftung* (Baden-Baden, Nomos,2013);European Patients Forum,'EUNETPAS' (2010,) www.eu-patient.eu/Projects/completed-projects/EUNetPaS.

[82] Pauli (n 81); C Linden-Lahti et al, 'Facilitators and Barriers in Implementing Medication Safety Practices Across Hospitals Within 11 European Union Countries' (2019) 17 *Pharmacy Practice* 1583.

[83] See Pauli (n 81).

[84] The European Network for Patient Safety (EUNetPaS), 'Use of Patient Safety Culture: Instruments and Recommendations' (2010), seguridaddelpaciente.sanidad.gob.es/proyectos/participacionInternacional/docs/WP1-REPORT__Use_of__PSCI_and_recommandations_-_March__2010.pdf.

[85] EUNetPaS, 'Patient Safety Culture Report: Focusing on Indicators' (2010), seguridaddelpaciente.sanidad.gob.es/proyectos/participacionInternacional/docs/WP1-Eunetpas-patient_safety_culture-report_focusing_on_indicators.pdf.

[86] Council Recommendation of 9 June 2009 on patient safety, including the prevention and control of healthcare associated infections [2009] OJ C 151/1.

[87] ibid recital (4).

[88] See generally Council Recommendation on patient safety (n 86).

[89] The Standing Committee of European Doctors (CPME), 'Patient Safety and Quality of Care Joint Action (PaSQ) 2012–2016', www.cpme.eu/policies-and-projects/projects/patient-safety-and-quality-of-care-joint-action-pasq.

recommendation on patient safety.[90] In 2014, the Council adopted conclusions on patient safety and quality of care asking Member States to 'intensify their efforts in implementing' the Council's Patient Safety Recommendation.[91] In addition to the focus on implementing and strengthening patient safety measures, the conclusions called for the establishment of patient safety standards and guidelines.[92]

As well as the role it played in the broader European patient safety efforts, the IOM's 1999 report also sparked national interest in the systems approach to improving patient safety in Germany.[93] By 2001, the issue of medical errors was increasingly gaining the attention of both the German public and the healthcare industry.[94] The Federal Health Monitoring Report disseminated, for the first time, a statistical analysis of medical errors in Germany.[95] The report addressed the impact of organisational errors, finding that curing organisational deficits would have prevented a significant number of medical errors.[96] It also noted that organisational errors were becoming more prominent topics in medical malpractice proceedings.[97] Finally, the report echoed the IOM's call for a systems approach to medical error prevention, calling it 'a task for society as a whole'.[98]

In 2002, the German Medical Centre for Quality in Medicine (*Ärztliches Zentrum für Qualität in der Medizin*; ÄZQ) established a Patient Safety Expert Group to address the problem of medical errors.[99] The group developed a plan to raise awareness for error prevention in the medical community, establish expert groups to discuss error management and prevention, develop principles and common data sets to use in error analysis, and improve quality assurance to address medical errors with a systems approach.[100] That same year, the Berlin Health Prize focused on projects that offered innovative approaches to medical error prevention.[101] The award's presenters, the Berlin Chamber of Medicine and the AOK public health insurer, sought to galvanise a culture of safety with the

[90] ibid.

[91] Council of the European Union, 'Council conclusions on patient safety and quality of care, including the prevention and control of healthcare associated infections and antimicrobial resistance' (Employment, Social policy, Health and Consumer affairs Council meeting, Brussels, 1 December 2014), www.consilium.europa.eu/uedocs/cms_data/docs/pressdata/en/lsa/145976.pdf.

[92] ibid.

[93] See Pauli (n 81).

[94] ML Hansis and D Hart, *Gesundheitsberichterstattung des Bundes, Medizinische Behandlungsfehler* (Robert Koch-Institut, Berlin, Paul Fieck KG, 2001), www.gbe-bund.de/pdf/Behand.pdf.

[95] ibid.

[96] ibid.

[97] ibid.

[98] ibid.

[99] See Pauli (n 81).

[100] ibid.

[101] AOK-Bundesverband, AOK Berlin and Ärztekammer Berlin, 'Fehlervermeidung und Sicherheitskultur in Medizin und Pflege – Deutschland ist noch Entwicklungsgebiet' Press Release (27 March 2003), www.presseportal.de/pm/8697/433102.

ability to identify and eliminate structural weaknesses in Germany's healthcare industry.[102]

In 2003, the German Advisory Council for Concerted Action in Healthcare included the topic of medical errors in its biannual report:[103] 'The Council consider[ed] the analysis of conditions under which medical errors arise and the development and implementation of more effective and efficient prevention strategies to be a pillar of quality assurance in the health care system.'[104] The report noted that errors were caused by failures in the many layers that comprise a complex healthcare delivery system, including at the individual, team, facility, and system levels.[105] It discouraged punishing individual providers for reporting errors and encouraged the establishment of sanction-free near-miss error-reporting systems.[106] Interestingly, although the report found that error prevention was more important than patient compensation for damages caused by medical errors, it also viewed medical error claims to be a valuable source of information for reducing errors and encouraged healthcare providers to disclose medical errors to patients.[107]

According to Dr Günter Jonitz, former President of the Berlin Chamber of Physicians, 2005 was 'the year of patient safety in Germany'.[108] That year, the German Medical Assembly (*Deutscher Ärztetag*) unanimously declared that 'medical ethics and social responsibility of doctors in Germany are the foundation to take action on patient safety'.[109] The year 2005 also saw the birth of the German Coalition for Patient Safety (*Aktionsbündnis Patientensicherheit*; APS).[110] APS is an interdisciplinary network of representatives from medical insurance, legal, government, and patient organisations with the single focus of improving patient safety.[111] Jonitz praises APS's work as a 'bottom-up' approach that offers practical solutions developed using the expertise of practitioners affected at the ground level rather than impractical administrative measures offered by politicians.[112] APS's work ranges from participation in international patient safety campaigns (like the World Health Organization (WHO)'s High

[102] ibid.

[103] See Advisory Council for the Concerted Action in Health Care, 'Health Care Finance, User Orientation and Quality (Report 2003 Summary)', www.svr-gesundheit.de/fileadmin/Gutachten/Gutachten_2003/Kurzfassung_engl_2003.pdf.

[104] ibid.

[105] ibid.

[106] ibid.

[107] ibid.

[108] G Jonitz, 'Medical Success Leads to Medical Error: How Health Professionals Accept Responsibility for Safety' (Plenary Session at the International Forum on Quality and Safety in Health Care, 19 March 2009) (on file with author and the Bundesärztekammer in Berlin).

[109] 'Beschlussprotokoll des 108 Deutschen Ärztetages' (3–6 May 2005), www.bundesaerztekammer.de/fileadmin/user_upload/_old-files/downloads/Beschluesse108.pdf.

[110] See Aktionsbündnis Patientensicherheit (APS), 'Das APS im Kurzportrait', www.aps-ev.de/kurzportrait; G Jonitz and S Barth, 'Etablierung von Patientensicherheit – national und international' (2013) 15 *Trauma und Berufskrankheit* 154.

[111] ibid.

[112] Jonitz and Barth (n 110).

5s project, which aimed to reduce five major patient safety issues in five countries over five years), to collaboration on national projects (like the Clean Hands Campaign, designed to reduce treatment-associated infections), to development of regional projects (like Safe in the Hospital, a pilot project designed to improve patient communication in Hessian hospitals), to research designed to better integrate patient safety concepts into medical, pharmaceutical, and psychotherapeutic education.[113]

Later in 2005, ÄZQ organised Germany's Critical Incident Reporting System (CIRS) with sponsorship from the National Association of Statutory Health Insurance Physicians and the German Medical Association.[114] The CIRS network encompasses systems that allow institutional, regional, and nationwide analysis of error reports as well as discipline-specific systems.[115] CIRS has enabled healthcare institutions in Germany to target organisational deficiencies through near-miss error reporting and analysis.[116] APS's project CIRS *forte*, funded by the Innovation Fund of the Federal Joint Committee, developed resources to support the implementation of error reporting and learning systems in outpatient settings.[117]

In 2009, APS established the Institute for Patient Safety (*Institut für Patientensicherheit*; IfPS) at Bonn University, which became the first institution in Germany dedicating academic research to patient safety.[118] Although IfPS's initial mission was to evaluate the implementation and effectiveness of APS's recommendations for action, the Institute's research and teaching activities have since expanded to encompass patient safety research, innovation, practical recommendations, and training at national and international levels.[119]

On 26 February 2013, Germany's Patients' Rights Act (*Patientenrechtegesetz*) was enacted to address growing public concern regarding medical errors.[120] The Act includes measures that attempt to both improve patient safety and strengthen patients' rights.[121] The law requires providers to implement risk and quality management and patient complaint systems.[122] The Patients' Rights Act also mandates internal near-miss error-reporting systems and offers financial

[113] See APS, 'Aktionsbündnis Patientensicherheit', www.aps-ev.de.

[114] See Jonitz (n 108) (regarding the establishment of APS); Bundesärztekammer, 'CIRSmedical.de – Critical Incident Reporting System', www.cirsmedical.de.

[115] Bundesärztekammer, 'Netzwerk CIRSmedical.de', www.cirsmedical.de/cirs.

[116] Jonitz (n 114).

[117] APS, 'CIRSforte', www.cirsforte.de/.

[118] Pauli (n 81).

[119] See Jonitz and Barth (n 110); Universitätsklinikum Bonn, 'Institut für Patientensicherheit (IfPS)', www.ukbonn.de/ifps.

[120] Gesetz zur Verbesserung der Rechte von Patientinnen und Patienten (25 February 2013) Bundesgesetzblatt (BGBl) I 277.

[121] See Deutscher Bundestag, 'Antwort der Bundesregierung auf die Kleine Anfrage der Abgeordneten Maria Klein-Schmeink, Elisabeth Scharfenberg, Kordula Schulz-Asche, weiterer Abgeordneter und der Fraktion BÜNDNIS 90/DIE GRÜNEN' (Drucksache 18/10022, 2016), dserver.bundestag.de/btd/18/102/1810203.pdf.

[122] Sozialgesetzbuch V (SGB V) 20 December 1988 BGBl I, as amended, § 135a.

incentives for participation in cross-facility error-reporting systems, both of which enable organisational learning from adverse events.[123] IfPS reported a drastic increase in the number of hospitals with internal CIRS from 2010 to 2015, signalling that the Patients' Rights Act's legislative mandate had a positive impact on the uptake of error reporting and learning systems as an organisational learning mechanism in German hospitals.[124]

At the global level, the WHO first addressed patient safety on a global scale at its 2002 World Health Assembly.[125] Noting that avoidable adverse events were a significant cause of human suffering, it passed resolution WHA55.18 on 'Quality of care: patient safety', urging Member States 'to pay the closest possible attention to the problem of patient safety'.[126] Since then, the WHO has leveraged its global network to bring together all stakeholders in the healthcare industry for the purpose of improving patient safety and managing healthcare risks.[127] In 2004, it launched the World Alliance for Patient Safety (WAPS) to unite Member States and pool their resources to advance an international patient safety agenda.[128] Like the IOM, the WAPS accepts that most adverse events are caused by organisational and systemic deficiencies and recommends preventive measures that change the system instead of those that target individual practices or products.[129] At its inception, the WAPS framed the international task of improving patient safety as follows:

> Enhancing the safety of patients includes three complementary actions: preventing adverse events; making them visible; and mitigating their effects when they occur. This requires: (a) increased ability to learn from mistakes, through better reporting systems, skillful investigation of incidents and responsible sharing of data; (b) greater capacity to anticipate mistakes and probe systemic weaknesses that might lead to an adverse event; (c) identifying existing knowledge resources, within and outside the health sector; and (d) improvements in the health-care delivery system itself, so that structures are reconfigured, incentives are realigned, and quality is placed at the core of the system. In general, national programmes are built around these principles.[130]

[123] See SGB V § 135a (mandate); SGB V § 137 (financial incentives).

[124] J Lauterberg, 'ABSCHLUSSBERICHT: Befragung zum Einführungsstand von klinischem Risiko-Management (kRM) in deutschen Krankenhäusern' (IfPS, 2012), www.aps-ev.de/wp-content/uploads/2016/08/KRM_Abschlussbericht_final_0.pdf (2010 statistics); F McDermott et al, 'Deutschlandweite Befragung zum Einführungsstand des klinischen Risikomanagements' (IfPS, 2016), www.aps-ev.de/wp-content/uploads/2016/08/ifps-beitrag-3.pdf (2015 statistics).

[125] World Health Organization (WHO), 'Resolutions', www.who.int/teams/integrated-health-services/patient-safety/policy/resolutions.

[126] WHO, 'Quality of Care: Patient Safety' (WHA55.18, 18 May 2002), apps.who.int/gb/archive/pdf_files/WHA55/ewha5518.pdf?ua=1&ua=1.

[127] See generally WHO, 'Patient safety: making health care safer' (2017), iris.who.int/items/43678287-6384-4947-a07b-ab07fbb4eaa4.

[128] WHO, 'World Alliance for Patient Safety' (27 October 2004), www.who.int/news/item/27-10-2004-world-alliance-for-patient-safety.

[129] WHO, 'World Alliance for Patient Safety: Forward Programme' (October 2004), iris.who.int/server/api/core/bitstreams/02e18d2b-517e-41f6-814c-09789b75e8bb/content.

[130] ibid.

In 2005, the WHO launched its first Global Patient Safety Challenge, an initiative to identify a patient safety risk and collaborate with international leaders to propose solutions.[131] The challenges have thus far addressed infections, surgery risks, and medication safety.[132] In 2005, the WHO also released its draft guidelines for adverse event reporting and learning systems. These guidelines identify voluntary error reporting as a valuable tool for organisational learning and error prevention.[133] The WHO continues to promote error reporting and learning systems by providing tools that facilitate error reporting and analysis such as the Minimum Information Model for Patient Safety, and updated guidelines for reporting and learning systems.[134]

Other WHO patient safety initiatives include: (1) Global Ministerial Summits on Patient Safety, which promote patient safety at the political level; (2) the Global Patient Safety Network, which collects and shares evidence from international stakeholders to encourage development and maintenance of patient safety guidelines and best practices; (3) the Global Knowledge Sharing Platform for Patient Safety, which provides an online platform for sharing systemic analysis and response to adverse events; (4) patient safety education and training resources, including the Multi-professional Patient Safety Curriculum Guide and the Educational Councils Network; (5) checklists that minimise patient safety risks, including the WHO Safe Childbirth Checklist and the WHO Surgical Safety Checklist; (6) Patients for Patient Safety, which provides a patient advocacy network for patients and their families; and (7) the development of tools and metrics for measuring patient safety.[135]

The Organisation for Economic Co-operation and Development (OECD) has also turned its attention to the global problem of medical errors.[136] In a 2017 working paper, the OECD estimated that the annual global health, financial, and economic costs of patient harm caused by treatment errors amount to trillions of dollars.[137] It also concluded that systemic and organisational changes were needed to prevent errors and reduce resulting patient harm.[138] Like the IOM, the OECD recognised that modern healthcare systems are complex and dynamic, and as a result, require complex and dynamic interventions to prevent medical errors.[139] These interventions, it argued, must take a

[131] See generally C Kilpatrick et al, 'WHO First Global Patient Safety Challenge: Clean Care Is Safer Care, Contributing to the Training of Health-Care Workers Around the Globe' (2010) 7 *International Journal of Infection Control*.

[132] WHO (n 127) 5.

[133] WHO, 'WHO Draft Guidelines for Adverse Event Reporting and Learning Systems: From Information to Action' (2005), www.who.int/publications/i/item/WHO-EIP-SPO-QPS-05.3.

[134] WHO (n 127) 11.

[135] ibid.

[136] L Slawomirskii et al, 'The Economics of Patient Safety: Strengthening a Value-Based Approach to Reducing Patient Harm at National Level' (2017) OECD Health Working Papers No 96, www.oecd-ilibrary.org/social-issues-migration-health/the-economics-of-patient-safety_5a9858cd-en.

[137] ibid.

[138] ibid.

[139] ibid.

systems perspective and focus on creating an organisational culture that fosters patient safety.[140]

2.2 THE IMPORTANCE OF CLINICAL RISK MANAGEMENT

As the modern healthcare delivery system becomes more complex, new avenues for medical errors emerge. Quick emphasises, however, that concern for patient safety is not new; the fundamental principle of 'do no harm' has long guided medical practice.[141] What is a relatively new development is the shift in thinking about medical errors as individual failings of medical professionals to thinking about medical errors within the larger narrative of patient safety.[142] Quick welcomes this shift in perspective, noting that 'the language of safety' is concerned with protecting patients (rather than regulating providers).[143] Existing literature is ripe with error taxonomies that help us understand the causes of errors and how they might be prevented.[144] Whether errors are rooted in matters of knowledge, perception, skill, or another source, one thing is clear: they are fundamentally human. Medical errors result then from well-known and entirely foreseeable limitations of human cognition. Patient safety is therefore defined not only as the absence of individual errors, but as the presence of activities and culture that aim to prevent risks.[145]

Healthcare institutions face a broad array of risks relating not only to the provision of healthcare treatment, but also to financial, managerial, and external activities.[146] Andrea Pauli defines risk in healthcare using the following formula: R (risk) = P (probability of a negative event occurring) × L (consequences of the negative event).[147] For jurists, this definition of risk has an unavoidable connection to American Judge Learned Hand's definition of negligence, which he describes as occurring when B (the burden of preventing an accident) is less than P (the probability of the accident) multiplied by L (the magnitude of the loss).[148] The inextricable connection between the definition of risk itself and liability for risks that materialise in healthcare must be observed, because as Ofri unenthusiastically points out, some level of risk acceptance is necessary.[149] Ofri compares the risk–benefit analysis involved with a daily activity like crossing a busy street to get a fresh bagel (the chance and degree of harm associated with being hit by a car and the necessity of breakfast) with the dozens of medical decisions

[140] ibid.
[141] Quick (n 4).
[142] ibid.
[143] ibid.
[144] ibid.
[145] ibid.
[146] See Pauli (n 81).
[147] ibid.
[148] *United States v Carroll Towing Co* 159 F 2d 169 (2d Cir 1947).
[149] D Ofri, *When We Do Harm: A Doctor Confronts Medical Error* (Boston, Beacon Press, 2020).

made hourly by healthcare providers 'trellised across the dizzying intricacies of the human body'.[150] Briner observes that: 'Risks associated with patient care can never be completely eliminated, therefore, clinical risk management plays a crucial role in enabling hospitals to enhance patient safety.'[151] However imperfect risk management efforts are at eliminating patient harm, reasonable efforts to identify and eliminate risks that can injure patients should be standard operating procedure in healthcare organisations.

Clinical risks are those specifically related to the quality and safety of patient care.[152] Managing clinical risks occurs at the organisational level through the process of clinical risk management.[153] Clinical risk management is defined 'as all structures, processes, instruments and activities that enable hospital employees to identify, analyze, contain and manage risks while providing clinical treatment and patient care'.[154] It seeks to eliminate risk of patient harm by identifying, analysing, and taking measures to prevent activities and processes that have the potential to harm patients during the treatment process.[155] Effective clinical risk management 'integrates both proactive and reactive approaches and frames the hospital as a system, instead of focusing on individuals and their potential for committing errors'.[156]

Hart describes treatment as only one element in the broader medical treatment process.[157] While medical treatment is carried out by individual medical providers and governed by medical standards, he distinguishes the medical treatment process as 'the organisational and institutional framework within which the medical treatment is carried out'.[158] This process is governed by interdisciplinary standards guided by medicine, law, and organisational science.[159] In order to effectively prevent medical errors, clinical risk management must look beyond medical treatment to the broader treatment process to develop an interdisciplinary and organisationally focused error prevention strategy.[160] In the Luxembourg Declaration on Patient Safety, the EU Commission found that 'A precondition for risk management is an open and trusting working environment with a culture that focuses on learning from near-misses and adverse events as opposed to concentrating on individual 'blame and shame' and subsequent punishment.'[161] The IOM's report became an important catalyst for shifting the

[150] ibid.
[151] M Briner, 'Assessing Hospitals' Clinical Risk Management: Development of a Monitoring Instrument' (2010) 10 *BMC Health Services Research* article no 337.
[152] See Pauli (n 81).
[153] ibid.
[154] Briner (n 151).
[155] WHO, 'Patient Safety Curriculum Guide: Multi-Professional Edition' (2011), www.who.int/publications/i/item/9789241501958.
[156] Briner (n 151).
[157] D Hart, 'Patientensicherheit nach dem Patientenrechtegesetz' (2013) 31 *Medizinrecht* 159.
[158] ibid.
[159] ibid.
[160] Briner (n 151).
[161] European Commission (n 77).

international medical community's focus from blaming individual providers for medical errors to creating an organisational culture of safety conducive to successful clinical risk management.

Preventing errors through a systems approach is not a singular task, but rather one that requires the cooperation of all stakeholders in the healthcare system.[162] The IOM identified internal factors (organisational leadership and culture) and external factors (safety-promoting knowledge and tools, professional leadership, legislative and regulatory action, and demand for improvement from purchasers and consumers), which combine to impact patient safety.[163] A detailed discussion of recommended improvements in the internal environment is beyond the scope of this book, as are the external factors regarding national research goals or the roles of consumers and purchasers. Instead, this book focuses on expanding the view of the legislative and regulatory factors that influence patient safety, specifically by looking at the topic of medical errors within the theoretical and operational workings of the medical liability system.

The ideal role of the external environment in propelling systemic change is to make errors costly enough to induce internal investment in patient safety.[164] The idea is that legislative and regulatory actions can create minimum safety standards that, if violated, would result in sanctions for the healthcare organisation.[165] The IOM posited that enforcing these standards across the industry would 'level [the] playing field' by requiring all healthcare organisations to make the same minimum investment in patient safety.[166] It broadly defined regulation and legislation to include, 'any form of public policy or legal influence, such as licensing or the liability system'.[167] In terms of licensing, accreditation, and professional standards, the IOM recommended the creation of minimum patient safety standards.[168] The IOM stopped short, however, of recognising the liability system's role in enforcing these minimum safety standards. Rather, its treatment of the liability system as an external influence was limited to the system's chilling effect on the disclosure and discussion of errors by providers who feared malpractice litigation.[169] To combat this problem, the IOM recommended federal peer-review protection for patient safety data in error-reporting systems that would shield providers' disclosure and analysis of non-injury-causing medical errors and enable the development of successful error-prevention strategies.[170] There is, however, a bigger, more central role that the medical liability system has in the larger patient safety agenda, namely, its ability to hold

[162] See generally IOM (n 5).
[163] ibid.
[164] ibid.
[165] ibid.
[166] ibid.
[167] ibid.
[168] ibid.
[169] ibid.
[170] ibid.

organisations legally responsible for preventing and minimising errors through the process of clinical risk management.

In a perfect world, healthcare organisations could take on the task of organisational improvement through clinical risk management for purely altruistic reasons with no concern for the liability consequences or implementation costs. In reality, as Ofri points out, 'bottom line is a powerful motivator', and healthcare organisations will respond to external influences that levy legal and financial consequences for failure to reasonably manage risks that can cause patient harm.[171] As discussed in this chapter, modern error prevention research shows that many of those risks stem from deficiencies buried in the belly of the organisational beast. In their review of 889 claims of malpractice involving an injury caused by one or more medical errors, Mello and Studdert found that system factors contributed to patient injuries in 56 per cent of the cases.[172] The system factors identified in their study included those related to communication, supervision, personnel management, staffing, distractions, fatigue, ergonomic failures, and technology failures.[173] Mello and Studdert called for patient safety interventions that 'require the commitment of organisational leadership, centralized planning, and the mobilization of resources at the organizational level'.[174] This means that risk management efforts, or lack thereof, can have a direct impact on medical error rates within the organisation. There are well researched and widely available clinical risk management tools and resources that enable organisations to identify and eliminate (or at least mitigate) those risks, making the healthcare system safer for patients. The medical liability system can act as a positive external influence by holding healthcare organisations responsible for complying with reasonable clinical risk management standards of care.

2.3 DIGITALISATION, ARTIFICIAL INTELLIGENCE AND PATIENT SAFETY

Health technologies are an integral part of increasingly digitalised healthcare systems.[175] Modern healthcare offers a broad range of medical technologies for diagnosis and treatment, from digital diagnostics[176] and patient monitor-

[171] Ofri (n 149).

[172] MM Mello and DM Studdert, 'Deconstructing Negligence: The Role of Individual and System Factors in Causing Medical Injuries' (2008) 96 *Georgetown Law Journal* 599.

[173] ibid.

[174] ibid.

[175] A Bodnari and J Travis, 'Scaling Enterprise AI in Healthcare: The Role of Governance in Risk Mitigation Frameworks' (2025) 8 *npj Digital Medicine* 272.

[176] See, eg Y Shi et al, 'The Value of Machine Learning Approaches in the Diagnosis of Early Gastric Cancer: A Systematic Review and Meta-Analysis' (2024) 22 *World Journal of Surgical Oncology* article no 40; R Lindsey et al, 'Deep Neural Network Improves Fracture Detection by Clinicians' (2018) 115 *Proceedings of the National Academy of Sciences* 11591.

ing[177] to AI-driven clinical support[178] and robotic surgery systems.[179] Healthcare organisations also use technologies to improve the efficiency and efficacy of healthcare delivery and administrative processes, including electronic systems for maintaining and sharing health records, communicating with patients, transmitting medical orders, organising staff, and monitoring equipment.[180] These technologies are designed to deliver benefits that improve healthcare quality and access, but whether those benefits are realised in practice depends heavily on how they are integrated into the complex organisational processes that underly healthcare delivery. Physician experiences with electronic medical records highlight how the same technology designed to improve healthcare delivery can, when poorly implemented, source new risks.[181] The more physicians struggle to record and locate clinical information across multiple, potentially incompatible, electronic records systems, the more likely they are to miss something important.

Interoperability, usability, resource and infrastructure challenges present common integration barriers for new technologies that can only be overcome by robust organisational processes for technology selection, implementation, training, oversight, reporting, and maintenance.[182] Bodnari and Travis warn that 'AI models rely heavily on the data they are trained on, and if this data is incomplete, biased, or unrepresentative, the resulting predictions or recommendations can be flawed' and that 'implementation risks emerge when AI systems are integrated into healthcare workflows without sufficient planning and oversight'.[183] Technology that is difficult to use, poorly integrated, or inadequately monitored can introduce new error pathways, disrupt clinical workflows, and erode trust between clinicians, patients, and systems.[184] AI-driven technologies add new complexity to the processes required for safe technology integration. While traditional medical technologies performed predictable and mechanistic functions, making failure detection and response technologically (though perhaps not culturally) straightforward, complex AI-driven software can introduce less predictable and less understandable failure modes. This complexity means that AI-systems are more dynamic, which sources both benefits and risks

[177] See generally R Sinha, 'The Role and Impact of New Technologies on Healthcare Systems' (2024) 3 *Discover Health Systems* article no 96.

[178] See, eg M Elhaddad and S Hamam, 'AI-Driven Clinical Decision Support Systems: An Ongoing Pursuit of Potential' (2024) 16 *Cureus* e57728.

[179] See, eg JK Wah, 'The Rise of Robotics and AI-Assisted Surgery in Modern Healthcare' (2025) 19 *Journal of Robotic Surgery* 311.

[180] D Nasef et al, 'Integrating Artificial Intelligence in Clinical Practice, Hospital Management, and Health Policy: Literature Review' (2025) 9 *Journal of Hospital Management and Health Policy* online; T Davenport and R Kalakota, 'The Potential for Artificial Intelligence in Healthcare' (2019) 6 *Future Healthcare Journal* 94.

[181] DC Classen et al, 'Inpatient EHR User Experience and Hospital EHR Safety Performance' (2023) 6 *JAMA Network Open* e2333152.

[182] Bodnari and Travis (n 175).

[183] ibid.

[184] ibid.

to patient safety,[185] depending largely on how organisations govern their integration and use.[186] Bodnari and Travis note that organisational safeguards for validating and continually assessing AI model performance and data quality are indispensable for managing risks of AI-driven medical technologies. They also call for 'clear implementation protocols' to avoid risks of misuse and overreliance on AI-driven systems.[187] The lack of such safeguards and protocols creates the latent conditions that Reason's Swiss Cheese Model identifies as organisational design failures, which can align with other factors to cause patient harm. This highlights that organisational behaviour can influence whether AI-driven technologies have an overall positive or negative impact on patient safety.

The complexity of AI-driven technologies also introduces new liability concerns that amplify the need for greater focus on healthcare organisations' risk management activities in the medical liability system. As discussed in chapter one, while AI-driven technologies might mimic human behaviour, they cannot be negligent and thus cannot anchor vicarious liability claims against the healthcare organisations that deploy them. This creates a risk that individual providers will become a 'liability sink' for AI-related medical injuries, even in the absence of provider negligence.[188] Of course, increasing blame for individual providers in response to growing complexity in the healthcare system will only aggravate the negative impacts on patient safety already caused by individual-focused liability. Additionally, AI integration in the healthcare system can scale risk management failures, causing them to impact more patients and cause more injuries, further supporting an approach to organisational liability that can target upstream risk management activities.

Healthcare technologies also become embedded within the complex sociotechnical systems that underly healthcare delivery, creating more challenges for safe integration. Quick provides crucial insight into 'cultural deficits' in the healthcare system, explaining that 'the myth of infallibility; a closed hierarchical system; the fear of blame and punishment; the normalisation of errors, a reluctance to speak up about safety, and a pragmatic "mend and make do" mentality' result in poor safety culture.[189] When organisational design failures manifest in clinical practice, this 'blame' culture can make it difficult for individual providers to voice concerns about poorly functioning technology without appearing incompetent or obstructionist.[190] Instead, providers often adapt to environments with technology failures by using workarounds to 'circumvent

[185] See MN Duffourc, 'Malpractice by the Autonomous AI Physician' (2023) 2023 *Illinois Journal of Law, Technology & Policy* 1.

[186] See Quick (n 4).

[187] Bodnari and Travis (n 175).

[188] T Lawton et al, 'Clinicians Risk Becoming "Liability Sinks" for Artificial Intelligence' (2024) 11 *Future Healthcare Journal* 100007.

[189] Quick (n 4).

[190] Leape (n 2).

or temporarily "fix" perceived workflow hindrances'.[191] This adaptation mentality shifts responsibility for managing system deficiencies to individual providers, leaving the latent conditions in the system design unaddressed.[192] Workarounds signal system failures, and when organisations allow them to persist, they can introduce patient safety risks and prevent organisations from correcting system design defects.[193] Unsurprisingly, there are numerous organisational and work process factors that trigger workarounds; Debono et al identified staffing workloads, productivity pressures, negative culture, lack of leadership and clear delineation of roles and responsibilities, mismatches between organisational processes and technology, insufficient resources and information, and inadequate equipment and working environments.[194] Koppel et al found that similar organisational factors influenced workarounds related to the use of barcoded medication administration systems.[195] They recommend points for organisational redesign and highlight that evaluation of new technology should be continuous because 'New workarounds will emerge in response to changes in technology, workflow, and patient types.'[196]

Robust clinical risk management is essential for addressing technology-related patient safety risks. To make matters more complex, new technologies can be used to improve the risk management process itself. Ferrara et al highlight how AI-driven technologies, when properly implemented, can help predict the risks of hospital-acquired infections, prevent diagnostic and medication errors, and improve errors reporting systems.[197] Responsibly addressing the risks of new technologies through the process of clinical risk management and using new technologies to improve clinical risk management processes is an admittedly formidable task, but also one that is indispensable in a complex digitalised healthcare system. Since organisational behaviour constitutes a critical variable for determining whether new technologies improve or undermine patient safety, the impetus for realigning the medical liability system to facilitate, or even promote, behaviour that increases patient safety is stronger than ever.

[191] DS Debono et al, 'Nurses' Workarounds in Acute Healthcare Settings: A Scoping Review' (2013) 13 *BMC Health Services Research* 175.

[192] ibid.

[193] See JR Halbesleben et al, 'Rework and Workarounds in Nurse Medication Administration Process' (2010) 35 *Health Care Management Review* 124.

[194] Debono et al (n 191).

[195] R Koppel et al, 'Workarounds to Barcode Medication Administration Systems: Their Occurrences, Causes, and Threats to Patient Safety' (2008) 15 *Journal of the American Medical Informatics Association* 408.

[196] ibid.

[197] M Ferrara et al, 'Risk Management and Patient Safety in the Artificial Intelligence Era: A Systematic Review' (2024) 12 *Healthcare* 549.

Part II

The Medical Liability System

3

Medical Liability Framework

THE MEDICAL LIABILITY system is designed to resolve disputes between individuals and healthcare providers involving harm caused by the provision of healthcare. Medical liability in both the United States (US) and Germany developed within the general framework of private law, and both jurisdictions adopt a fault-based approach to medical liability.[1] This chapter examines the fault-based medical liability frameworks in the US and Germany and their capacity to deter the kinds of organisational behaviours that chapter two identified as the primary causes of preventable medical injuries.

3.1 COMPARING FAULT-BASED MEDICAL LIABILITY SYSTEMS

Although both the US and German medical liability systems operate using remarkably similar fault-based principles, there are two notable distinctions. First, the two countries use different systems of law – the US is a common law jurisdiction while Germany is a civil law jurisdiction. Second, the US typically approaches medical negligence as a tortious cause of action, while Germany usually takes a contract-based approach.

Turning first to the system of law distinction, legal rules develop differently in common and civil law jurisdictions. In common law jurisdictions, legal rules are generally derived from case law, while legal rules in civil law jurisdictions are generally derived from statutes.[2] This source-of-law distinction also impacts the development of law in the two systems. In civil law jurisdictions, legal scholars have a significant impact on the codification and, later, the interpretation of legal rules.[3] In Germany, this enables a mutually beneficial relationship between academic writers and German courts through which academics develop and

[1] M Stauch, *The Law of Medical Negligence in England and Germany: A Comparative Analysis* (Oxford, Hart Publishing, 2008); B Watson-Dunham, *Medical Malpractice Law and Litigation* (Clifton Park, Delmar Cengage Learning, 2006). Private law generally governs medical liability in the US and Germany regardless of whether the hospital is a state or private institution. D Giesen, *International Medical Malpractice Law: A Comparative Law Study of Civil Liability Arising from Medical Care* (Tübingen, JCB Mohr (Paul Siebeck), 1988); A Pauli, *Risikomanagement und CIRS als Gegen stand der Krankenhaushaftung* (Baden-Baden, Nomos, 2013).

[2] Stauch (n 1).

[3] ibid.

revise legal theories in response to judicial criticism, and courts adopt legal theories put forth by academics.[4] In common law jurisdictions, lawyers and judges are the main forces propelling changes in the controlling case law.[5] In the US, this means that while legal scholars might influence the interpretation of legal rules by appellate courts, they generally play a minor role in the development of case law by judges in the courts of first instance. Nevertheless, the application of legal rules to specific cases in both systems requires judicial interpretation of the broader legal rules, whether they are found in cases or statutes.[6] Mark Stauch notes that, 'Ultimately, any legal rule – be it contained in a code, statute, or judicial decision – must be subject to further interpretation in the course of its application to settle a given dispute.'[7] Indeed, Jörg Fedtke credits the role of German judges as 'oracles of the law' for the stability of the German Civil Code (*Bürgerliches Gesetzbuch*; BGB) over the past century and beyond.[8] He describes German judges as 'no less influential with respect to the development of the [private] law than their Anglo-American counterparts'.[9]

The system of law distinction has less practical importance in the context of US and German medical liability law because medical liability law in both jurisdictions was largely developed by judges who applied the general rules in the law of obligations to decide medical liability disputes.[10] According to Dieter Giesen:

> [M]edical malpractice law, then, not only in the Common Law tradition, but also in all the principal Civil Law countries, remains judge-made law. In the case of Civil Law countries, this takes the form of a "vast gloss overlaying a few exiguous Code articles."[11]

Pauli described German medical liability law as 'an independent area of law which developed in the second half of the 20th century from the principles of contract and tort law and is decisively shaped by the guidelines of the judicial decisions issued in this area (judge's law)'.[12] There is, however, one recent development in German medical malpractice law that echoes Germany's civil law roots. In 2013, Germany passed the Patients' Rights Act, which introduced the 'treatment contract' (*Behandlungsvertrag*) into the German Civil Code. The Patients' Rights Act regulates the rights and duties of physicians and patients regarding consent, obligations to provide information, treatment documentation requirements, inspection of medical records, and the burden of proof

[4] B Markesinis et al, *The German Law of Torts: A Comparative Treatise*, 5th edn (Oxford, Hart Publishing, 2021).
[5] Stauch (n 1).
[6] ibid.
[7] ibid.
[8] J Fedtke, 'The Culture of German Tort Law' (2012) 3 *Journal of European Tort Law* 183.
[9] ibid.
[10] Stauch (n 1).
[11] Giesen (n 1).
[12] Pauli (n 1).

in medical malpractice cases.[13] Still, because the Patients' Rights Act is largely a codification of the existing medical liability case law,[14] the system of law distinction remains less of an obstacle in a comparative analysis of medical liability in the US and Germany. This is because while the Patients' Rights Act codified medical malpractice law in Germany to some extent, practically, the adjudication of medical malpractice disputes operates under the same legal principles originally developed in the German case law. Crucially, the principles that control findings of fault, causation, and damages in medical liability cases in German law are comparable to those used by US courts. The Patients' Rights Act, through its designation of the treatment contract as the liability-controlling instrument, highlights the second jurisdictional distinction in the US and German medical liability systems.

Turning to the second distinction, basing liability claims in tort versus contract law reflects a fundamental difference in how the two jurisdictions conceptualise the legal relationship between patients and providers. Although both jurisdictions recognise concurrent contractual and tortious claims for medical malpractice, the US favours the application of tort law, while Germany favours contract law.[15] Like the civil–common law distinction, there are several reasons why this tort–contract distinction has limited significance in a comparative analysis of American and German medical liability law.

The broadest reason is taken from Sanne Taekema's theory of pragmatist interactionism, which posits that 'the legal assessment of cases of tort and contract is largely based on the normative force of interactional expectancies'.[16] According to Taekema, formal rules governing contract and tort law do not operate in isolation but rather within the framework of more flexible standards influenced by the expectations of social interactions.[17] As a result, the rigid tort–contract distinction in medical malpractice claims is mitigated by the application of broader standards informed by the expectations of participants in the healthcare system.

Additionally, regardless of whether a medical malpractice lawsuit is based on tort or contract law, both jurisdictions rely upon a fault-based model of liability. In both jurisdictions, the imposition of liability on healthcare providers who breach a legal duty of care, regardless of whether that duty is grounded in contract or tort, will follow similar negligence-based principles. As Giesen explains:

> [T]here is little difference in practice in the possible consequences of a physician's breach of his contractual duties in the field of medical law or his duty of care in the tort of negligence. Obligations are meant to be fulfilled, promises are meant to be kept. And

[13] Bürgerliches Gesetzbuch (BGB) 18 August 1896 RGBl I, as amended, §§ 630a–h.

[14] See D Hart, 'Patientensicherheit nach dem Patientenrechtegesetz' (2013) 31 *Medizinrecht* 159.

[15] See Giesen (n 1).

[16] S Taekema, 'Private Law as an Open Legal Order: Understanding Contract and Tort as Interactional Law' (2014) 43 *Netherlands Journal of Legal Philosophy* 140.

[17] ibid.

> contractual terms implied by law are usually identical with duties arising in tort from one party's 'undertaking' to act for another, as in the case of professional services.[18]

As a result, the fault-based law of negligence dominates the assessment of medical liability under either tort or contract in both the US and Germany.[19]

In the US, the law of negligence holds a person who fails to act reasonably under the circumstances liable for injury that this substandard conduct causes to another.[20] As the nineteenth century saw rapid development in medical science and the emergence of medicine as a profession, the liability system also began to hold medical practitioners accountable for patient injuries under general negligence principles.[21] In 1855, the Supreme Court of Maine articulated the standard by which medical professionals should be held:

> The law implies an undertaking on the part of apothecaries and surgeons, that they will use a reasonable degree of care and skill in the treatment of their patients. They are held responsible for injuries resulting from a want of ordinary care and skill.[22]

Although US courts have recognised that implied contractual duties arise from a treatment relationship between a doctor and a patient, they nevertheless view medical malpractice as a tort action for negligence. The Maryland Court of Appeals, in responding to a litigant's argument that contract law venue provisions were applicable in a medical malpractice case, stated that:

> While it may be as appellant argues that a physician impliedly contracts with those who employ him that he possesses and will exercise a reasonable degree of care, skill and learning . . . malpractice is predicated upon the failure to exercise requisite medical skill and, being tortious in nature, general rules of negligence usually apply in determining liability . . . The great majority of courts that have considered the question have concluded that medical malpractice actions sound in tort, and not in contract.[23]

Negligence also features prominently in the German Civil Code to assess both tort and contract claims. German law defines negligence as, 'the failure to observe the socially required level of care'.[24] In tort, BGB §823(1) provides a legal cause of action for those injured by negligent conduct of another. In contract, BGB §§ 276(1) and 280(1) provide a cause of action for negligent performance of a contract. The German Federal Supreme Court (*Bundesgerichtshof*; BGH) has confirmed the unity of contractual and tortious duties of care in the provision of medical treatment, stating:

[18] Giesen (n 1).

[19] ibid (civil liability in civil and common law countries is largely based on negligence, unless superseded by a no-fault or strict liability scheme).

[20] Watson-Dunham (n 1).

[21] ibid.

[22] *Simonds v Henry* 39 Me 155 (Me 1855).

[23] *Benson v Mays* 227 A2d 220 (Md Ct App 1967).

[24] Stauch (n 1).

> The Defendant owed the claimant a duty in both contract and tort to provide appropriate medical care. These duties, deriving respectively from the treatment contract and from the positive assumption in tort of the task of treating the claimant, were in effect identical.[25]

A final reason for the diminished importance of the tort–contract distinction is the fact that German medical liability law developed primarily under a tort law regime.[26] This is because, prior to 2002, awards for pain and suffering (*Schmerzengeld*) were not available in contract and the patient had to rely upon a concurrent tort claim to recover non-economic damages.[27] Mark Stauch observed that, 'until recently tort law continued to have an important, indeed arguably dominant, role in medical malpractice actions [in Germany]'.[28] In sum, despite their differences, both US and German medical liability systems operate under similar negligence-based principles developed within the larger framework of tort law.

3.2 DETERRENCE AS A GOAL OF FAULT-BASED LIABILITY

Since both the US and Germany take a fault-based approach to medical liability, the two systems share, in differing measures and with varying success, common goals. These goals include compensation and deterrence.[29] Though several critics of the medical liability system, particularly in the US, describe the system as punitive, punishment is generally not a recognised goal of modern tort law outside of rare instances in which punitive damages for particularly egregious conduct are allowed.[30] Compensation is regarded as the 'central purpose' for awarding damages in medical malpractice litigation.[31] Though some legal scholars regard compensation as the *only* legitimate goal of the tort system,[32] most

[25] Bundesgerichtshof (BGH) 20 September 1988 NJW 1989, 767.
[26] Stauch (n 1).
[27] ibid.
[28] ibid.
[29] D Shuman, 'The Psychology of Deterrence in Tort Law' (1993) 42 *University of Kansas Law Review* 115; MM Mello and DM Studdert, 'The Medical Malpractice System: Structure and Performance' in WM Sage and R Kersh (eds), *Medical Malpractice and the US Health Care System* (Cambridge, Cambridge University Press, 2006); European Group on Tort Law, *Principles of European Tort Law: Text and Commentary* (Vienna, Springer, 2005).
[30] See BS Markesinis, 'Tort' (Britannica.com, last updated 18 February 2026), www.britannica.com/topic/tort. ('Most authors would probably agree that punishment and appeasement are no longer major aims of tort law.'); Legal Information Institute, 'Tort' Cornell Law School, www.law.cornell.edu/wex/tort. ('In contrast, tort law addresses private wrongs and has a central purpose of compensating the victim rather than punishing the wrongdoer.').
[31] Giesen (n 1). But see TA Heller, 'An Overview of Medical Malpractice Law in the United States Including Legislative and the Health Care Industry's Responses to Increased Claims' (2017) 10 *Medicine Law & Society* 139 (the primary purpose of tort law is to prevent accidents and compensation is a corollary goal).
[32] RA Posner and WM Landes, 'The Positive Economic Theory of Tort Law' (1980) 15 *Georgia Law Review* 851.

recognise deterrence as a secondary goal of tort law, particularly for fault-based liability. For example, Howard Latin maintains that 'Litigation is a very expensive method for accident loss allocation, and the transaction costs of the tort system would not be warranted unless liability achieves some commensurate increase in social utility.'[33]

The measure of the medical liability system's effect on social utility lies in its ability to deter negligent conduct that causes patient injuries.[34] However, the capacity of a fault-based liability system to deter socially unacceptable behaviour is the subject of much interdisciplinary debate. The first question that must be examined is whether deterrence is a recognised goal of the medical liability system in both jurisdictions. Second is the question of whether deterrence is a feasible goal considering both economic and psychological influences on behaviour. Although there is a stronger case in the literature for recognising deterrence as an explicit goal of the US medical liability system, there is evidence that the German system also accepts deterrence as a legitimate goal.

Since the US medical liability system exists as a subset of tort law and deterrence is an often-recognised, albeit hotly debated, goal of modern US tort law, there is little question that deterrence is recognised as a goal of the US medical liability system.[35] In 1970, Guido Calabresi observed that tort law had the ability to affect behaviour of tortfeasors and victims in a way that could result in the reduction of accidents and their costs.[36] Forty-one years later, Andrew Popper vehemently defended deterrence as a virtue of the tort system.[37] Popper maintained that the threat of liability affects how actors behave.[38] Tort law's ability to deter behaviour finds support from prominent American legal minds like Judge Richard Posner as well as from lesser-known judges from all around the country, who discuss the goal of deterrence in their legal decisions.[39] Other academics, like George Priest, who criticises the means that modern tort law uses to achieve deterrence aims, still embrace accident reduction as a legitimate goal. Priest declared that deterrence

> command[s] widespread acceptance [because] [a]ll citizens share the goal of reducing the accident rate both, on moral grounds, because no personal injury can ever be fully compensated and, on economic grounds, because reducing accidents conserves valuable and productive resources in human capital.[40]

[33] H Latin, 'Problem-Solving Behavior and Theories of Tort Liability' (1985) 73 *California Law Review* 677.

[34] See Heller (n 31) (deterrence in tort law is 'a form of social control').

[35] Mello and Studdert (n 29) ('Deterrence is the primary theoretical rationale for the tort liability system.').

[36] RA Posner, 'Guido Calabresi's "The Costs of Accidents": A Reassessment' (2005) 64 *Maryland Law Review* 12; see also Latin (n 33).

[37] AF Popper, 'In Defense of Deterrence' (2012) 75 *Albany Law Review* 101.

[38] ibid.

[39] See Posner and Landes (n 32).

[40] GL Priest, 'Modern Tort Law and Its Reform' (1987) 22 *Valparaiso University Law Review* 1.

While scholars launch reasonable attacks on the actual ability of tort law to deter undesirable behaviour, it is crucial to recognise that those attacks are launched against a generally accepted belief, in practice if not in academia, that deterrence is a legitimate goal of tort law, and hence, a legitimate goal of the American medical liability system.

When considering the goal of deterrence in the German medical liability system, a brief return to the tort–contract distinction is necessary. Of the two private law liability mechanisms, tort law is primarily concerned with prevention of harmful conduct in society generally, while contract law is primarily concerned with compensating an individual for damages incurred because of a broken promise. Giesen explains more thoroughly:

> The *law of contract* primarily exists for the purpose of vindicating an individual interest, for instance, in having the promises of others performed. If the promisor fails, or fails properly, to perform his obligation, the law of contract will award the promise damages for breach of contract in order to put him, so far as possible, in as good a position as if the promise had been kept, or to compensate him for the disappointment of his legally protected expectations under the contract. The *law of torts* (or delict), on the other hand, aims first of all at the prevention of wrongful harm caused by others and if things go wrong, at compensating injuries or distributing losses thereby suffered.[41]

While it is true that contract law is generally less concerned with prevention as a goal, the merging of contract and tort law principles in the fault-based German medical liability system encompasses the goal of deterrence. In principle fault-based liability systems only compensate victims who are damaged by behaviour that needs deterring, ie, negligent behaviour.[42] In other words, a fault-based system has no interest in compensation when the behaviour causing the injury is not the kind of behaviour that society wishes to prevent. From this perspective, while compensation might be a primary goal of medical malpractice liability, in either contract or tort, the compensatory role of any negligence-based system cannot exist without at least a secondary goal of deterring undesirable behaviour. Otherwise, a legal system would opt for a no-fault scheme for compensating medical injuries, such as the one adopted in New Zealand.[43] Indeed, the German Medical Law Association rejected a no-fault scheme for medical injuries partly because it wished to 'preserve a deterrent effect' by subjecting medical conduct to the court system.[44]

Two additional features of Germany's medical liability system support a goal of deterrence. First, the legislative history for the Patients' Rights Act discusses

[41] Giesen (n 1).
[42] Shuman (n 29).
[43] Giesen (n 1).
[44] Stauch (n 1).

the goal of improving patient safety by preventing medical errors.[45] Although the Act's provisions were not adopted exclusively in the Civil Code, this general legislative intent implies that deterrence is a valid goal of the German medical liability system in private law. Second, as already discussed, Germany's medical liability law primarily developed under tort law principles, which implies that the generally recognised goals of tort law, including deterrence, remain relevant in Germany's modern medical liability system, despite its modern contractual anchor.[46]

The second question of whether any fault-based liability regime can effectively deter undesirable behaviour has long attracted the interest of not only legal scholars, but also economists and psychologists. This discussion primarily occurs within the context of the American economic theory of tort law but is also found in the German economic efficiency model of tort law. Additionally, the unique inner workings of the healthcare system influence the extent to which fault-based medical liability can prevent harm-causing behaviours within healthcare organisations.

Turning to the general ability of tort law to deter undesirable behaviour – and dredging up the first, and likely only, time American law students encounter algebra – I begin with Judge Learned Hand's definition of negligence: $B < P \times L$.[47] According to Hand, if the burden of precaution necessary to prevent the accident (B) is less than the probability of the accident (P) multiplied by the magnitude of the loss (L), then the relevant standard of care is breached and the defendant is negligent.[48] This formula, named for Judge Hand, has since been adapted by proponents of a positive economic theory of tort law to define an economic standard of negligence assigning marginal, rather than absolute, values to the Hand Formula.[49] According to Posner, 'This means that it is negligent to use a level of care at which the marginal cost of accident avoidance is less than the marginal benefit from avoidance.'[50]

Tort law's capacity to deter negligent behaviour is rooted in this economic approach and, according to Posner, can be traced back to Oliver Wendell Holmes's 1881 writing *The Common Law*.[51] Influenced by Arthur Pigou's concept of social-cost internalisation and Ronald Coase's idea that common law could be used to internalise social costs, Posner developed an economic theory of tort law, in which deterrence is not only recognised as an effect of tort law, but a feasible goal.[52]

[45] See Deutscher Bundestag, 'Antwort der Bundesregierung auf die Kleine Anfrage der Abgeordneten Maria Klein-Schmeink, Elisabeth Scharfenberg, Kordula Schulz-Asche, weiterer Abgeordneter und der Fraktion BÜNDNIS 90/DIE GRÜNEN' (Drucksache 18/10203, 2016), dip21.bundestag.de/dip21/btd/18/102/1810203.pdf.

[46] See H Kerkmeester and L Visscher, 'Learned Hand in Europe: A Study in the Comparative Law and Economics of Negligence' (2003) *German Working Papers in Law and Economics* Paper 6.

[47] *United States v Carroll Towing Co* 159 F2d 169 (2d Cir 1947).

[48] ibid.

[49] Posner and Landes (n 32).

[50] ibid.

[51] ibid.

[52] ibid.

The economic theory of deterrence relies on an expected utility maximisation model, which presumes that people will make choices that have the highest chance of maximising their expected income or wealth.[53] Under this model, a rational actor will increase his level of care until an additional increase in care fails to yield a reduction in expected damages greater than the cost of the increased care.[54] It continues that an actor's expectation of damages is directly affected by the potential for tort liability. As a result, liability determinations in tort law should theoretically deter future accidents by inducing the liable actor or similarly situated actors to increase their levels of care in response to the clear risk of tort liability.[55] According to Latin, 'virtually all social engineering and "law and economics" analyses share one central behavioral assumption – that imposition of liability substantially affects how categories of actors respond to the risks they create or confront'.[56] Popper finds it 'hard to conceive of a healthy economic model where rational actors ignore clear warning signs and thus render themselves vulnerable to sanctions or punishment'.[57] While Popper and other advocates of deterrence admit that the tort law system does not have a perfect record of deterring harmful behaviour, they maintain that, overall, the system 'positively affects the safety and efficiency of goods and services'.[58]

Although this economic model of deterrence developed in the common law tradition, it has also found acceptance in some civil law jurisdictions. According to Heico Kerkmeester and Louis Visscher, 'the Law and Economics approach in Europe has received attention especially in Germany'.[59] The Hand formula echoes in German courts, where judges consider both the cost of preventive measures and expected losses when deciding whether a defendant was negligent, ie failed to exercise a socially acceptable level of care.[60] According to Claus Ott and Hans-Bernd Schäfer, the German court system develops efficient standards of care over time, despite the fact that individual courts do not assume the explicit task of setting the applicable standard of care in every case.[61] The process, they argue, develops organically when courts evaluate the social gain of the precaution taken by the tortfeasor and precaution proposed by the victim in individual cases.[62] The courts measure social gain of the precaution by subtracting the cost of prevention from the social gain of the activity 'appl[ying] criteria related to economic efficiency like the Learned Hand test' and choose

[53] ibid.
[54] ibid.
[55] Popper (n 37).
[56] Latin (n 33).
[57] Popper (n 37).
[58] ibid.
[59] Kerkmeester and Visscher (n 46).
[60] ibid.
[61] See generally C Ott and HB Schäfer, 'Negligence as Untaken Precaution, Limited Information, and Efficient Standard Formation in the Civil Liability System' (1997) 17 *International Review of Law and Economics* 15.
[62] ibid.

the preventive measure that has the higher social gain to measure negligence in an individual case.[63] As an example, Ott and Schäfer discuss a case in which a builder of an attic was sued after the homeowners discovered dry rot a year and a half after the attic was completed.[64] While the builder argued that there were no signs of dry rot during the attic construction, the court agreed with the plaintiff that the builder should have noticed and investigated rotten planks, which he could have done at very little cost and which would have revealed the dry rot.[65]

Under the social gain approach, once a German court chooses a precaution with a higher social gain, it follows that the negligent tortfeasor will presumably adjust his behaviour by subsequently adopting the favoured precaution or another precaution with at least the same social gain to avoid future liability.[66] As a result, individual cases will continue to shape the standards of care as plaintiffs continue to challenge the sufficiency of precautions taken by defendants and courts continue to apply the social gain balancing test.[67]

Some legal scholars criticise the law-and-economics-based model of deterrence. Legal realists often reject the 'magical character' that the positive economic theory ascribes to tort law.[68] They cast doubt on tort law's ability to simultaneously compensate victims, internalise costs, pre-empt private retributive justice, prevent accidents, and hold wrongdoers accountable.[69] They dismiss its ability to deter harmful conduct and, instead, credit safe practices to 'private morality, market pressures, self-protection instincts, and existing governmental regulation'.[70] Others, like Priest, accept tort law's capacity to prevent accidents, but contend that modern American tort law must be 'vastly reorganized' to accomplish this goal.[71] Priest claims that tort law has 'done a scandalously poor job of controlling the accident rate' partly because courts have accepted that product and service providers are in a better position than consumers to prevent accidents.[72] Priest is especially sceptical of strict liability regimes that hold product and service providers liable in the absence of fault, and suggests that liability should only attach to defendants when accidents could have been prevented.[73] When no practical preventive measure existed prior to the accident, Priest claims that 'attaching liability will not affect the accident rate'.[74]

[63] ibid.
[64] ibid.
[65] ibid.
[66] ibid.
[67] ibid.
[68] SD Sugarman, 'A Comparative Law Look at Pain and Suffering Awards' (2006) 55 *DePaul Law Review* 399.
[69] ibid.
[70] ibid.
[71] Priest (n 40).
[72] ibid.
[73] ibid.
[74] ibid.

Howard Latin accepts deterrence as a valid goal of tort law but calls for a liability system that targets only 'problem-solving actors' to achieve this goal.[75] His approach focuses not on who is most causally connected to the injury, but rather on the actor's accident prevention potential.[76] He criticises the notion that all actors are 'rational utility maximizers' with the information and ability to rationally engage in a cost-benefit analysis. Instead, he argues that:

> [T]he assumption that liability rules influence most people's risk-avoidance behaviour in most accident contexts is unproven and appears unwarranted. In many settings, people lack sufficient information and expertise to assess risks properly; they are inattentive to known risks; they do not understand the applicable liability doctrines; and compelling nonlegal incentives shape their behaviour.[77]

As a result, Latin proposes classifying actors according to their attention level and only imposing liability on high-attention actors, who have the capacity to prevent accidents.[78]

Shuman argues for a psychological, rather than economic, approach to deterrence in tort law. According to him, 'economic analysis of tort law proceeds on many behavioral assumptions that are either not validated, or have been disproved by empirical research'.[79] As an example, he posits that organisational decision-makers rarely engage in a cost–benefit analysis and rarely prioritise profit maximisation when making decisions.[80] Shuman further argues that, according to mainstream behaviour theory, certainty of punishment, which the current tort system lacks, is crucial for deterring undesirable conduct.[81] He complains that in a system that doles out sanctions according to the quality of the injury, rather than the conduct, it becomes difficult to predict which conduct will lead to sanctions.[82] Ultimately, Shuman admits that despite the theoretical and practical difficulties of deterrence, tort law plays some role, however cloudy, in shaping the safety behaviour of American business.[83] He further acknowledges that 'deliberative behaviour is more readily deterred by the tort system'.[84]

Turning more specifically to the medical liability system, it has thus far struggled to effectively deter medical errors. Stauch, in his examination of the medical liability system in England and Germany, observed that, 'while it may suppress the number of claims for compensation, the litigation system does not by itself do enough to promote accident prevention'.[85] Similarly in the US,

[75] Latin (n 33).
[76] ibid.
[77] ibid.
[78] ibid.
[79] Shuman (n 29).
[80] ibid.
[81] ibid.
[82] ibid.
[83] ibid.
[84] ibid.
[85] Stauch (n 1).

'There is little evidence that the system actually deters negligence in medicine or improves the quality of care.'[86] One possible reason for the system's weak deterrent signal is its continued focus on individual providers' behaviour rather than organisational behaviour, including clinical risk management.

Physician Danielle Ofri describes a quality that warrants attention to the difference between individual healthcare providers (doctors, physician's assistants, nurses, etc) and other actors in the fault-based liability system at-large (drivers, business owners, mechanics, etc):

> We all want our patients to do well. No clinician with a detectible heartbeat wants her patient to get a hospital-acquired infection, or have surgery on the wrong side of the body, or receive a delayed diagnosis of cancer. Threats of lawsuits are not necessary to instill this priority.[87]

As a result, economic-driven theories of deterrence that may operate in the tort system at-large fail at the individual provider level in the medical liability system because doctors and nurses generally do not need financial incentives to avoid patient injuries. The primacy of the provider–patient relationship and Hippocratic oath are already at the ethical forefront of the medical profession, and 'the vast majority of errors are committed unintentionally by otherwise conscientious doctors and nurses'.[88]

The medical malpractice insurance environment can also affect deterrence in the medical liability system. Malpractice insurance can dull the system's deterrent signal because insurance companies, not healthcare providers, are largely responsible for the costs of medical liability.[89] However, in the US, 'the incentive-dampening effect of insurance is a less serious problem [for hospitals] than for individual physicians because insurance premiums for hospitals, but not for individual providers, are experience rated'.[90] In Germany, rising medical malpractice claims expenses resulted in increased premiums and the need for higher liability limits, especially for providers practicing in high-risk specialties.[91] In response, some German insurers withdrew from the medical liability market altogether.[92] While German professional regulations require individual providers to carry medical malpractice insurance,[93] the law does not

[86] Mello and Studdert (n 29).

[87] D Ofri, *When We Do Harm: A Doctor Confronts Medical Error* (Boston, Beacon Press, 2020).

[88] ibid.

[89] Mello and Studdert (n 29).

[90] ibid.

[91] D Püster, *Entwicklungen der Arzthaftpflichtversicherung* (Berlin, Springer, 2013) 71–97; D Pohl, 'Arzthaftpflicht: Der Markt schrumpft weiter' (2013) 110 *Deutsches Ärzteblatt* 18; Norddeutscher Rundfunk, 'Haftpflichtschutz belastet Kliniken in Schleswig-Holstein' *Versicherungsbote* (23 August 2013), www.versicherungsbote.de/id/4781109/Haftpflichtschutz-Kliniken-Schleswig-Holstein-Behandlungsfehler-NDR.

[92] See Püster (n 91); see also O Bergmann and F Kienzle, *Krankenhaushaftung: Organisation, Schadensverhütung und Versicherung - Leitfaden für die tägliche Praxis* (Düsseldorf, Deutsche Krankenhaus, 2003).

[93] See Bergmann (n 92) (citing Berufsordnung für Ärzte (BOÄ) § 8).

impose the same insurance requirement on hospitals, leaving larger healthcare organisations with the option of being self-insured or obtaining policies with high deductibles.[94] Similarly, many US hospitals have historically exercised the option to be self-insured, though the current trend is for hospitals to maintain insurance with high self-insured retentions.[95] Self-insurance, policies with high self-insured retentions, and uninsured claims can undermine the protection that insurance might otherwise offer tortfeasors.[96] As a result, while insurance can decrease deterrence, healthcare organisations that bear some liability costs directly should still respond to the threat of liability.

Non-economic factors such as emotion, stress, and time commitment to litigation can also deter negligent behaviour.[97] Indeed, healthcare providers who commit medical errors are often labelled 'second victims' because of the emotional toll they suffer themselves in the aftermath of medical errors.[98] Ofri describes how healthcare providers who commit medical errors experience a 'powerful enough dose of grief, shame, and awareness of the error' without a lawsuit. However, those who are sued suffer further from 'clinical judicial syndrome' which can lead to depression, anxiety, isolation, and loss of trust in the doctor-patient relationship.[99]

Unfortunately, for individuals, this fear of litigation, leads to what Mello and Studdert label 'mutant deterrence', more commonly known as defensive medicine, which describes 'assurance and avoidance behaviors that are induced by apprehension about liability and are of little benefit (compared to their cost), no benefit, or outright harmful'.[100] Although defensive medicine developed as a concept in the US, it is also a recognised, albeit not as prevalent, practice in Germany.[101] One view of defensive medicine is that it results from the medical liability system's efforts to deter medical malpractice by targeting primarily individual providers. Given the Institute of Medicine (IOM)'s report regarding the ineffectiveness of blaming individual healthcare providers as an error prevention

[94] ibid.

[95] See JR Posner, 'Trends in Medical Malpractice Insurance, 1970–1985' (1986) 49 *Law and Contemporary Problems*, 37; C Cheney, 'Hospitals Need to Brace for Upward Trend in Malpractice Claims' healthleaders (2 December 2019), www.healthleadersmedia.com/clinical-care/hospitals-need-brace-upward-trend-malpractice-claims.

[96] Shuman (n 29).

[97] ibid.

[98] See DB Schwappach, 'Nach dem Behandlungsfehler: Umgang mit Patienten, Angehörigen und dem involvierten Personal' (2015) 58 *Bundesgesundheitsblatt* 80; J Barnes et al, 'When Things Go Wrong: Responding to Adverse Events' (Massachusetts Coalition for the Prevention of Medical Errors, March 2006), www.macoalition.org/documents/respondingToAdverseEvents.pdf.

[99] Ofri (n 87).

[100] Mello and Studdert (n 29).

[101] Bergmann (n 92); J von Dohanyi, 'Bauchentscheidung' BertelsmannStiftung (30 September 2015), www.bertelsmann-stiftung.de/de/themen/aktuelle-meldungen/2015/september/bauchentscheidungen; R Brilla et al, 'Are neurology residents in the United States being taught defensive medicine?' (2006) 108 *Clinical Neurology and Neurosurgery*, doi.org/10.1016/j.clineuro.2005.05.013.

strategy, it should come as no surprise that the medical liability system's mutant deterrent signal, which is targeted towards individual healthcare providers, has failed to 'incentiviz[e] quality improvements' in the healthcare system more broadly.[102]

As discussed in chapter two, modern error prevention research reveals that focusing on individual provider's actions, negligent or otherwise, will not identify the systemic deficiencies that are largely responsible for medical errors. As a result, even if individual provider actions are deterred through the medical liability system, it will do little to reduce patient harm caused by systemic defects. This is because those latent systemic defects will continue to induce different individuals to commit similar medical errors.[103]

While the healthcare organisation may be responsible for implementing effective clinical risk management to make the healthcare system safer, as long as individual providers are the primary liability targets, the deterrence signal will be misdirected and manifest as defensive medicine. As a result, deterrence will fail as an error prevention mechanism because the actions targeted by the medical liability system are not the actions most capable of preventing future medical errors. Even worse, the systemic problems that are at the root of medical errors are less likely to be reported internally by providers who fear individual persecution from the medical liability system. According to Mehlman:

> The system is highly punitive; it not only makes wrongdoers pay damages but also makes the process of being found liable for malpractice an extremely negative punishing experience. The experience is so unpleasant that it gives clinicians no incentive to admit their mistakes. The resulting culture of silence makes it very difficult for the system to carry out its deterrence function because it produces little information about why mistakes occur or how they can be prevented in the future.[104]

This problem is known as 'cloaking behaviour': the reluctance of healthcare providers to participate in error reporting and learning systems for fear that the reported information will later be used against them in medical malpractice litigation.[105] Although the US medical liability system is generally regarded as more liberal in terms of filings and compensation, Germany's healthcare system is no stranger to the culture of silence, and legal threats are also a recognised barrier to medical error reporting in Germany.[106]

[102] See Mello and Studdert (n 29).

[103] See Institute of Medicine (IOM) Committee on Quality of Health Care in America, *To Err is Human: Building a Safer Health System* (LT Kohn, JM Corrigan and MS Donaldson eds, Washington DC, National Academies Press, 2000).

[104] MJ Mehlman, 'Promoting Fairness in the Medical Malpractice System' in WM Sage and R Kersh (eds), *Medical Malpractice and the US Health Care System* (Cambridge, Cambridge University Press, 2006).

[105] Mello and Studdert (n 29).

[106] K Loewenbrück et al, 'Disclosure of Adverse Outcomes in Medicine: A Questionnaire Study on Voice Intention and Behaviour of Physicians in Germany, Japan and the USA' (2016) 30 *German Journal of Human Resource Management* 313; but see MN Duffourc, 'Filling Voice Promotion

3.3 REFORMING A FAULT-BASED MEDICAL LIABILITY SYSTEM

In addition to compensation and deterrence, an overarching goal of the medical liability system, as in any system of law, is fairness.[107] As Heller observes, 'Society will not long respect the legal system if it does not perceive it as fundamentally fair to everyone.'[108] One aspect of fairness in a legal system manifests in the notion that it should 'not unduly harm or hinder useful economic activities'.[109] When a system is perceived as fundamentally unfair, calls for reform ensue.

The US and German medical liability systems are no strangers to calls for reform. As early as the 1960s, an increase in medical malpractice claims in Western societies triggered criticism for its perceived role in increasing healthcare cost and decreasing healthcare quality by encouraging the practice of defensive medicine, damaging the patient-physician relationship, and discouraging physicians from entering high-risk specialties.[110] Experts attributed the increase in malpractice claims to a variety of factors including the increase in litigation generally, rapid advances in medical science and technology, deterioration of the traditional patient-physician relationship, pro-plaintiff litigation attitudes, urbanisation, and increased patient autonomy and awareness.[111]

In the US, the frequency and costs of claims increased significantly. Malpractice claims rose from approximately 1.6 claims per 100 physicians in the period 1956–63 to 10 claims per 100 physicians by 1985.[112] In terms of costs, one prominent medical malpractice insurer reported a 95 per cent increase in paid

---

Gaps in Healthcare Through A Comparative Analysis of Error Reporting and Learning Systems and Open Communication and Disclosure Policies in the United States and Germany' (2018) 44 *American Journal of Law and Medicine* 579, noting that Germany's conservative discovery and evidentiary rules as well as federal regulations that require error reporting data to remain anonymous help mitigate liability-based fears for German physicians.

[107] See Heller (n 31) (noting that tort law aims not only to compensate victims and prevent accidents, but to 'foster notions of fairness and predictability').

[108] ibid.

[109] ibid.

[110] See Stauch (n 1) (regarding increase in malpractice claims in Western societies and the widespread assumption that the practice of defensive medicine occurs in Germany and claims that malpractice litigation undermines trust and confidence in the physician-patient relationship); DM Studdert et al, 'Claims, Errors and Compensation Payments in Medical Malpractice Litigation' (2006) 354 New England Journal of Medicine 2024 (study finding one quarter of litigation outcomes not concordant with the merits); L Hafemeister and JH Porter, 'The Health Care Reform Act of 2010 and Medical Malpractice Liability: Worlds in Collision or Ships Passing in the Night' (2011) 64 *Southern Methodist University Law Review* 735 (discussing the practice of defensive medicine and rising insurance premiums in the US); see also Heller (n 31) (insurers withdrew from high-risk practice areas).

[111] See Stauch (n 1) (explaining causes of increased malpractice claims); see also P Danzon, 'The Frequency and Severity of Medical Malpractice Claims: New Evidence' (1986) 49 Law and Contemporary Problems 57 (identifying factors explaining increase in medical malpractice claims); Bergmann (n 92) (identifying reasons for sharp rise in medical malpractice claims expenses in Germany).

[112] R Olsen, 'The Reform of Medical Malpractice Law: Historical Perspectives' (1996) 55 *American Journal of Economics and Sociology* 257.

claims costs from 1979 to 1983.[113] This increase in US malpractice litigation was so drastic that it attracted international attention.[114] In 1980, an English judge warned:

> Take heed of what has happened in the United States . . . Experienced practitioners are known to have refused to treat patients for fear of being accused of negligence. Young men are even deterred from entering the profession because of the risks involved. In the interests of all, we must avoid such consequences in England.[115]

The change in the medical malpractice claims landscape was thus deemed a 'crisis' and politicians began advocating for reform.

State legislatures in the US responded to the 'crisis' by implementing a variety of tort reform measures, including shortened statutes of limitations, damages caps, and pre-litigation screening mechanisms.[116] Nevertheless, the system still faces criticism for its inability to fairly adjudicate claims. Other reform proposals included abolition of legal doctrines of joint and several liability, *res ipsa loquitur*, and the collateral source rule; schedules for non-economic damages; regulation of malpractice insurers; limits on attorney's fees; health courts; alternative dispute resolution; and adoption of a no-fault liability system.[117]

Although Germany did not experience a medical malpractice 'crisis', it too saw a sharp increase in medical malpractice lawsuits around the same time as the US.[118] In Germany, litigation increased from a handful of medical malpractice claims per year before the 1960s to 6,000 claims per year by the end of the 1970s.[119] By 2005, medical malpractice claims in Germany were estimated to be 20,000–35,000 per year.[120] Germany also experienced claim cost increases. 'In Germany, the average expenses per insurer per claim . . . trebled from 1981–2001; in some sub-areas the rise has been more than six-fold.'[121] Like in the US, this increase in medical malpractice filings and costs in Germany spurred calls for reform.

Discussions among academics and practitioners regarding radical reform to medical malpractice law dominated the German Medical Assembly in 1978. Also, in the mid-1970s, at the same time that some US states were implementing medical review panels to screen malpractice claims, the German regional medical boards (*Ärztekammern*) established medical arbitration bodies to encourage pre-trial

[113] Danzon (n 111) (identifying factors explaining increase in medical malpractice claims).

[114] Olsen (n 112) (conceding that prior to 1960 the medical malpractice insurance market was stable).

[115] *Whitehouse v Jordan* [1980] 1 All ER 650, CA.

[116] See generally Heller (n 31).

[117] Mehlman (n 104). See generally Heller (n 31).

[118] See Stauch (n 1) (Germany did not experience 'US-style malpractice crises', but the increase in medical malpractice claims 'generated a disproportionate amount of concern'.).

[119] ibid.

[120] ibid.

[121] ibid.

resolution of claims.[122] There are still calls for reform in Germany. Bergmann et al believe that, absent reforms, increasing malpractice filings and claims payouts will lead to a 'crisis about the insurability of physicians' services'.[123] On the other hand, patients' rights advocates in Germany seek reforms that improve patients' access to court and ability to recover damages and strengthen error disclosure duties in the Patients' Rights Act.[124] One plaintiff's lawyer in Germany calls for a strict liability system and higher pain and suffering awards.[125]

The ongoing calls for change on both sides demonstrate a deeper dissatisfaction with the medical liability system's ability to achieve its goals of fairness, accident prevention, and compensation. While it is outside of the scope of this book to comment on the wisdom of each of the various proposals for reforming the medical malpractice system in the US and Germany, it is notable that both jurisdictions have retained negligence-based systems to govern liability for medical injuries. However, these negligence-based systems often inhibit the healthcare industry's approach to error prevention, as discussed in chapter two. Mello and Studdert note:

> [T]he tort approach to safety regulation – which is punitive in orientation, individualistic in focus, and adversarial in process – is in serious conflict with the nonpunitive, systems-focused, cooperative approach of the 'patient safety movement.'[126]

Thus, finding ways to harmonise the existing medical negligence system with the patient safety movement to accomplish a common goal of medical error prevention is a task that remains. This book proposes that recognising and defining a duty to clinical risk management will help achieve that task.

Reform efforts within a negligence-based medical liability system are more likely to be successful if they help shift the system's focus from the actions of individual providers to the actions of healthcare organisations – the same paradigm shift that the IOM ignited in the healthcare industry's approach to medical error prevention.[127] A medical liability system that requires healthcare organisations to reduce medical errors through the process of clinical risk

[122] See Stauch (n 1).

[123] Bergmann (n 92).

[124] See generally T Hommel, 'Riesige Baustellen links liegen gelassen' G+G – Gesundheit und Gesellschaft (2016), archiv.gg-digital.de/imperia/md/gug/archiv/g+g_4_16.pdf (interview with M Klein-Schmeink, a German Bundestag Member from the Green Party, discussing challenges encountered by victims of medical errors); M Albrecht et al, 'Studie zu den Wirkungen des Patientenrechtegesetzes (IGES Institut, 2016), www.researchgate.net/profile/Martin-Albrecht-3/publication/310242975_Studie_zu_den_Wirkungen_des_Patientenrechtegesetzes/links/5848816e08ae95e1d1665d7c/Studie-zu-den-Wirkungen-des-Patientenrechtegesetzes.pdf (discussing criticism by patients rights advocates of the Patients' Rights Law's disclosure obligations).

[125] See AT Schäfer, 'Plädoyer für einen besseren Schutz der Patienten: 10 Forderungen zur Reform der Haftung bei Behandlungsfehlern' (2 October 2013), www.yumpu.com/de/document/view/21187574/pladoyer-fur-einen-besseren-schutz-der-patienten-rechtsanwalt-dr-.

[126] Mello and Studdert (n 29).

[127] C Burkle, 'Medical Malpractice: Can We Rescue a Decaying System?' (2011) 86 *Mayo Clinic Proceedings* 326.

management holds promise for restoring the goals of the tort system generally in reliably compensating patients (by encouraging individual provider error reporting) and preventing medical errors (by deterring negligent risk management conduct of healthcare organisations). Although no reform is likely to transform the medical liability system into a perfect deterrent, various deterrence theories support the idea that focusing liability on organisational actors can strengthen the system's deterrence signal.

First, there is evidence that healthcare institutions – as opposed to individual providers – may modify behaviours in response to threats of legal or regulatory sanctions.[128] Latin cautions that 'liability rules will promote social engineering objectives only to the extent that prospective injurers and victims can, and typically do, undertake informed problem-solving behavior with respect to the risks for which they may be liable.'[129] Studies aimed at testing the deterrent effect of medical negligence on healthcare providers suggest that while individual providers are likely not deterred by the risk of medical liability, hospitals might improve care in response to medical malpractice claims.[130] Although the studies supporting this conclusion have been criticised as 'limited and . . . vulnerable to methodological criticism', they provide some support for the idea that organisations are more likely deterred by the threat of liability than individual providers.[131] Crucially, deterrence at the organisational level is more likely to translate to error reduction. Although, as discussed further in chapter five, both the US and Germany recognise direct liability for organisational errors, the duties of care in the current law do not clearly encompass a broader duty to clinical risk management. As a result, the US and German medical liability systems still look primarily to individual providers as the main source of liability for treatment errors, further encouraging defensive medicine and concealing systemic defects. However, as Goldbach notes, expanding organisational liability to include a duty to conduct clinical risk management will 'lead to a reduction in liability cases in the long term' because 'increased systematics and transparency of treatment procedures should even partially relieve physicians and hospital operators of the fear of increasing liability pressure and thus lead to a decrease in defensive medicine'.[132]

Another problem is that the system does not reliably identify medical errors, because claims filed in the system are both over- and under- inclusive and thus do not accurately reflect the true nature and rate of medical errors.[133] For example, while American patients who are injured because of negligent care are

[128] Ofri (n 87).
[129] Latin (n 33).
[130] Mello and Studdert (n 29).
[131] ibid.
[132] C Goldbach, *Risikomanagementsysteme im Krankenhaus nach dem Patientenrechtegesetz: Sozialrechtliche Pflicht und haftungsrechtlicher Standard* (Kassel, Kassel University Press, 2014).
[133] See Studdert et al (n 110).

more likely to file a lawsuit than those who are injured during non-negligent treatment, 'most instances of negligence never give rise to a malpractice claim, and many malpractice lawsuits are brought and won by patients even though expert reviewers can identify no evidence of negligent care'.[134] There is a similar disconnect in Germany between medical malpractice claims and the occurrence of medical errors. There is evidence that a large number of medical errors do not result in claims.[135] And for those that do, experts often determine that there was no error. In 2020, the medical arbitration boards (*Gutachterkommissionen* and *Schlichtungsstellen*) – pre-litigation review panels composed of medical experts and a judge – found no medical error (or breach of a standard of care) for 4,876 (69.1 per cent) of the 7,055 claims decided.[136] Similarly, treatment error statistics from Medical Service of the National Association of Health Insurance Funds (*Medizinischer Dienst des Spitzenverbandes Bund der Krankenkassen*; MDS) – a service that provides insureds with free expert opinions regarding suspected medical errors – reveals similar results: no error in 9,943 (70.8 per cent) of the 14,042 cases reviewed.[137] Regardless of the reasons for unreported claims or expert findings of no error in claims reported, this disconnect between malpractice claims and the occurrence of medical error signals a deeper problem with medical liability system's ability to sufficiently identify, and thus deter, injury-causing behaviour. Compounding the problem in the US is that healthcare providers perceive no rational relationship between medical negligence and the likelihood of being sued.[138] If future system reforms focus on healthcare organisations and the process of clinical risk management, they can help align the medical liability system with the industry's patient safety goals by connecting a hidden source of medical errors (systemic defects) in the healthcare system to a mechanism for accident prevention (deterrence) in the legal system.

Second, under a utility maximisation perspective, healthcare organisations are more likely to increase systems-based error prevention measures through clinical risk management in response to a clear risk of organisational liability. Focusing liability on healthcare organisations, who are in the best position to

[134] Mello and Studdert (n 29).

[135] Medizinischer Dienst des Spitzenverbandes Bund der Krankenkassen (MDS), 'Behandlungsfehler-Begutachtung der Gemeinschaft der Medizinischen Dienste: Jahresstatistik 2020' (2020), md-bund.de/fileadmin/dokumente/Pressemitteilungen/2021/2021_10_12/4_FIN_-_MD_BEHANDLUNGSFEHLER_BF.pdf.

[136] Bundesärztekammer, 'Statistische Erhebung der Gutachterkommissionen und Schlichtungsstellen für das Statistikjahr 2020' www.aerztekammern-schlichten.de/fileadmin/user_upload/Gutachterkommissionen_und_Schlichtungsstellen/Behandlungsfehler-Statistik/Behandlungsfehler-Statistik_2020.pdf (statistics compiled for the purpose of helping identify causes of medical errors showing no findings of organisational errors, presumably because the expert commissions and arbitration boards do not consider organisational errors); see also H Liebermiester, 'How to Avoid Liability Litigation in Courts – Suggestions from a German Example' (2010) 8 *German Medical Science* 3 (error confirmation rate is consistently around one-third).

[137] MDS (n 135).

[138] Mello and Studdert (n 29).

identify and correct systemic deficiencies, also satisfies Latin's approach of assigning tort liability 'whenever possible to categories of actors who do, in reality, think about accident prevention, loss spreading, and the effects of legal rules, and whose behaviour may therefore be significantly influenced by potential liability'.[139] Recognising a legal duty to conduct clinical risk management would not entirely relieve individual providers of legal consequences for patient harm caused by individual treatment errors. It would, however, properly orient 'financial and administrative responsibility' for systemic failures to the organisation by demanding reasonable clinical risk management from the parties that are able to

> diversify liability risk across a range of specialties and services, insure or self-insure that risk at manageable cost, engage in coordinated injury reduction activities, and enter into efficient contractual arrangements downstream with patients and upstream with health insurers regarding claims for compensation.[140]

Third, under Latin's actor taxonomy, healthcare organisations would be classified as high-attention actors susceptible to being deterred by the threat of liability because they 'specialize in limited problem elements, are able to adapt their decisions in response to experience derived from many similar choices, and are subject to performance monitoring systems that aim to control pecuniary costs including potential tort damages'.[141] On the other hand, contrary to Latin's approach, which would apply strict liability to disputes between healthcare organisations and patients, maintaining a negligence-based system would decrease errors without decreasing participation in the risky activity, here the provision of healthcare.[142] This approach would also satisfy Priest's concern that deterrence is only effective when liability attaches to behaviour that can be prevented.[143]

In summary, fault-based liability in both systems requires substandard behaviour, ie, negligence. However, focusing liability for harm caused by medical errors on individual providers' behaviour does not effectively deter future medical negligence. Instead, because individual healthcare providers respond to threats of legal liability by practicing defensive medicine, the medical liability system, in its capacity as an external influencing factor on patient safety, inhibits systems-based error prevention efforts. On the other hand, focusing liability on organisational actions and deficiencies is more likely to achieve the goal of preventing medical errors. Additionally, because organisational deficiencies are best detected and resolved through the process of clinical risk management, the medical liability system should impose liability on healthcare organisations for patient injuries caused by negligent risk management.

[139] Latin (n 33).
[140] WM Sage, 'Malpractice Reform as a Health Policy Problem' in WM Sage and R Kersh (eds), *Medical Malpractice and the US Health Care System* (Cambridge, Cambridge University Press, 2006).
[141] Latin (n 33).
[142] Posner and Landes (n 32).
[143] Priest (n 40).

4

Establishing Medical Liability

THE MEDICAL LIABILITY system in both the United States (US) and Germany recognises three general categories of errors: (1) consent or information errors,;(2) treatment errors; and (3) organisational errors.[1] Consent and information errors occur when a physician fails to obtain patient consent for medical treatment or properly disclose information regarding the risks of medical treatment.[2] Liability for consent and information errors is rooted in the protection of autonomy, bodily integrity, and self-determination.[3] As a result, failure to obtain the requisite consent to treat a patient is a legal transgression regardless of whether the treatment itself was 'appropriate and carried out skill-fully'.[4] Because competency of the medical treatment is not a factor in determining liability for consent or information errors, those errors, strictly speaking, do not constitute 'medical malpractice' but rather 'disclosure malpractice'.[5] As such, a discussion of consent errors falls outside of the scope of this book. The duty to conduct clinical risk management to prevent medical errors occurs primarily at the intersection of treatment errors and organisational errors, both of which will be the focus of this chapter. This chapter describes how treatment errors occur when either the provision or failure to provide medical treatment by individual medical providers violates the applicable standard of care in both jurisdictions.[6] It

[1] See ML Hansis and D Hart, *Gesundheitsberichterstattung des Bundes, Medizinische Behandlungsfehler* (Robert Koch-Institut, Berlin, Paul Fieck KG, 2001), www.gbe-bund.de/pdf/Behand.pdf; A Pauli, *Risikomanagement und CIRS als Gegenstand der Krankenhaushaftung* (Baden-Baden, Nomos, 2013); see generally SD Hodge and MZ Steinhaus, 'The Ever-Changing Landscape of Informed Consent and Whether the Obligation to Explain a Procedure to the Patient May Be Delegated' (2019) 71 *Arkansas Law Review* 727 (discussing the doctrine of informed consent in the US); SA Adelman and J Robertson, 'Emerging Trends in Healthcare Liability' (AHLA Seminar Materials, 19 June 2000), perma.cc/Q8VG-6FXF.

[2] EL Raab, 'The Parameters of Informed Consent' (2004) 102 *Transactions of the American Ophthalmological Society* 225; M Stauch, *The Law of Medical Negligence in England and Germany: A Comparative Analysis* (Oxford, Hart Publishing, 2008).

[3] ibid.

[4] Raab (n 2). See *Ehrlich v Sorokin*, 165 A3d 812 (NJ Super AD 2017) ('Informed consent is generally unrelated to the standard of care for performing medical treatment.'); SA Sommer et al, 'Medical Liability and Patient Law in Germany: Main Features with Particular Focus on Treatments in the Field of Interventional Radiology' (2016) *188 RoFo: Fortschritte auf dem Gebiete der Röntgenstrahlen und der Nuklearmedizin* 353 ('Without an effective consent the treatment is considered illegal whether it was free of treatment error or not.').

[5] Raab (n 2); D Giesen, *International Medical Malpractice Law: A Comparative Law Study of Civil Liability Arising from Medical Care* (Tübingen, JCB Mohr (Paul Siebeck), 1988).

[6] See Pauli (n 1); *Russell v May*, 400 P3d 647 (Kan 2017) (finding that the physician's duty to the patient obligates him to use a certain standard of care).

also discusses how organisational errors occur when the healthcare organisation itself breaches standards governing the medical treatment process.[7]

4.1 THE ELEMENTS OF MEDICAL LIABILITY

Medical liability attaches when a healthcare provider causes a legally cognisable harm through negligent conduct. A patient might experience two types of harm during the course of medical treatment.[8] First, a patient may experience harm that is caused by the patient's underlying medical condition. In this case, treatment aimed at curing the patient's underlying condition may fail, and upon such failure, the natural progression of the patient's medical condition can harm the patient.[9] Second, a patient might experience a harm that is caused by the medical treatment itself. This type of harm is called an 'iatrogenic injury'.[10] Within both categories of harm, negligence is required before liability can be imposed on a healthcare provider for an unintentional medical injury. For example, a healthcare provider might be liable for harm caused by the natural progression of a patient's medical condition if they negligently failed to diagnose or misdiagnosed the patient's condition. On the other hand, a healthcare provider will not be liable for patient harm, even harm caused by medical treatment, if the provider rendered treatment with reasonable care. Giesen notes that 'neither in contract nor in torts can a conclusion be drawn as to negligence on part of the acting physician from the mere fact that an accident happened or the result was not in accordance with expectation'.[11]

In the US, the question is whether, according to the particular facts of the case, the 'physician has performed his duties with reasonable care and skill'.[12] The Maine Supreme Court explains:

> The law also implies that, in the treatment of all cases which they undertake, they will exercise reasonable and ordinary care and diligence. They are also bound always to use their best skill and judgment in determining the nature of the malady and the best mode of treatment, and in all respects to do their best to secure a perfect restoration of their patients to health and soundness. But physicians and surgeons do not impliedly warrant the recovery of their patients, and are not liable on account of any failure in that respect, unless through some default of their own duty, as already defined.[13]

[7] See YK Puig, 'Liability Overview: New Theories and Challenges' (AHLA Seminar Materials, 2001), https://perma.cc/KPQ8-95XW (citing *Welsh v Bulger*, 698 A2d 581, 585 (Pa 1997); Pauli (n 1).
[8] Stauch (n 2).
[9] ibid.
[10] ibid.
[11] Giesen (n 5).
[12] ibid.
[13] *Patten v Wiggin*, 51 Me 594 (Me 1862).

German law similarly limits liability for medical injuries. Pauli explains that failed medical treatments, natural disease progressions, and unavoidable undesirable events and complications that occur during the course of medical treatment are not indicative of medical errors for which a healthcare provider will be held liable under German law, but rather are risks that the patient assumes when obtaining medical treatment.[14] In a reference decision distributed to medical malpractice litigants by the Saarbrücken Regional Court (*Saarbrücken Landgericht*), the Court reminds the parties of the complexities associated with the provision of medical care:

> The physician does not owe any treatment success, but only a treatment according to the rules of the medical art. The mere fact that the desired healing success has not occurred or that undesirable complications and risks have materialised cannot be taken to mean that the doctor has acted incorrectly. This is because each person is an individual with his or her own anatomical characteristics. For example, a disease that causes certain symptoms in one person may have completely different symptoms in another. Conversely, certain symptoms can have very different causes. For this reason, even the correct diagnosis is associated with particular difficulties. The mere fact that a doctor does not make the correct diagnosis or does not make it immediately does not necessarily mean that a treatment error has occurred. Moreover, it is not certain in advance whether a particular therapy will be successful for this particular patient. While some patients respond to a certain therapy, the same therapy does not succeed in other patients.[15]

In reality, it can be difficult to determine whether a provider's negligence is responsible for a patient injury since the provision of both reasonable and unreasonable care can combine in various ways to produce harm.[16] However, when a healthcare provider fails to exercise reasonable care, ie, is negligent, a treatment error occurs, and when that error causes patient harm, then the provider has committed medical malpractice.

Medical malpractice in both jurisdictions requires the same core elements: fault, causation, and damage. In the US, the medical liability system developed as part of tort law and is governed primarily by the common law principles of negligence.[17] Tort liability for negligence exists in the US when: (1) a duty of care owed by the defendant to the plaintiff; (2) is breached; and (3) causes (4) damage.[18] The German Civil Code allows medical malpractice claims under

[14] Pauli (n 1).

[15] Landgericht (LG) Saarbrücken, Hinweisbeschluss, 12 December 2010.

[16] Hansis and Hart (n 1).

[17] B Watson-Dunham, *Medical Malpractice Law and Litigation* (Clifton Park, Delmar Cengage Learning, 2006); MM Mello and DM Studdert, 'The Medical Malpractice System: Structure and Performance' in WM Sage and R Kersh (eds), *Medical Malpractice and the U.S. Health Care System* (Cambridge, Cambridge University Press, 2009).

[18] See *Elam v Coll Park Hosp*, 132 Cal App 3d 332 (Cal Ct App 1982); *Jennings v Badgett*, 230 P3d 861 (Okla 2010) (discussing the elements of a medical malpractice claim in the US).

both contract and tort law.[19] Since the German medical treatment contract is a contract for services, liability will only be imposed when the provider is negligent in the performance of those services.[20] As a result, the elements of malpractice under a contract for negligent performance merge with those under tort for negligent conduct.[21] Giesen explains the this merger between duties in contract and duties in tort in the context of medical liability:

> [C]ontractual duties do not, then, affect the true nature of medical liability, which remains in all countries essentially the legal duty, the breach of which will normally lead that kind the legal liability which exists either in the presence or absence of the contract, and which can properly be described as tortious or delictual lability in all jurisdictions under review. [22]

Tort liability will arise under the German Civil Code when the following exist: (1) a protected right or interest; (2) unlawful interference with that right or interest; (3) causation; and (4) damage.[23]

4.1.1 The Duty of Care

Before liability is imposed on a wrongdoer in either jurisdiction, they must be under a legal duty or obligation to act with a certain level of care. Generally, the relationship between a healthcare provider and their patient requires the provider to act with reasonable care in treating the patient.[24] Giesen depicts the patient-physician relationship as follows:

> Thus, a person who is a medical professional, or who holds himself out as ready to give medical advice or treatment, impliedly undertakes that he is possessed of skill and knowledge for the purpose, and when consulted by a patient will owe him a duty of care, namely in deciding whether to undertake the case, in taking a proper case history, in making careful diagnosis, in properly informing his patient about any proposed treatment or operation and inherent risks of treatment and no treatment, in obtaining a patient's consent to such treatment and in his administration of that treatment or the performance of that operation, and, at all stages, in answering questions where he knows or ought to know that the patient intends to rely on his answer.[25]

[19] Stauch (n 2).
[20] ibid.
[21] See Giesen (n 5).
[22] Giesen (n 5).
[23] B Markesinis et al, *The German Law of Torts: A Comparative Treatise*, 5th edn (Oxford, Hart Publishing, 2021).
[24] Giesen (n 5) (discussing the duty of care generally and in medical malpractice cases in common and civil law jurisdictions).
[25] ibid.

US courts rely specifically on this relationship to anchor medical liability. In Germany, medical liability can stem from both the medical treatment contract and a more general duty to refrain from interfering with a patient's legally protected interest in life, body, and health.

In the US, the patient-physician relationship creates a legal duty owed by the individual healthcare provider to the patient.[26] A Maryland appellate court explains:

> We have long recognized, as have most courts, that, except in those unusual circumstances when a doctor acts gratuitously or in an emergency situation, recovery for malpractice 'is allowed only where there is a relationship of doctor and patient as a result of a contract, express or implied, that the doctor will treat the patient with proper professional skill and the patient will pay for such treatment, and there has been a breach of professional duty to the patient.'[27]

Although determining whether a patient-physician relationship exists is a fact-specific inquiry, it is usually established, 'when the professional services of a physician are accepted by another person for the purposes of medical or surgical treatment'.[28] In the absence of direct contact between the physician and patient, a the relationship can be implied when 'the doctor takes affirmative action to participate in the care and treatment of a patient', for example, by directing a patient's care over the phone.[29] However, mere consultation with a treating physician, who retains ultimate medical decision-making authority, will usually not establish a patient-physician relationship between the patient and the consulting physician.[30] Some American courts have also found that physicians can owe a duty to non-patient third parties when the third party's injury stems from the patient's medical care, including cases in which third parties contract infections from patients or are injured by a physically or mentally incapacitated patient.[31]

In Germany, legal obligations can stem from both the medical treatment contract and a more general duty to refrain from interfering with a patient's legally protected interest in life, body, and health. The treatment contract obliges the provider to deliver non-negligent care.[32] This is because German law classifies a contract for medical treatment as a contract for services (*Dienstvertrag*) as

[26] *McNulty v City of New York*, 792 NE2d 162 (NY 2003) ('Generally, a doctor only owes a duty of care to his or her patient.'); *Betesh v US*, 400 F Supp 238 (DDC 1974).

[27] *Dingle v Belin*, 749 A2d 157 (Md 2000).

[28] SE Pegalis, 2 *American Law of Medical Malpractice* § 2:3, 3rd edn, Thomson Reuters Westlaw (database updated June 2025); K Gelein, 'Are Online Consultations a Prescription for Trouble? The Unchartered Waters of Cybermedicine' (2000) 66 *Brooklyn Law Review* 209.

[29] *Sterling v Johns Hopkins Hosp*, 802 A2d 440 (Md Spec App 2002).

[30] ibid.

[31] Pegalis (n 28) § 3:16.

[32] KO Bergmann et al, 'Krankenhaushaftung un Versicherung' in KO Bergmann and HF Kienzle (eds), *Krankenhaushaftung: Organisation, Schadensverhütung und Versicherung – Leitfaden für die tägliche Praxis* (Düsseldorf, Kohlhammer Verlag, 2015).

opposed to a contract for work (*Werkvertrag*) guaranteeing a particular result.[33] In ambulatory settings, the treatment contract in the majority of cases will be concluded between the patient and the individual physician providing the treatment.[34] Inpatient treatment contracts can take several forms. The default rule for patients with statutory health insurance is the total hospital admission contract (*Totaler Krankenhausaufnahmevertrag*), wherein the contract is concluded solely between the hospital and the patient.[35] As a result, the hospital alone has a contractual obligation to provide medical treatment and is held vicariously liable pursuant to German Civil Code (*Bürgerliches Gesetzbuch*; BGB) § 278(1) for individual healthcare providers' treatment errors.[36] Other types of inpatient contracts include the split hospital admission contract (*Gespaltener Arzt-Krankenhaus-Vertrag*) and the hospital admission contract with an additional physician contract (*Totaler Krankenhausaufnahmevertrag mit Arztzusatzvertrag*), wherein the patient contracts with both the hospital and the physician.[37] When both the hospital and physician are contractual obligors, they can be held jointly and severally liable, depending on the circumstances of the treatment arrangement, the physician's employment relationship, and the negligence alleged.[38]

In addition to contractual liability, tort liability can arise under German law when a protected interest, including life, body, and health, under BGB § 823 is implicated.[39] As a result, individual healthcare providers can be liable under tort principles for the negligent provision of medical care that results in an injury.[40] German tort law also allows recovery by injured third parties, but limits damages in such cases to those relating to funeral costs and loss of financial support when the patient is deceased.[41]

4.1.2 Breaching the Standard of Care

Once an established legal duty or obligation flows from the healthcare provider to the patient, negligence occurs when the healthcare provider breaches the applicable standard of care. In the US, negligence is generally defined as the failure to act reasonably under the circumstances.[42] German law defines negligence

[33] Stauch (n 2). There are, however, situations in which a contract for medical products or devices will be viewed as a contract for sale and subject the physician to a stricter form of liability when the materials or products used during medical treatment cause harm. See Giesen (n 5) for more.

[34] See Bürgerliches Gesetzbuch (BGB) § 630a.

[35] Bergmann et al (n 32).

[36] ibid.

[37] ibid.

[38] ibid.

[39] Markesinis et al (n 23).

[40] FM Petry, 'Medical Liability in Germany' in BA Koch (ed), *Medical Liability in Europe: A Comparison of Selected Jurisdictions* (Berlin, De Gruyter, 2011).

[41] BGB §§ 844, 845.

[42] See Watson-Dunham (n 17).

(*Fahrlässigkeit*) as the failure to 'exercise reasonable care'.[43] To interpret this standard, German courts look to 'the notional conduct of a careful person engaging in the same sphere of activity as the defendant'.[44] It follows that, in both jurisdictions, the duty or obligation that a healthcare provider owes to a patient is a duty to use reasonable care.[45]

In the US, the standard of care for medical professionals requires them to 'exercise the amount of care, skill, and diligence exercised generally in the community by doctors engaged in the same field'.[46] US courts have made clear that, 'the standard of care for physicians is an objective one—physicians must have and employ the same skill and knowledge typically used by physicians in the medical profession, and must keep themselves informed of contemporary developments in the profession'.[47] As a result, an individual physician's best judgement or good faith is irrelevant when determining whether they breached the applicable standard of care.[48] By the same token, some American jurisdictions hold junior doctors to the same standard of care as more experienced ones.[49]

Although objective, US courts allow for some flexibility in the applicable standard of care. The US First Circuit Court of Appeals explained that:

> [T]he standard of care for medical doctors is not static or rigid. It is a standard that changes depending on many factors, including a doctor's specialty, the resources available, and the advances of the medical profession at the time of the alleged negligent act.[50]

The Pennsylvania Supreme Court recognised that more than one course of treatment can meet the applicable standard of care and that doctors who choose a course 'advocated by a considerable number of his professional brethren in good standing in his community' will not be held liable.[51] US courts also allow variances in the standard of care based upon the availability of equipment and resources in different localities despite the overall trend of moving toward a

[43] BGB § 276(2).

[44] Stauch (n 2).

[45] ibid; Giesen (n 5).

[46] *Betesh*, 400 F Supp 238 (DDC 1974).

[47] *Pringle v Rapaport*, 980 A2d 159, 170 (Pa Sup Ct 2009).

[48] See Morlino v Med Ctr of Ocean Cty, 706 A2d 721 (NJ 1998) ('The physician's exercise of judgment is to be evaluated not on the basis of the physician's good faith or honesty, but solely on whether it falls below an objective standard of care.'); Shumaker v Johnson, 571 So 2d 991 (Ala 1990) (noting that a growing number of jurisdictions have abandoned the 'good faith' rule in recent years); Hirahara v Tanaka, 959 P2d 830 (Haw 1998) ('The jury must focus on whether the physician breached the standard of care. His or her exercise of "best judgment" is superfluous to this determination.').

[49] *St Germain v Pfeifer*, 637 NE2d 848 (Mass 1994) (citing *Centman v Cobb*, 581 NE2d 1286 (Ind App 1991) and *Jenkins v Clark*, 454 NE2d 541 (Ohio App 3d 1982)); but see *Jistarri v Nappi*, 549 A2d 210 (Pa 1988) (holding an orthopaedic resident to a standard of care, 'higher than that for general practitioners but less than that for fully trained orthopaedic specialists').

[50] *Heinrich v Sweet*, 308 F3d 48 (1st Cir 2002).

[51] *Duckworth v Bennett*, 181 A 558 (Pa 1935).

national standard of care for medical practice.[52] The Mississippi Supreme Court articulated the national standard of care with a 'resources-based caveat' as follows:

> As a result of its resources-based component, the physician's non-delegable duty of care is this: given the circumstances of each patient, each physician has a duty to use his or her knowledge and therewith treat through maximum reasonable medical recovery, each patient, with such reasonable diligence, skill, competence, and prudence as are practiced by minimally competent physicians in the same specialty or general field of practice throughout the United States, who have available to them the same general facilities, services, equipment and options.[53]

US courts generally require expert testimony to establish both the applicable standard of care and a breach of that standard.[54] The exception to this general rule is when a healthcare provider's 'want of skill and lack of care is so apparent so as to be understood by a layman, and requires only common knowledge and experience to understand it'.[55] The Alabama Supreme Court articulated various situations that might fall within this exception:

> 1) where a foreign instrumentality is found in the plaintiff's body following surgery; 2) where the injury complained of is in no way connected to the condition for which the plaintiff sought treatment; 3) where the plaintiff employs a recognized standard or authoritative medical text or treatise to prove what is or is not proper practice; and 4) where the plaintiff is himself or herself a medical expert qualified to evaluate the doctor's allegedly negligent conduct.[56]

As a result, unless an exception applies, a plaintiff in the US must present expert testimony to establish the standard of care applicable to the defendant provider based on what is generally expected by the medical community in the relevant field of expertise and that the defendant's conduct fell below that objective standard.

German law requires physicians to provide medical treatment that accords with 'medical standards . . . generally recognised at the time of treatment'.[57] The standard of care applicable to the treatment contract is the same as the standard of care in tort.[58] The German Federal Court of Justice (BGH) has found that

[52] Pegalis (n 28) § 3:5; see Estate of Hagedorn ex rel Hagedorn v Peterson, 690 NW2d 84 (Iowa 2004) ('the facilities, personnel, services, and equipment reasonably available to a physician continue to be circumstances relevant to the appropriateness of the care rendered by the physician to the patient'); Birchfield v Texarkana Meml Hosp, 747 SW2d 361 (Tex 1987) ('The purpose of the locality rule is to prevent unrealistic comparisons between the standards of practice in communities where resources and facilities might vastly differ.').

[53] *Hall v Hilbun*, 466 So 2d 856 (Miss 1985), superseded by statute on other grounds, Miss Code Ann § 85–5–7, as recognised in *Narkeeta Timber Co, Inc v Jenkins*, 777 So 2d 39 (Miss 2000).

[54] See *American Law Reports*, 81 ALR2d 597 (originally published in 1962) ('The overwhelming weight of authority supports the view that ordinarily expert evidence is essential to support an action for malpractice against a physician or surgeon.').

[55] *Lloyd Noland Found, Inc v Harris*, 322 So 2d 709 (Ala 1975).

[56] *Holt v Godsil*, 447 So 2d 19 (Ala 1984).

[57] BGB § 630a.

[58] Bergmann et al (n 32).

doctors must demonstrate the standard of care of a respectable and conscientious medical professional of average expertise in the relevant field.[59] While a subjective approach may operate in German law to hold more knowledgeable physicians to a higher standard of care, the threshold level of care that all physicians must provide is objective and not influenced by a doctor's experience level or personal circumstances.[60] Applying this objective standard of care, the BGH ruled that a junior doctor 'owes that same duty of skill and care to the patient as any other doctor'.[61]

German courts also reject a singular or fixed standard of care and opt to define the applicable standard of care based upon the circumstances of each case. According to Stauch:

> [T]he [medical] 'standard' in question will derive from a combination of scientific knowledge, medical experience and professional acceptance. In so doing, it serves to particularise 'required care' in relation to a given set of circumstances . . . often a single universally accepted practice does not exist [and] the law will need to leave room for rival schools of thought, with the courts functioning 'as a form of border control' ('*in einer Art Grenzkontrolle*') in checking if particular method involved undue risks, or was carelessly executed.[62]

The BGH has found that the applicable standard of care can vary based upon the hospital size, specialty, and available staff and equipment.[63] Bergmann et al affirm that the case law establishes that the standard of medical care 'must take into account the fact that the standard of staffing and equipment in a regional or district hospital is generally lower than in a university hospital'.[64] For example, the BGH found that there was no breach of the standard of care when a plaintiff underwent a laparoscopic tubal sterilisation using monopolar high-frequency current despite the fact that the same operation using lower-risk bipolar high-frequency current was available in another hospital.[65] The BGH observed that:

> [T]he rapid progress in medical technology and the associated acquisition of ever new experience and knowledge mean that there are inevitably differences in quality in the treatment of patients, depending on whether they go to a larger university hospital or a special clinic with particularly well-equipped staff and equipment, or to a general care hospital. Within limits, therefore, the medical standard to be demanded varies depending on the personnel and equipment available. It can be maintained in a medium-sized or smaller hospital, if at least the basic equipment meets modern medical requirements.[66]

[59] Bundesgerichtshof (BGH) 13 June 1960 NJW 1961, 600.
[60] Stauch (n 2).
[61] See Stauch (n 2) (citing BGH 27 September 1983 NJW 1984, 655).
[62] ibid.
[63] BGH 22 September 1987 NJW 1988, 763.
[64] Bergmann et al (n 32).
[65] BGH 22 September 1987 NJW 1988, 763.
[66] ibid.

On the other hand, when a hospital did not have the facilities and equipment to accommodate the need for an emergency caesarean section during childbirth, the Zweibrücken appellate court noted that hospitals with limited resources cannot avoid liability for failing to provide the minimum requirements necessary to organise basic and functional care. In this case, the court noted that the minimum requirements for operating an obstetrics department set forth by the German Society for Gynecology and Obstetrics meant that the hospital had to provide facilities and equipment for normal and high-risk births 'as any normal birth can develop into a high-risk birth at any time'.[67] This case demonstrates that healthcare providers must meet minimum standards regardless of resources; however, as long as the treatment provided 'corresponds to the current state of medicine', failing to provide the best possible treatment will not result in a breach of the standard of care.[68]

In Germany, experts must testify regarding the applicable standard of care.[69] However, as Stauch points out, German courts are more critical of expert testimony and will not absolve a defendant physician merely because an expert has testified that the standard of care was met when the courts find that the 'socially required care' was not observed.[70] Bergmann et al describe the court's reliance upon medical experts as follows:

> In the final instance, it is the courts that have to decide on the required care, on the standard in cases of liability, usually after expert advice. But the standards are also legal, judicial standards of judgment for deciding legal disputes. The standards are ultimately medical guidelines, because the law cannot of itself determine what is possible and necessary on the part of physicians. This is where the relevant expert steps into his or her rights. In the core medical areas of diagnosis, indication and therapy, the courts are dependent on medical expertise and medical experts. Through them, it is the physicians themselves who determine the standard . . . [T]he standard of due care is a necessary, but not an absolutely binding, tool to determine the treatment required.[71]

Consequently, while German courts rely on the medical knowledge of experts to determine the applicable legal standard, they are still the ultimate arbiters of negligence. In fact, because of the information asymmetry between plaintiffs and defendant healthcare providers in medical negligence cases, German courts take on a greater investigatory role in an attempt to ensure equality of arms between the parties.[72]

[67] Oberlandesgericht (OLG) Zweibrücken 27 March 2012, 5 U 7/08.
[68] See BGH 22 September 1987 NJW 1988, 763.
[69] Stauch (n 2) (citing BGH 17 September 1985 VersR 1985, 1187; BGH 2 March 1993 NJW 1993, 2378).
[70] ibid.
[71] Bergmann et al (n 32).
[72] Petry (n 40).

4.1.3 Causation

For liability to attach to a healthcare provider who breached a standard of care, that breach must have caused the plaintiff's alleged injury.[73] Because medical malpractice plaintiffs initially seek medical care for a pre-existing medical condition, proving that the provider's breach, rather than the condition itself, caused harm 'represents the greatest hurdle for a patient in a medical malpractice lawsuit'.[74] In both jurisdictions, the general rule requires medical expert testimony to support a causation finding.[75] Additionally, causation in both US and German law has two parts, both of which must be met: (1) factual causation, or *äquivalenter Kausalzusammenhang*; and (2) legal causation, or *adäquater Kausalzusammenhang* and *schutzzwecklehre*.[76] Giesen describes factual causation as a 'preliminary filter eliminating the irrelevant'.[77] Damage is not factually caused by negligence unless it would not have occurred without the precedent negligent act or omission.[78] Determining factual causation is fairly straightforward using the common law 'but-for' test or the civil law '*condicio sine qua non*' formula.[79] Legal causation, on the other hand, has long been the subject of wrangling amongst legal scholars and judges.[80] This is because legal causation goes beyond the logic underlying factual causation to create a 'legal policy filter' that limits liability for negligence as demanded by justice and fairness.[81] The US reasonable foreseeability test and the German adequacy and protective purpose tests generally guide courts' legal causation determinations, which, according to Giesen, entail 'a test on the balance of probabilities . . . to establish that some conduct or event caused or materially contributed to the injury'.[82] Thus, both jurisdictions require that the negligent conduct be both a 'but-for' cause of the injury and satisfy some criteria by which liability is considered fair under the circumstances.

[73] *Pearson v Parsons*, 757 P2d 197 (Idaho 1988); T Voigt in *BeckOGK BGB* (Beck online, 1 February 2026) BGB § 823 paras 1084–94.

[74] LG Saarbrücken, Hinweisbeschluss, 12 December 2010.

[75] See *Ashland Hosp Corp v Lewis*, 581 SW3d 572 (Ky 2019) (causation in medical malpractice cases requires expert testimony); *Morisch*, 653 F3d 522 (n 90); Bergmann et al (n 32) (noting that main tasks of an expert in German medical malpractice cases is to determine whether there was a treatment error and whether the error caused the resulting damage).

[76] See Stauch (n 2) (identifying two-part causation in Germany); see also *O'Neal v Saint John Hospital & Medical Center*, 791 NW2d 853 (Mich 2010) ('These two prongs are respectively described as "cause-in-fact" and "legal causation.'); M Infantino and E Zervogianni, 'The European Ways to Causation' in M Infantino and E Zervogianni (eds), *Causation in European Tort Law* (Cambridge, Cambridge University Press, 2017) (noting that both *Adäquanztheorie* and *Schutzzwecklehre* are used to determine legal causation in Germany).

[77] Giesen (n 5).

[78] ibid.

[79] ibid.

[80] ibid.

[81] ibid.

[82] ibid.

In the US, some courts interpret the term 'proximate cause' broadly to encompass both cause-in-fact and legal causation.[83] Other US courts distinguish proximate cause from cause-in-fact.[84] Nevertheless, most courts agree that the causation element of a medical malpractice claim must satisfy two prongs of causation: factual causation and legal causation. To determine whether the factual causation prong is satisfied, courts traditionally apply the 'but-for' test to determine whether, '"but for" the defendant's actions, the plaintiff's injury would not have occurred'.[85] However, some courts also allow factual causation to be determined under a more lenient 'substantial factor' test that asks whether the defendant's breach was 'a substantial factor in bringing about the injury'.[86] The 'substantial factor' test is favoured when more than one action or omission caused the plaintiff's alleged injury.[87] This is particularly common in medical malpractice cases because a plaintiff's pre-existing medical condition is often cited as a contributing cause of the alleged injury.[88] For example, the Supreme Court of Pennsylvania found that a doctor's failure to diagnose a cancerous breast mass could have been a substantial factor in increasing the plaintiff's health risks despite the defendant's position that the plaintiff was 'already suffering from cancer' and the failure to diagnose the tumour had no adverse impact on her existing condition.[89]

Legal causation focuses on the foreseeability of a particular action or omission in causing the injury sustained.[90] The legal causation requirement serves

[83] See *Craig ex rel Craig v Oakwood Hospital*, 684 NW2d 296 (Mich 2004) ('"Proximate cause" is a legal term of art that incorporates both cause in fact and legal (or "proximate") cause'); *McKellips v Saint Francis Hospital*, 741 P2d 467 (Okla 1987) ('Proximate cause consists of two elements: cause in fact and legal causation.'); *Marvelli v Alston*, 100 SW3d 460 (Tex App 2003) ('To establish proximate cause, the plaintiff must prove: (1) foreseeability, and (2) cause-in-fact.'); *Turcios v DeBruler*, 32 NE3d 1117 (Ill 2015) ('The term "proximate cause" embodies two distinct concepts: cause in fact and legal cause.').

[84] See *Kilpatrick v Bryant*, 868 SW2d 594 (Tenn 1993) ('Causation (or cause in fact) is a very different concept from that of proximate cause.'); *Peterson v Reeves*, 727 SE2d 171 (Ga Ct App 2012) ('analysis of the issue of proximate cause . . . [is] distinguished from cause in fact'); *Ploch v Hamai*, 213 SW3d 135 (Mo Ct App 2006) ('To establish causation in a medical malpractice action, the plaintiff must show that the physician's conduct was the cause-in-fact and the proximate cause of the plaintiff's damages.').

[85] *O'Neal*, 791 NW2d 853.

[86] *Bustamante v Ponte*, 529 SW3d 447 (Tex 2017).

[87] See *Newberry v Martens*, 127 P3d 187, 191 (Idaho 2005) (noting that the but-for test is appropriate when there is one possible cause, but the substantial factor test should be used in cases with multiple causes of damage).

[88] See *Scafidi v Seiler*, 574 A2d 398, 403 (NJ 1990) (noting that a majority accept the 'substantial factor' test to determine cause-in-fact in medical malpractice cases involving pre-existing medical conditions).

[89] *Jones v Montefiore Hospital*, 431 A2d 920 (Penn 1981) (finding that the trial court erred in failing to properly instruct the jury on causation based on the substantial factor test).

[90] See *Morisch v United States*, 653 F3d 522 (7th Cir 2011) ('[T]o prove legal cause, a plaintiff must also show that an injury was foreseeable as the type of harm that a reasonable person would expect to see as a likely result of his or her conduct.'); *Easterling v Kendall*, 367 P3d 1214 (Idaho 2016) ('[T]o prove legal cause, a plaintiff must also show that an injury was foreseeable as the type of harm that a reasonable person would expect to see as a likely result of his or her conduct.').

to limit the scope of liability to exclude negligent actions that may have been a cause-in-fact of a plaintiff's injury but are too far removed from the type of injury that the plaintiff ultimately suffered.[91] Foreseeability is judged from the perspective of an ordinary reasonable person under the circumstances.[92] According to a Texas court of appeals, 'foreseeability exists if the actor, as a person of ordinary intelligence, should have anticipated the dangers his negligent act creates for others'.[93] In Illinois, the foreseeability inquiry is 'whether the injury sustained is one that a reasonable person would consider to be a likely consequence of his conduct'.[94] In *Morisch v US*, the Seventh Circuit Court of Appeals agreed with the trial court that there was no proximate cause in a medical malpractice case when the plaintiff's stroke was 'not a foreseeable result' of the hospital's failure to immediately relay test results.[95]

US courts are split on the issue of fault apportionment for tortfeasors who simultaneously and independently cause medical injuries. Concurrent (or simultaneous) causes exist when the negligent conduct of two or more separate tortfeasors or two or more actions (or omissions) by one tortfeasor was each independently capable of producing the resulting damage.[96] Some states impose joint and several liability on tortfeasors who 'act in concert' to cause harm.[97] Others take a comparative fault approach to hold tortfeasors responsible only for damages corresponding with their per centage of fault.[98]

In the case of successive or intervening causes, which occur subsequent to an actor's negligent conduct, a prior actor will generally not be relieved of liability

[91] Some US courts view foreseeability as a factor limiting the scope of a legal duty rather than one affecting the causation injury. See *American Law Reports*, 100 ALR2d 942 (originally published in 1965) (noting that although foreseeability is generally considered to determine liability for negligence, courts are in sharp disagreement regarding whether foreseeability should be considered to determine legal duty versus causation). Some US courts view foreseeability as an element of both duty and causation. See *Macias v Summit Management*, 220 A3d 363 (Md Ct App 2019); *Westin Operator v Groh*, 347 P3d 606 (Colo 2015); *Kerns v Independent School District No 31 of Ottawa County*, 44 F Supp 3d 1110 (ND Okla 2014) (applying Oklahoma law).

[92] *MJS & Associates v Master*, 501 SW3d 751 (Tex App 2016); *Winchell v Guy*, 857 NE2d 1024 (Ind Ct App 2006).

[93] *Scurlock v Pennell*, 177 SW3d 222 (Tex App Houston 1st Dist 2005).

[94] *Atchley v University of Chicago Medical Center*, 64 NE3d 781 (Ill App 1 Dist 2016).

[95] *Morisch*, 653 F3d 522 (n 90).

[96] See Giesen (n 5).

[97] *Woods v Cole*, 693 NE2d 333 (Ill 1998) ('The general principle that tortfeasors who negligently act in concert are held jointly and severally liable for the damages which they cause has been recognized in Illinois for over 100 years.'); see *Velez v Tuma*, 821 NW2d 432 (Mich 2012) ('The same comprehensive tort-reform legislation, however, also specifically retained "joint and several liability" in medical malpractice cases.'); *Palmer v Comprehensive Neurologic Services*, 864 NE2d 1093 (Ind Ct App 2007) (noting that medical malpractice cases are exempt from Indiana's comparative fault law).

[98] *Volz v Ledes*, 895 SW2d 677 (Tenn 1995) (applies doctrine of comparative fault, rather than joint and several liability, in medical malpractice case); *Dumas v State ex rel Department of Culture, Recreation & Tourism*, 828 So 2d 530 (La 2002) ('The comparative fault article, La. C.C. art. 2323, makes no exceptions for liability based on medical malpractice.'); *Gardner v Oregon Health & Sciences University*, 461 P3d 222 (Or 2020) (recognising the application of comparative fault in a medical malpractice case).

if he should have anticipated the negligent intervening act or if the intervening act was a 'normal consequence of the situation created' by the prior actor and is not 'extraordinarily negligent'.[99] For example, the Ohio Supreme Court found that a doctor's admitted negligence in failing to promptly treat a patient with preeclampsia upon receiving a nurse's report of high blood pressure was not enough to sever the nurse's failure to recognise preeclampsia and/or give the physician a full report of the patient's condition.[100]

German law also takes a 'bifurcated approach' to causation.[101] The first prong of causation considers whether the 'conduct played some role in bringing about the Plaintiff's hurt', a consideration comparable to cause-in-fact inquiry in US law.[102] The second prong, similar to legal causation in US law, undertakes a normative evaluation of whether conduct that meets the first prong should result in legal liability.[103] However, unlike US law, German law has another, deeper layer that underlies the causation analysis: it distinguishes between causation that establishes liability (*haftungsbegründende Kausalität*) and causation that completes liability (*haftungsausfüllende Kausalität*).[104] Stauch describes the distinction between the two as follows:

> The first of these, 'liability grounding causation', denotes the link from the defendant's faulty conduct and *initial* harm to the claimant (in the form of invasion of one of his abstract protected interests). By contrast, the latter, 'liability-completing causation', refers to the subsequent link between that invasion and the further, tangible injuries suffered by the claimant (which form the subject of his claim for substantial damages).[105]

Infantino and Zervogianni describe *haftungsbegründende Kausalität* as a question of causation concerned with the existence of liability and *haftungsausfüllende Kausalität* as a question of causation concerned with the scope or extent of the liability.[106]

Although some scholars characterise this causation distinction as theoretical or philosophical rather than practical, Stauch observes that the distinction can nevertheless be important in medical negligence cases because once the patient establishes liability-grounding causation, liability-completing causation is held to a lower standard of proof.[107] The BGH confirmed that this evidentiary effect could have 'led to a different, more favourable result for the plaintiff' in a case involving an undiagnosed finger fracture that was discovered one month later when

[99] Restatement (Second) of Torts § 447 (American Law Institute 1965).
[100] *Berdyck v Shinde*, 613 NE2d 1014 (Ohio 1993).
[101] Markesinis et al (n 23).
[102] ibid.
[103] ibid.
[104] A Spickhoff, 'Kausalität' in A Spickhoff (ed), *Medizinrecht*, 4th edn (CH Beck, 2022); BGB § 276, para 17.
[105] Stauch (n 2).
[106] Infantino and Zervogianni (n 76).
[107] Stauch (n 2).

the patient re-fractured his finger and was diagnosed with Sudeck's syndrome.[108] Here, the BGH explained that the standard of proof under ZPO § 286 requiring 'a degree of certainty useful for practical life' governs the determination of liability that gives rise to the injury (failure to diagnose and properly treat the initial fracture).[109] However, since the standard of proof under ZPO § 287 requiring only a 'preponderance of probability' governs liability-filling causation (the second fracture and development of Sudeck's syndrome), the court remanded the case for a causation redetermination applying the lower standard.[110]

To determine factual causation, German courts use a '"*condicio sine qua non*" formula . . . [that] is identical to the "but for" test in common law'.[111] To determine whether a defendant's conduct is a 'but for' cause or *condicio sine qua non* of the plaintiff's injury, German courts generally rely on two methods to evaluate causation: (1) 'the method of elimination (*Hinwegdenken*)' for negligent actions; and (2) the method of 'total substitution' for negligent omissions.[112] Generally, the the method of elimination is used to determine whether a defendant's actions caused an injury, and considers whether the same injury would have resulted if the defendant's acts are 'eliminated in thought'.[113] When a defendant's omissions allegedly caused an injury, the court will usually apply the total substitution method to eliminate the wrongful omission and substitute in the non-negligent conduct that the defendant should have taken, and ask whether the injury would have still occurred.[114] In both cases, an affirmative answer to the question results in no factual causation.[115] Conversely, if eliminating or substituting the defendant's actions also eliminate the injury, then factual causation exists.[116] A common negligent omission in medical malpractice cases – failure to diagnose – will trigger the total substitution method.[117]

There are instances when both elimination or substitution methods fail to provide an acceptable solution to causation, for example, in the case of simultaneous independent causes of the same harm.[118] Markesinis et al give the example of two motorcycles that simultaneously pass a horse and make it bolt. Assuming that each motorcycle alone would have made the horse bolt, a strict application of the 'but-for' test would lead to no liability for either motorcyclist.[119] While Markesinis et al advocate for the adoption of the US 'substantial factor' test

[108] BGH 12 February 2008, VI ZR 221/06, r+s 2008, 214.
[109] ibid.
[110] BGH 12 February 2008, VI ZR 221/06, r+s 2008, 214 (noting that the OLG applied a standard of proof for liability-filling causation of 'probability bordering on certainty', which is even stricter than what even § 286 ZPO requires).
[111] Stauch (n 2).
[112] Markesinis et al (n 23).
[113] ibid.
[114] ibid.
[115] ibid.
[116] ibid.
[117] Petry (n 40).
[118] Markesinis et al (n 23).
[119] ibid.

discussed above, they conclude that German courts will consider the conduct of both motorcyclists as a 'condition' of the harm at the cause-in-fact stage of the analysis.[120] Thus, tortfeasors who simultaneously and independently cause an injury are jointly and severally liable,[121] unless the resulting harm is divisible and each harm can be clearly attributed to a particular cause.[122] In the case of medical treatment, it is not unusual for several healthcare providers to have concurring duties to a patient to prevent the same harm. For example, the BGH found that both the hospital's nursing staff and the surgeon had a duty to monitor the placement of an indwelling cannula during a patient's post-operative care, and thus both were liable when the cannula became detached, causing a patient injury.[123]

In the case of successive or intervening causes in Germany, the first tortfeasor will be relieved of liability for the final harm only in rare instances. Unless the subsequent tortfeasor was grossly negligent[124] or the second negligent act is outside of the scope of risk created by the first negligent act,[125] the first actor will remain jointly and severally liable for the ultimate injury.[126] For example, the BGH held that a family physician's refusal to conduct a home visit for a patient was still a cause-in-fact of an injury caused by delayed treatment even though the plaintiff subsequently consulted with an emergency physician whose negligence may have also caused the delay.[127] In this case, the family physician, who had information about the patient's history and recent complaints, and thus should have suspected that the patient had an emergent condition, refused the patient's request for an immediate home visit.[128] After this refusal, an emergency physician responded to the plaintiff's request, diagnosed the condition, and recommended the proper treatment, but failed to convey the seriousness of the risk (leg amputation) to the patient.[129] As a result, the patient's delay in seeking the recommended treatment led to a leg amputation.[130] The Court found that the family physician's refusal to conduct a home visit was still a cause of the patient's injury, noting that:

> [A] subsequent medical treatment error [by the emergency physician] . . . would not have been so remote from the outset that it could no longer be imputed to the defendant. The summoned emergency physician, who unlike the treating general

[120] ibid.
[121] ibid.
[122] T Voigt in *BeckOGK BGB* (Beck online, 1 February 2026), BGB § 823 paras 1021–24 (noting that if it is possible to clearly delineate the contribution of a cause to a particular portion of the damages, then the physician will only be responsible for the portion of damages they caused).
[123] BGH 1 October 1984 NJW 1984, 1400.
[124] Stauch (n 2).
[125] BGH 20 September 1988 NJW 1989, 767.
[126] Stauch (n 2).
[127] BGH 28 January 1986 NJW 1986, 2367.
[128] ibid.
[129] ibid.
[130] ibid.

> practitioner lacks knowledge of the patient's medical history and personality, who perhaps also does not have the necessary specialist knowledge, who finally does not enjoy the same trust of the patient as the general practitioner from the outset, can be at a disadvantage compared with the general practitioner when making a diagnosis and advising the patient . . . Even if Dr. P. [the emergency physician] had told the plaintiff with the necessary seriousness and emphasis everything that had to be done from the medical point of view to save the leg, it remains open whether this eliminated all effects of the treatment error to be blamed on the defendant on the further course of the disease. Even then, as long as nothing else is actually established, the possibility remains that the defendant, who would have been obligated to act on his own and who had not given the treatment, would have succeeded differently and better than Dr. P. in convincing the plaintiff that he had to go to a hospital immediately.[131]

This means that an act of medical negligence will likely be deemed sufficient to cause an injury if the injury would not have occurred in the course of treatment rendered in accordance with the applicable standard of care, even if the act or omission was not the sole or even primary cause of the injury.[132]

Legal causation in Germany is determined by applying both the adequacy theory (*adäquater Kausalzusammenhang*) to determine the likelihood of the conduct to cause the injury and a second test to determine whether the injury falls within the protective scope of the relevant law or norm (*schutzzwecklehre*).[133] As in the US, the tortfeasor's subjective state of mind does not impact legal causation; German courts use the objective 'optimal observer' standard to assess legal causation.[134] The adequacy theory is satisfied when the defendant's negligent conduct was 'generally apt' to bring about the type of damage suffered by the plaintiff.[135] Stauch notes that the adequacy theory for legal causation is stricter than the common law reasonable foreseeability test and typically only excludes liability in cases of mere 'coincidence'.[136] As a result, German courts supplement the adequacy theory with a test that requires the injury to fall within the protective purpose of the law or norm prohibiting the defendant's conduct.[137] Although most injuries caused by medical treatment will fall within the scope of protecting a patient's bodily health and integrity, some will not. For example, the OLG Naumburg found that the unwanted birth of a child resulting from the failure to diagnose a pregnancy at a gynaecological visit, during which there was no discussion of a suspected pregnancy or desire to prevent pregnancy, was not within the protective purpose of the law governing treatment.[138]

[131] ibid (translation from German).
[132] T Voigt in *BeckOGK BGB* (Beck online, 1 February 2026); BGB § 823, paras 1021–24.
[133] Stauch (n 2).
[134] Giesen (n 5).
[135] Stauch (n 2); see Giesen (n 5).
[136] ibid.
[137] ibid.
[138] OLG Naumburg 26 May 1998, 11 U 2100/97, r+s 1999, 67.

The concept of *schutzzwecklehre* in German causation as applied here is most analogous to what US courts consider when determining the scope of a defendant's legal duty. The Louisiana Supreme Court, in *Faucheaux v Terrebonne*, explained the relevance of a legal rule's protective purpose in the duty–scope analysis:

> The scope of the duty inquiry is ultimately a question of policy as to whether the particular risk falls within the scope of the duty. Rules of conduct are designed to protect some persons under some circumstances against some risks. The scope of protection inquiry asks whether the enunciated rule extends to or is intended to protect this plaintiff from this type of harm arising in this manner.[139]

In the *Faucheaux* case, a fisherman suffered a fatal heart attack when a closing waterway gate collided with his boat. The court first recognised that the parish government had, and breached, a duty to provide warnings of waterway obstructions, including 'adequate signing, marking and warnings to alert boat operators traveling on the canal to unusual, perilous and unexpected hazards'.[140] In addressing whether the fisherman's injury was within the scope of the parish's duty, the court determined that:

> The duty to warn of the danger presented by the descending gate weighing several thousand pounds clearly encompassed the risk that a boat might collide with or be caught by the descending gate and that property damage and personal injury might result from the collision.[141]

4.1.4 Damage

When, under the principles articulated above, a treatment error causes patient harm, the medical liability system seeks to compensate the injured party for the damage sustained.[142] In both jurisdictions, damages can be separated into two broad categories: economic (or special); and non-economic (or general).[143] Economic damages are those subject to calculations that can be used to assign a monetary value to the damage sustained.[144] Examples of economic damages include past and future medical expenses, lost wages, and funeral costs. Non-economic damages are those that cannot be easily reduced to a monetary value, including pain and suffering, loss of enjoyment of life, and loss of consortium.[145]

[139] *Faucheaux v Terrebonne Consolidated Government*, 615 So2d 289 (La 1993).
[140] ibid.
[141] ibid.
[142] See Giesen (n 5) ('The central purpose of damages for medical malpractice in all jurisdictions under review is to compensate that patient for his loss.').
[143] ibid.
[144] ibid.
[145] ibid.

Both US and German medical liability law compensate medical malpractice patients for past and future medical (and related) expenses, past lost wages and future loss of earnings, and past and future physical and mental pain and suffering;[146] however, the jurisdictions diverge regarding the form of recoverable damages, quantum valuation of non-economic damages, and recognition of loss of chance as a recoverable item of damages.[147] First, in Germany, future economic damages are generally paid by quarterly pension while non-economic damages are typically paid in a lump sum.[148] As a general rule in the US, all damages awards are paid as a lump sum with future economic damages paid at the present-day value.[149] Second, awards for general damages in the US are much higher than those for similar injuries in Germany.[150] However, recent American tort reform efforts have led states to impose damages caps in an attempt to control general damages awards described as 'enormously more generous than other legal systems'.[151] Third, damages for a patient's loss of chance for a better outcome, commonly following a failure to diagnose or misdiagnosis, are recoverable in some US jurisdictions, but not in Germany.[152]

Finally, Germany's strong social insurance system provides an overarching policy reason for differences in damages awards in the US and Germany.[153] Ninety per cent of Germans receive health insurance coverage under the country's statutory health insurance system.[154] The system ensures that each member, regardless of income, receives the same medical benefits, including care for prevention and treatment of diseases.[155] In addition to medical care through statutory health insurance, the broader German social insurance system also provides statutory long-term care insurance, statutory accident insurance, statutory pension insurance, and statutory unemployment insurance.[156] Germany's comprehensive social insurance scheme impacts recovery of damages caused by medical malpractice because Germans, unlike Americans, do not need to rely upon medical malpractice lawsuits to pay for their past and future medical care, home care, rehabilitation. It also limits compensation for past or future lost

[146] See generally ibid (discussing the approaches of various jurisdictions to heads of recoverable loss in medical malpractice cases).

[147] See generally ibid (regarding form of damages and pain and suffering awards); Stauch (n 2) (regarding loss of chance in Germany).

[148] Giesen (n 5).

[149] ibid.

[150] See generally SD Sugarman, 'A Comparative Law Look at Pain and Suffering Awards' (2006) 55 *DePaul Law Review* 399.

[151] ibid.

[152] Stauch (n 2) (no awards for loss of chance in Germany); see B Casaceli, 'Losing A Chance to Survive: An Examination of the Loss of Chance Doctrine Within the Context of A Wrongful Death Action' (2014) 9 *Journal of Health & Biomedical Law* 521 (analysis of loss of chance doctrine in the US).

[153] See J Fedtke, 'The Culture of German Tort Law' (2012) 3 *Journal of European Tort Law* 183 ('The German Social Security system is the single most relevant influence on the German legal system.').

[154] Deutscher Ärzte-Verlag, *The Healthcare System in Germany: A Short Introduction* (2012) 1, 3–8.

[155] ibid.

[156] ibid.

wages. As a result, the German insurance system protects healthcare providers and their insurers from the kind of exorbitant awards for future medical costs, life care plans, and lost wages seen in the US.

4.2 PROVING LIABILITY

The US and Germany both require the plaintiff to bear the burden of proving liability, provide avenues for the plaintiff to obtain evidence needed to meet this burden, and employ burden-shifting mechanisms to either lessen or eliminate the plaintiff's burden of proof in certain circumstances. However, the jurisdictions have rules that diverge in each of these areas of proof as discussed below.

4.2.1 The Burden and Standard of Proof

The default position in both the US[157] and Germany[158] is that the plaintiff bears the burden of proving medical malpractice. Also, as a general rule, both jurisdictions require expert testimony to prove both a breach of the applicable standard of care and that the breach caused the alleged damages.[159] The jurisdictions diverge, however, on the standard of proof required to meet the plaintiff's burden.

In the US, the plaintiff must prove both breach of the applicable standard of care and causation by a preponderance of the evidence.[160] *Black's Law Dictionary* defines 'preponderance of the evidence' as follows:

> The greater weight of the evidence, not necessarily established by the greater number of witnesses testifying to a fact but by evidence that has the most convincing force; superior evidentiary weight that, though not sufficient to free the mind wholly from all reasonable doubt, is still sufficient to incline a fair and impartial mind to one side of the issue rather than the other. This is the burden of proof in most civil trials, in which the jury is instructed to find for the party that, on the whole, has the stronger evidence, however slight the edge may be.[161]

US courts have further explained that proof of a fact by a preponderance of the evidence requires it to be proven more probably true than not true or its existence more likely than not.[162]

[157] GL Blum et al, 61 *American Jurisprudence Physicians* Surgeons, and Other Healers § 309 (2d ed) Thomson Reuters Westlaw (database updated February 2026).

[158] Stauch (n 2).

[159] See Bergmann et al (n 32) (regarding Germany); Pegalis (n 28) § 8:1.

[160] See La Stat Ann § 9:2794; *Evans v DeKalb City Hospital Authority*, 267 SE2d 319 (Ga Ct App 1980); *Todd v United States*, 570 F Supp 670 (DSC 1983); *Klug v Ramirez*, 830 SW2d 801 (Tex App 1992).

[161] 'Preponderance of the Evidence' in BA Garner (ed), *Black's Law Dictionary*, 11th edn (Saint Paul, Thomson Reuters, 2019).

[162] *James v McHenry*, 828 So 2d 94 (La App 2 Cir 2002); *Cook v Michael*, 330 P2d 1026 (Or 1958); *Matter of Briscoe Enterprises*, 994 F2d 1160 (5th Cir 1993); *Nauheim v City of Topeka*, 432 P3d 647 (Kan 2019); *Herman & MacLean v Huddleston*, 459 US 375 (1983).

One adjustment to the preponderance of evidence standard in medical malpractice cases is the requirement by some jurisdictions that expert testimony establishing breach of the applicable standard of care and causation be given 'to a reasonable degree of medical certainty'; however, there are inconsistent judicial interpretations of this standard.[163] In Pennsylvania, expert opinions in medical malpractice cases do not meet the requisite standard if they are expressed in terms of possibility, likelihood, or even high probability.[164] On the other hand, Virginia courts equate the 'reasonable degree of medical certainty' standard with the 'preponderance of evidence' standard.[165] Similarly, other jurisdictions use the 'reasonable degree of medical probability' standard for expert testimony and interpret it as having the same effect as the 'preponderance of evidence' standard, which is to exclude mere speculation or possibility.[166]

In Germany, the standard of proof is governed by the Civil Code of Procedure, which requires the court, 'to decide, at its discretion and conviction, and taking account of the entire content of the hearings and the results obtained by evidence being taken, if any, whether an allegation as to fact is to be deemed true or untrue'.[167] Stauch expresses this standard as requiring the court to be, 'overwhelmingly convinced of the facts', which he notes is higher than the common law 'more likely than not' standard.[168] The BGH has explained the standard of proof as requiring 'Full judicial conviction in the form of a degree of certainty that silences doubts for practical purposes, even if it does not eliminate them entirely.'[169] However, the BGH has also noted that requiring a standard of 'probability bordering on certainty' is stricter than what the Code requires.[170]

German courts aim to sculpt proof rules to create an 'equality of arms' between the litigants.[171] The German Federal Court observes the competing interests that medical malpractice cases invoke:

> On the one hand, there is the patient's need for proof, who must in principle prove that the doctor made a mistake as the basis for a claim, but who has only limited insight into the doctor's actions, and often no insight at all, for example due to anesthesia. On the other hand, the physician is confronted with the difficulty that incidents, which as a rule indicate medical malpractice, can in many areas, as a result

[163] *Morisch*, 653 F3d 522 (n 90); *Griffin v University of Pittsburgh Medical Center-Braddock Hospital*, 950 A2d 996 (Pa 2008).

[164] See *Griffin*, 950 A2d 996 (n 163) (noting that reasonable degree of medical certainty standard is not met by an expert opinion rendered in 'more likely than not' terms).

[165] *Hoffman v Carter* 648 SE2d 318 (Va Ct App 2007).

[166] *Morsicato v Sav-On Drug Stores*, 111 P3d 1112 (Nev 2005) (expert's speculative testimony failed to meet standard); *American Radiology Services v Reiss*, 236 A3d 518 (Md Ct App 2020) (expert's opinion must be based upon 'more than speculation or conjecture')

[167] *Zivilprozessordnung* (ZPO), 12 September 1950, BGBl I 1950, 533, as amended, § 286.

[168] Stauch (n 2). Stauch notes that the higher standard of proof is related to the inquisitorial nature of civil law jurisdictions, wherein the court seeks to uncover the truth rather than just judging the stronger case as presented by advocates.

[169] ibid (citing BGH 17 February 1970 BGHZ 53, 245).

[170] BGH 12 February 2008 VI ZR 221/06.

[171] See Bergmann et al (n 32).

> of the unpredictability of the living organism, exceptionally also occur as a result of fate; that the latter was the case, he could only prove with sufficient certainty if he secured every detail of his actions as evidence by documentation and the presence of witnesses.[172]

To balance the competing interests of patients and providers at the proof level, the burden of producing evidence in German medical malpractice cases is slightly modified by shifting the initial burden of production to the defendant provider. German law requires the defendant provider to first produce information, usually in the form of medical records, regarding the patient's course of medical treatment. [173] As a result, the plaintiff's burden of producing evidence is relaxed to accommodate for their information deficiency and lack of expert medical knowledge.[174]

4.2.2 Burden of Proof Modifications

Both jurisdictions allow for some modification of the default burden of proof rules. US courts are more willing to ease the burden of proof for a plaintiff by observing legal inferences or presumptions of negligence in medical malpractice cases in certain circumstances, while German courts will relieve the plaintiff of their burden of proof by shifting the burden to the defendant in certain categories of cases.

In the US, the common law doctrine of *res ipsa loquitur* is the legal mechanism by which courts can ease the plaintiff's burden of proof. Meaning 'the thing speaks for itself', *res ipsa loquitur* creates an inference of negligence in tort cases when: (1) the injury does not ordinarily occur in the absence of negligence; (2) the agency or instrumentality of the injury is in the exclusive control of the defendant; (3) the plaintiff was not contributorily negligent; and (4) the defendant is in a superior position to explain the accident.[175]

Once a plaintiff invokes the doctrine of *res ipsa loquitur*, a rebuttable inference or presumption of negligence arises, and a burden of production shifts to the defendant to produce evidence that they are not negligent.[176] If the defendant can rebut this presumption, the plaintiff must prove that the defendant was negligent and that such negligence caused the plaintiff's injury.[177] Medical malpractice cases that are generally suited for application of the *res ipsa loquitur* doctrine include cases in which a surgeon operates on the wrong body part

[172] BGH 14 March 1978 VI ZR 213/76.

[173] ibid.

[174] See Bergmann et al (n 32).

[175] KK Ablin, 'Res Ipsa Loquitur and Expert Opinion Evidence in Medical Malpractice Cases: Strange Bedfellows' (1996) 82 *Virginia Law Review* 325.

[176] See *Chapman v Harner*, 339 P3d 519 (Colo 2014) (discussing 'the effect of *res ipsa loquitur* as a rebuttable presumption').

[177] See ibid.

or injury to a body part not involved in the surgery,[178] and cases in which foreign objects are found in a patient's body after surgery.[179]

All states, with the exception of Alabama, Alaska, Georgia, and South Carolina, allow plaintiffs to invoke the doctrine of *res ipsa loquitur* to ease their burden of proving negligence in medical malpractice cases.[180] Nevada, in addition to recognising the doctrine of *res ipsa loquitur* generally, has also codified rebuttable presumptions in medical malpractice cases involving a foreign body left in a patient following surgery, an explosion or fire during the course of treatment, an unintended burn during the course of treatment, injury to a body part not directly involved in the treatment, or a surgical procedure performed on the wrong patient, organ, or body part.[181] While the doctrine generally only gives rise to a rebuttable presumption of negligence, in Louisiana, the burden of proof shifts entirely to the defendant in medical malpractice cases where the court finds that the doctrine of *res ipsa loquitur* is applicable.[182]

The states diverge on the issue of whether plaintiffs can present expert testimony in medical malpractice cases that invoke the doctrine of *res ipsa loquitur*. Most states, in accordance with Comment D to Restatement (Second) of Torts,[183] allow expert testimony in medical malpractice cases to assist laypeople on the jury to determine whether the plaintiff's medical injury is the kind that necessitates an inference of negligence.[184] Eight states, however, refuse to allow expert evidence in medical malpractice cases that invoke the *res ipsa loquitur* doctrine, reasoning that the doctrine can only be applied in cases that allow lay jurors with common knowledge to infer negligence without any specialist knowledge or explanation.[185]

Like the doctrine of *res ipsa loquitur*, Germany's *Anscheinsbeweis* or prima facie *Beweis* doctrines can reduce a plaintiff's burden of proving negligence when

[178] *Long v Hacker*, 520 NW2d 195 (Neb 1994) (wrong vertebra); *Manax v Ballew*, 797 SW2d 71 (Tex App 1990) (wrong part of back); *Wick v Henderson*, 485 NW2d 645 (Iowa 1992) (operation for gallbladder, injury to left arm); *Dalley v Utah Valley Regional Medical Center*, 791 P2d 193 (Utah 1990) (caesarean, burn on calf); *Beaudoin v Watertown Memorial Hospital*, 145 NW2d 166 (Wis 1966) (vaginal polyp removed, burns on buttocks); *Simmons v Neuman*, 50 AD3d 666 (NY App Div 2d Dept 2008) (patient who allegedly suffered burns to her right thigh during surgery on her right shoulder sued her physician for medical malpractice); *Ceresa v Karakousis*, 210 AD2d 884 (NY App Div 4th Dep't 1994) (unusual compression fracture to arm and shoulder during surgery to remove tumour from lower spine); *Kerber v Sarles*, 151 AD2d 1031 (NY App Div 4th Dept 1989) (absence of front teeth which had been knocked out during foot surgery).

[179] *Tiller v Von Pohle*, 230 P2d 213 (Ariz 1951) (large cloth sack lodged in plaintiff's bowel after abdominal operation, inference that it was a result of the operation would be permitted); *Kambat v Saint Francis Hospital*, 678 NE2d 456 (NY App Div 2d Dept 1997) (18 × 18-inch towel or laparotomy pack); *Gravitt v Newman*, 114 AD2d 1000 ((NY App Div 2d Dept 1985) (tip of an internal vein stripper left in the patient's leg during surgery for varicose veins); *Critelli v Long Island Jewish-Hillside Medical Center*, 115 AD2d 632 (NY App Div 2d Dept 1985) (laparotomy pad left in abdomen).

[180] See *Sides v St Anthony's Medical Center*, 258 SW3d 811 (Mo 2008).

[181] Nev Rev Stat 41A.100.

[182] La Stat Ann § 9:2794.

[183] Restatement (Second) of Torts § 328D cmt m (American Law Institute 1965).

[184] *Sides*, 258 SW3d 811 (n 180).

[185] ibid.

their injury does not occur 'in the typical course of events' absent negligence.[186] However, for plaintiffs in medical malpractice cases, the Patients' Rights Act (*Patientenrechtegesetz; PRG*) codified more advantageous burden shifting mechanisms for certain categories of cases.[187]

The plaintiff's burden of proving negligence will shift to the defendant in two scenarios. First, the burden will shift when manifestation of a 'fully masterable' risk – a risk that was fully in the control of the defendant – caused the plaintiff's injury.[188] 'Fully masterable' risks include patient positioning, hygiene deficiency, and equipment insufficiency.[189] Second, the burden will shift when the treating party fails to document a medically necessary measure.[190] If a required medical measure is not documented, the court will presume that it was not carried out, and the burden of proof will shift to the defendant if it is 'sufficiently likely' that the missing measure would have revealed something relevant for the patient's medical treatment.[191] However, if the missing measure was omitted from the patient's treatment as a result of a treating physician's diagnostic error, the burden of proof will not shift to the defendant who failed to carry out the medically necessary measure.[192]

The plaintiff's burden of proving causation will shift to the defendant in two scenarios. First, in the case of 'beginners' errors' – when a provider is not qualified to carry out the treatment – the court will presume that the lack of qualifications caused the injury.[193] Second, the burden of proof on causation shifts to the defendant when the plaintiff's injuries are caused by 'gross errors'.[194] Gross errors are the primary reason for burden shifting in German medical malpractice cases.[195] According to the BGH, gross errors include those that occur, 'when a physician has definitely violated established medical treatment rules or latest medical knowledge and committed an error that no longer seems to be understandable from an objective point of view because it simply must not occur'.[196] Additionally, organisational errors can also be considered gross errors, for example, when the organisation of the admission process for new-born babies is 'severely' flawed and leads to an 'incomprehensible' and 'unacceptable' delay in treatment.[197]

[186] Stauch (n 2).
[187] See C Goldbach, *Risikomanagementsysteme im Krankenhaus nach dem Patientenrechtegesetz: Sozialrechtliche Pflicht und haftungsrechtlicher Standard* (Forum Wirtschaftsrecht, Band 16, 2014) 129 (noting that the PRG codified burden of proof rules previously developed by the case law).
[188] BGB § 630h(1).
[189] Bergmann et al (n 32).
[190] BGB § 630h(3); see Sommer et al (n 4).
[191] See Sommer et al (n 4).
[192] Bergmann et al (n 32).
[193] BGB § 630h(4); see Sommer et al (n 4).
[194] BGB § 630h(5).
[195] Bergmann et al (n 32).
[196] A Wienke, 'Errors and pitfalls: Briefing and accusation of medical malpractice – the second victim' (2013) 12 *GMS Current Topics in Otorhinolaryngology – Head and Neck Surgery* 1.
[197] OLG Bremen 13 January 2006, 4 U 23/05, MedR 2007, 660.

In the case of an erroneous failure to make a diagnostic finding, the burden of proof will shift with regard to causation if it is sufficiently probable that the diagnostic finding, had it been made, would have warranted a further response which, if not taken, would have constituted a gross error.[198] For example, the Koblenz Higher Regional Court found that the failure to investigate a patient's post-operative complaints was not itself a gross error, but it was highly probable that had the investigation occurred, a perforated ulcer, which ultimately caused the plaintiff's death, would have been discovered. Further, because failure to respond to the discovery of a perforated ulcer would have constituted a gross error, the plaintiff was entitled to a reversal of the burden of proof on causation.[199]

4.2.3 Obtaining Evidence of Malpractice

Both jurisdictions provide legal avenues for obtaining evidence of medical negligence. In the US, the adversarial process of pre-trial discovery dominates the evidence-seeking stage of litigation. Pre-trial discovery is a mechanism through which parties in litigation can obtain information and documents pertaining to the disputed matter. Generally, the pre-trial phase in US civil litigation civil litigation, which typically allows 'discovery regarding any nonprivileged matter that is relevant to any party's claim or defense and proportional to the needs of the case',[200] is more liberal and broader in scope than its German counterpart. The US Fifth Circuit Court of Appeals has observed that 'many foreign countries, particularly civil law countries, do not subscribe to our open-ended views regarding pretrial discovery, and in some cases may even be offended by our pretrial procedures'.[201] This is particularly true in Germany, where the concept of *nemo tenetur se ipsum accusare*, meaning 'no man has to accuse himself', provides an important limitation on the process of obtaining evidence in all legal proceedings. G Arthur Martin observes:

> In the German law of procedure – not only civil and criminal, but also administrative, labour, social, etc. – the rule '*nemo tenetur se ipsum accusare*' has been generally accepted for well over one century. It is based upon the ethical concept that the procedural interest in the exploration of the truth must stand back behind the higher valued interest of the individual to be protected from any coercion to self-incrimination.[202]

In medical malpractice litigation, evidence is primarily centred around documents relating to the plaintiff's medical treatment. While both jurisdictions

[198] OLG Koblenz 10 January 2008, NJW-RR 2008, 1055.
[199] ibid.
[200] Fed R Civ P 26.
[201] *In re Anschuetz & Company, GmbH*, 838 F2d 1362 (5th Cir 1988).
[202] GA Martin, 'The Privilege against Self-Incrimination under Foreign Law' (1960/61) 51 *Journal of Criminal Law, Criminology & Police Science* 161, 172.

provide plaintiffs with access to their medical treatment records, they also limit the types of documents that litigants can obtain in medical malpractice cases.

In the US, the Health Insurance Portability and Accountability Act of 1996 (HIPAA) provides patients with a right to request medical treatment records.[203] This includes medical treatment, billing, and insurance records as well as any records used 'to make decisions about individuals'.[204] However, patients are not entitled to 'Information compiled in reasonable anticipation of, or for use in, a civil, criminal, or administrative action or proceeding.'[205] Attorneys in medical malpractice litigation may obtain a plaintiff's medical records via a HIPAA-compliant authorisation to release records to a third party.[206] Additionally, the parties can obtain medical records from one another pursuant to procedural rules that allow litigants to request documents and electronic information in pre-trial discovery by 'describ[ing] with reasonable particularity each item or category of items to be inspected'.[207] Although US courts are split regarding whether plaintiffs are required to sign HIPAA authorisations allowing third-party access to medical records as part of pre-trial discovery,[208] HIPAA itself allows healthcare providers to provide medical records pursuant to a court order, subpoena, or discovery request 'in the course of any judicial or administrative proceeding'.[209]

There are two main privileges that protect documents from discovery in medical malpractice litigation in the US. First, the peer review privilege, which is codified in nearly every state,[210] excludes information developed by hospital peer review committees from pre-trial discovery.[211] Peer review committees are designed to evaluate both the competency of physicians and the quality of medical treatment provided in the hospitals to discover and correct deficiencies and improve the overall quality of care.[212] The Seventh Circuit Court of Appeals

[203] Health Insurance Portability and Accountability Act of 1996 (HIPAA), Pub L No 104–191, 110 Stat 1936 (codified as amended in scattered sections of 18, 26, 29, and 42 USC); the Department of Health and Human Services' privacy regulations, which implement s 264(c) HIPAA, are codified at 45 CFR §§ 164.500–164.534. See 45 CFR §§ 164.508; 45, 164.524, 164.526.

[204] 45 CFR § 164.501.

[205] 45 CFR § 164.524(a)(1)(ii).

[206] 45 CFR § 164.506.

[207] See Fed R Civ P 34(b)(1)(A). Although most medical malpractice cases are litigated in state courts, most states have adopted or closely model their civil procedure rules after the federal rules. See US Legal, 'State Rules of Civil Procedure', civilprocedure.uslegal.com/rules-of-civil-procedure/state-rules-of-civil-procedure.

[208] See *Wymore v Nail* No 5:14-CV-3493, 2016 WL 1452437 (WD La 13 April 2016) ('Rule 34, along with rule 37, empowers federal courts to compel parties to sign written authorizations consenting to the production of various documents'); *cf Chase v Nova Southeastern University*, No 11-61290-CIV, 2012 WL 1936082 (SD Fla 29 May 2012) (finding that the court does 'not possess the authority to routinely require a plaintiff to execute a release for medical records').

[209] 45 CFR § 164.512(e)(1).

[210] KR Kohlberg, 'The Medical Peer Review Privilege: A Linchpin for Patient Safety Measures' (2002) 86 *Massachusetts Law Review* 157, 157.

[211] See ibid.

[212] See KT Stukes, 'The Medical Peer Review Privilege After Virmani' (2002) 80 *North Carolina Law Review* 1860, 1862–63.

articulated the policy interests behind extending confidentiality to the peer review process:

> Candid and conscientious evaluation of clinical practices is a *sine qua non* of adequate hospital care. To subject these discussions and deliberations to the discovery process, without a showing of exceptional necessity, would result in terminating such deliberations. Constructive professional criticism cannot occur in an atmosphere of apprehension that one doctor's suggestion will be used as a denunciation of a colleague's conduct in a malpractice suit.[213]

Although the peer review privilege generally protects the entire peer review process, including investigation, deliberations, and decisions, from use in litigation, peer review information available from other sources is usually exempt from the privilege's protection.[214] Additionally, US courts have limited the privilege's scope depending on how closely connected the information was to the formal peer review committee process.[215]

The second discovery privilege that arises in US medical malpractice litigation is found in the Patient Safety and Quality Improvement Act, 2005 (PSQIA). The PSQIA promotes the development and use of patient safety organizations (PSOs) to analyse medical error reports from healthcare organisations and recommend preventive measures.[216] To encourage improvements in healthcare quality, the PSQIA provides a level of confidentiality for data and records, 'assembled or developed by a provider for reporting to a PSO'.[217] This category of data and information, referred to as Patient Safety Work Product (PSWP), is protected from pre-trial discovery.[218] However, similar to the peer review privilege, PSWP does not 'include information that is collected, maintained, or developed separately, or exists separately, from a patient safety evaluation system'.[219]

German law also provides avenues for medical malpractice plaintiffs to obtain their medical records. First, patients in Germany have a legal right to inspect their medical records.[220] Medical records subject to inspection include 'all data arising in connection with the patient's medical treatment', including incidents that occur 'within the scope of the treatment'.[221] Patients can request their medical records directly or seek assistance from their health insurance companies, who are obligated to assist them in the case of a suspected medical error.[222]

[213] *Memorial Hospital for McHenry County v Shadur*, 664 F2d 1058 (7th Cir 1981).
[214] See *American Law Reports*, 69 ALR 5th 559 (originally published in 1999).
[215] See ibid.
[216] 42 USC §299b-21–b-26 (2005); see also S Rep No, 108-196 (discussing the intent of the Act).
[217] See 42 USC § 299b-22; 42 USC § 299b-21(7).
[218] 42 USC § 299b-21(7).
[219] 42 CFR § 3.20 (2009).
[220] BGB § 630g.
[221] J Thüß, *Rechtsfragen des Critical Incident Reportings in der Medizin* (Heidelberg, Springer-Verlag Berlin, 2012) 116.
[222] See Sozialgesetzbuch (SGB) V § 66.

Second, medical malpractice plaintiffs can request medical records pursuant to their broader right to obtain documents during litigation. The German rules of civil procedure allow parties to request documents by describing the document, the facts the document intends to prove, the contents of the document, the circumstances under which the opposing party allegedly has possession of the document, and the legal ground supporting the opposing party's obligation to produce the document.[223]

Both avenues for obtaining medical records in Germany can exclude certain information related to a healthcare organisation's efforts to improve patient care.[224] German scholars observe that patients generally do not have a right to access records relating to organisational failures, though potentially relevant to a medical malpractice claim, because the information sought is not necessary for the plaintiff's medical treatment.[225]

4.3 ORGANISATIONAL LIABILITY

The preceding sections have examined medical liability primarily through the lens of individual provider negligence. This section turns to the liability of healthcare organisations themselves. Giesen describes proper medical treatment as 'an obligation inseparably owed by both physician and hospital, captain and ship'.[226] Both US and German law recognise two distinct bases for organisational liability: (1) vicarious liability, in which the organisation is held derivatively liable for the negligence of individual providers; and (2) direct organisational liability, in which the organisation is held independently liable for its own negligent conduct.

4.3.1 Vicarious Liability

Under the doctrine of vicarious liability, healthcare organisations can be liable for injuries caused by the negligence of individual providers if those providers were acting as employees or agents of the organisation.

Although hospitals historically enjoyed immunity from liability for patient injuries in the US, in 1957, the New York Court of Appeals in *Bing v Thunig* found that hospitals could be vicariously liable for the actions of individual healthcare providers employed by the hospital.[227] Following *Bing*, theories pursuant

[223] ZPO § 424.

[224] See LG Bonn 2 September 2009 MedR 2009, 573 (finding that a report concerning a patient's fall in the hospital hallway was not discoverable).

[225] See Thüß (n 221); Pauli (n 1).

[226] Giesen (n 5).

[227] *Bing v Thunig* 143 N.E.2d 3 (New York Court of Appeals, 1957).

to the doctrines of estoppel and apparent agency emerged and provided additional bases for holding hospitals vicariously liable for patient injuries caused by treatment errors of non-employee physicians.[228] Because vicarious liability operates independent of joint and several or comparative liability schemes, a physician or hospital that is vicariously liable for injury caused by another's negligence will remain responsible for the entirety of the damages attributable to the negligent provider, 'regardless of whether joint and several liability or several liability is the governing rule'.[229] However, a physician or hospital held vicariously liable for another's negligence is entitled to seek indemnity from the original tortfeasor to recover the amount it paid to compensate for their negligence.[230]

In Germany, hospitals can be vicariously liable for negligent actions or omissions of healthcare providers who render services to the patient in the hospital. This is true in contract pursuant to BGB §§ 611 and 278, and in tort, pursuant to BGB § 31 or § 831.[231] Under the total hospital admission contract (*Totaler Krankenhausaufnahmevertrag*), the hospital is held vicariously liable pursuant to BGB § 278(1) for individual healthcare providers' treatment errors, because the hospital alone has a contractual obligation to provide medical treatment.

Under BGB § 831, hospitals can be held vicariously liable in tort law for an individual provider's negligence because the individual provider will generally be viewed as an agent of the hospital.[232] Vicarious agents include 'anyone who is generally or specifically integrated into the sphere of control and organisation of another person and is bound by their instructions'.[233] For hospitals, this includes physicians providing care under the general time and scope set forth by the hospital despite the hospital operator's inability to control physicians' professional judgment and medical decision-making.[234] When vicarious liability applies, both the hospital and the individual provider would be jointly and severally liable for damages in tort.[235]

Tort liability for vicarious agents is not strict and can be avoided when the principal establishes either: (1) reasonableness in the selection, management, and supervision of the of the agent; or (2) that the damage would have occurred despite proper selection, organisation, and supervision.[236] However, the BGH sets standards for presenting exculpatory evidence sufficient to avoid vicarious

[228] See ibid.
[229] Restatement (Third) of Torts § 13 (American Law Institute 2000).
[230] ibid § 122.
[231] Giesen (n 5).
[232] See BGB § 831.
[233] A Laufs et al, *Arztrecht*, 8th edn (Munich, CH Beck, 2026) (citing BGH 30 June 1966 NJW 1966, 1807).
[234] Laufs et al (n 233).
[235] BGB § 840(1).
[236] See BGB § 831; Markesinis et al (n 23).

liability so high that Franz Petry opines that vicarious liability is akin to strict liability.[237] For example, the Schleswig-Holstein Higher Regional Court applied these standards to summarily reject a hospital's claim that it properly selected and monitored providers in a case involving a birth injury because the providers committed gross errors that delayed the delivery.[238] The Court explained that the hospital, which 'presented the actions of their staff as consistently flawless', could not escape vicarious liability because, 'If a hospital operator describes objectively incorrect behaviour on the part of its staff as correct in the process, it cannot be assumed that it has selected, monitored and instructed the staff correctly.'[239]

To further narrow (or eliminate) the Civil Code's exception to strict vicarious liability, German courts have also relied on an employee's right to indemnification by an employer under labour law, a broad interpretation of an entity's liability for 'duly appointed representatives' under BGB §§ 31 and 89 (which includes a chief physician), the expansion of direct liability for organisational defects under BGB I § 823 (discussed below), and contractual liability for persons used to fulfil the organisation's obligations under BGB § 278.[240]

While vicarious liability might result in financial burdens for healthcare organisations, it does not expose the organisation's own conduct to legal scrutiny. This is because vicarious liability claims stem from an individual provider's breach of the standard of care, with organisational liability resulting only as a technical legal consequence. Although vicarious liability can help achieve the liability system's compensatory goals, it does nothing in terms of effective deterrence of injury-causing organisational behaviour. As highlighted in the prior chapters, blaming individual providers for medical errors while ignoring the deep-seated systemic deficiencies in healthcare organisations is not an effective error prevention strategy.[241]

4.3.2 Direct Organisational Liability

Both US and German law recognise that hospitals can be directly and independently liable for their own organisational errors, distinct from vicarious liability for the negligence of individual providers. According to Giesen, 'the raison d'être of direct (corporate) hospital liability is to prevent substandard care in the health care system as a whole'.[242] Direct hospital liability does not

[237] Petry (n 40).
[238] OLG Schleswig 23 December 1998, 4 U 16/95.
[239] ibid.
[240] Markesinis et al (n 23); Petry (n 40) (a chief physician is an 'organ' of the hospital under BGB §§ 30–31).
[241] See Institute of Medicine (IOM) Committee on Quality of Health Care in America, *To Err is Human: Building a Safer Health System* (LT Kohn, JM Corrigan and MS Donaldson eds, Washington DC, National Academies Press, 2000).
[242] ibid.

relieve the individual provider of liability for its own negligence.[243] Rather, it takes into account the realities under which modern healthcare is provided. Both the physician and the hospital can be held jointly liable.[244]

In the US, while hospital liability was historically determined under strict vicarious liability doctrines,[245] courts now recognise that hospitals can be directly and independently liable for their own organisational errors.[246] Direct hospital liability first emerged as a legal concept in 1965 with the Illinois Supreme Court's opinion in *Darling v Charleston Community Memorial Hospital*.[247] In *Darling*, the plaintiff received treatment for a broken leg at the defendant hospital. After his leg was set in a cast, he was admitted for further treatment and observation.[248] During this time, his foot subsequently became swollen, discoloured, and numb, and he complained of excruciating leg pain, all of which was either observed by or reported to the hospital staff managing his care.[249] By the time his cast was removed, his leg had suffered necrosis, necessitating a below-the-knee amputation.[250] According to the orthopaedic surgeon, the necrosis 'resulted from interference with the circulation of blood in the limb caused by swelling or hemorrhaging of the leg against the construction of the cast', which should have been recognised and prevented with proper care management.[251] The *Darling* court recognised that the hospital owed a direct legal duty to the patient to ensure competent and adequate nursing staff, to review the course of treatment, and to require necessary consultation.[252] *Darling* also recognised that healthcare industry, state licensing, and hospital standards and regulations could be used to determine the legal standard of care that hospitals owed to their patients.[253] Now, the Joint Commission's accreditation standards are frequently used to set the applicable standard of care in organisational (or corporate) negligence cases.[254] After *Darling*, other states began to adopt the doctrine of corporate negligence to hold hospitals directly responsible to patients for the negligent provision of healthcare services.[255]

[243] Giesen (n 5).

[244] ibid.

[245] See *Bing v Thunig* 143 NE2d 3 (New York Court of Appeals, 1957).

[246] *Darling v Charleston Community Memorial Hospital* 211 NE2d 253 (Illinois Supreme Court, 1965).

[247] ibid.

[248] ibid.

[249] ibid.

[250] ibid.

[251] ibid.

[252] ibid.

[253] See MJ Wiet, 'Darling v. Charleston Community Memorial Hospital and Its Legacy' (2005) 14 *Annals Health Law* 399.

[254] See KA Kearney and EL McCord, 'Hospital Management Faces New Liabilities' (1992) 6 *Health Law* 1.

[255] See Priestley (n 227); see Kearney and McCord (n 254) (noting in 1992 that 22 states had adopted some form of corporate liability).

To prove corporate negligence in the US, a plaintiff must establish the following: (1) deviation from an accepted standard of care; (2) actual or constructive notice of the defects or procedures that created the harm; and (3) negligent conduct that was a substantial factor in bringing about the plaintiff's harm.[256] In medical negligence cases, legal theories of corporate negligence against a healthcare organisation primarily focus on administrative and managerial actions rather than medical decision-making.[257] In varying degrees, US jurisdictions have held hospitals directly liable for failing to select and retain competent physicians, failing to maintain appropriate facilities and equipment, failing to train and supervise employees, and failing to implement appropriate protocols and procedures.[258]

The majority of corporate negligence cases involve claims of negligent credentialing, which occurs when a hospital fails to exercise due care in granting hospital privileges to a physician who is not qualified to treat patients. The Texas Supreme Court found that a plaintiff had successfully pled a claim against a hospital for permitting a plastic surgeon to perform several surgeries at the hospital despite its knowledge of complaints that called the surgeon's qualifications in question.[259] In this case, the Court noted that 'Although neither the Hospital as an entity nor the credentialing board actually performed the surgeries on [the plaintiff], a doctor lacking credentials could not have performed surgery in that hospital.'[260]

Related to negligent credentialing, hospitals can also be held responsible for failing to maintain competent staff, which includes failing to train, supervise, and monitor all healthcare providers working in the hospital.[261] A Louisiana court of appeals found that a teaching hospital breached its duty to maintain competent staff when a patient, who suffered a bowel perforation, was never seen by an attending physician, and the medical team responsible for her care was inexplicably absent during 'her most critical time of need'.[262]

Since an individual provider commits the injury-causing act in cases involving negligent credentialing and failure to maintain competent staff, the injured

[256] See JA Gebauer et al, 3 *Summary of Pennsylvania Jurisprudence* § 37:45, 2nd edn, Thomson Reuters Westlaw (database updated January 2026); see also Puig (n 7).

[257] See *Essig v Advocate BroMenn Medical Center*, 33 NE3d 288 (Ill App 4th Dist 2015) ('Ordinarily, the hospital's institutional duty of care is "administrative or managerial in character".').

[258] See generally Adelman and Robertson (n 1); see Gebauer (n 256) § 37:45 (discussing theories of direct hospital liability).

[259] *Garland Community Hospital v Rose*, 156 SW3d 541 (Tex 2004) (finding that the plaintiff's claim against the hospital for negligent credentialing must be properly considered).

[260] ibid.

[261] See *Kirby v State ex rel Louisiana State University Board of Supervisors*, 174 So3d 1 (La App 1st Cir 2014); *Darling v Charleston Community Memorial Hospital* 211 NE2d 253 (Illinois Supreme Court, 1965); *Northern Trust Company v Louis A Weiss Memorial Hospital*, 493 NE2d 6 (Ill App 1st Dist 1986) (finding of hospital liability based upon a failure to have a specially-trained nurse in the nursery at all times).

[262] *Kirby*, 174 So3d 1 (n 261).

patient will generally have claims for both malpractice against the individual provider and corporate negligence against the hospital. This is because a failure to ensure provider competency 'is "inextricably interwoven" with delivering competent quality medical care to hospital patients'.[263] It then follows that, 'If the physician is not negligent, there is no negligent credentialing claim against the hospital.'[264]

The corporate negligence doctrine can also hold a hospital legally responsible for patient injuries in the absence of an individual provider's negligence based upon duties to maintain appropriate facilities and equipment, and to implement appropriate protocols, policies, and procedures.[265] The duty to maintain appropriate facilities and equipment does not require hospitals to employ the best available medical technology, but they must have the facilities and equipment necessary to safely provide the medical treatment offered to their patients.[266] For example, the Georgia Court of Appeals dismissed a claim of hospital negligence when the hospital treated a patient with an incubator that was not the newest model when there was no evidence that the incubator was defective or not reasonably suited for its intended purpose.[267] On the other hand, a hospital was negligent in failing to maintain proper equipment when a crash cart used in the patient's care did not have a functioning electrocardiogram machine or the right-size endotracheal tubes.[268]

Additionally, some US jurisdictions require hospitals to adopt policies and procedures designed to ensure patient safety, including duties to provide both quality medical care and sanitary facilities.[269] Hospitals have been held liable under the doctrine of corporate negligence for negligent policies and procedures governing the administration of oxygen to premature infants,[270] allowing an anaesthesia provider with its own negligent policies and procedures to treat hospital patients,[271] and failing to assist physicians in obtaining a specialist consultation in accordance with hospital bylaws.[272] While some states exclude

[263] *Bell v Sharp Cabrillo Hospital*, 212 Cal App 3d 1034 (Ct App 1989).

[264] *Hiroms v Scheffey*, 76 SW3d 486 (Tex App 2002).

[265] See Adelman and Robertson (n 1) (liability imposed on hospital management company); but see *In re Otero County Hospital Association*, 527 BR 719 (Bankr DNM 2015), on reconsideration in part, 11-11-13686 JL, 2018 WL 882394 (Bankr DNM 29 January 2018) (corporate negligence doctrine does not extend to hospital management companies). See also Kearney and McCord (n 254) (identifying duties imposed by the corporate negligence doctrine).

[266] See Adelman and Robertson (n 1); *Lauro v Travelers Insurance Company*, 261 So2d 261 (La App 4th Cir 1972) (finding that a hospital's duty is measured by the degree, care, and skill generally exercised by hospitals in the same community).

[267] *Emory v Porter*, 103 Ga App 752 (Ga App 1961).

[268] *Kirby*, 174 So3d 1 (n 261).

[269] See Kearney and McCord (n 254) (duty to formulate policies to ensure safety of medical care); *Sibley v Board of Supervisors of Louisiana State University*, 477 So 2d 1094 (La 1985) (duty to have procedures to ensure safety of building and grounds).

[270] *Air Shields v Spears*, 590 SW2d 574 (Tex Civ App—Waco 1979).

[271] See *Denton Regional Medical Center v LaCroix*, 947 SW2d 941 (Tex App—Fort Worth 1997).

[272] See *Johnson v Saint Bernard Hospital*, 399 NE2d 198 (Ill App 1st Dist 1979).

liability for failure to implement policies and procedures that control the actions of independent physicians,[273] others recognise that hospitals have a duty to ensure patient safety by using their administrative expertise to create, implement, and enforce adequate policies and procedures on a broader scale.[274] For example, the Kentucky Court of Appeals held that a hospital could be directly liable for allowing an uncertified nurse anaesthetist to administer anaesthesia without supervision in violation of the hospital's own anaesthesiology policies.[275] The Court, in rejecting the hospital's argument that it was not responsible for supervising non-employee anaesthesiologists practicing in the hospital, noted that:

> [T]he legal duty in the case at bar, which appellant claims the hospital owed him and which he claims is breached, is not the duty to supervise or review the medical treatment given him, but the duty to enforce its policies which, if followed, would have precluded his receiving any anesthetic treatment in the first place solely from an unqualified, uncertified, inexperienced nurse with temporary, limited staff privileges.[276]

Thus, while there are limitations on a hospital's ability to control individual providers' medical decision-making, the line between what qualifies as control over the individual provider and control over a patient's medical care more broadly is not always easy to discern.

Hospitals in Germany can also be held directly liable for organisational negligence.[277] Giesen describes how this direct liability stems from the hospital's 'non-delegable duty to organise and ensure what can be called a safe hospital system'.[278] German courts have consistently acknowledged that the activities of the physicians and the hospital are inextricably tied, such that the hospital should be responsible for patient injuries that occur on its premises.[279] In 1985, the BGH expressed a broad view of direct hospital liability:

> It [the hospital operator] operates the hospital and makes its staff and facilities available to those citizens who need clinical treatment as patients. As a result, it becomes the guarantor for the protection of patients from avoidable harm in the use of its hospital and in the treatment and care it provides. It is thus obligated not only in contract, but also in tort, to do everything reasonable within its power to avert possible dangers to patients.[280]

[273] See *Gafner v Down E Community Hospital*, 735 A2d 969 (Me 1999).
[274] See *Williams v Saint Claire Medical Center*, 657 SW2d 590 (Ky App 1983); Johnson, 399 NE2d 198 (n 272).
[275] ibid.
[276] ibid.
[277] See Goldbach (n 187) (discussing statutory bases for direct organisational liability in Germany).
[278] See Giesen (n 5).
[279] See ibid.
[280] BGH 18 June 1985 NJW 1985, 2189.

Thus, organisational liability in Germany arises when: (1) a hospital is obliged under principles of both contract and tort to protect its patient from harm; (2) it fails 'to make all reasonable efforts required to provide the best possible medical care to the patient and to protect the patient from inadequate and erroneous treatment measures'; and (3) damage is caused by such failure.[281] To avoid liability, hospitals in Germany must maintain 'proper hospital communication and organisation'.[282] This includes the maintenance and enforcement of organisational standards that ensure adequate personnel, facilities, and equipment.[283]

Regarding the adequate provision of hospital personnel, the BGH demands that hospitals exercise due diligence in the selection, training, and supervision of hospital employees.[284] For example, when a patient suffered syringe paralysis after a nursing assistant, rather than a nurse, administered intramuscular injections, the BGH found the hospital was subject to liability for failing to properly select, instruct and supervise its staff concerning the administration of such injections.[285] In support of this finding, the Court noted that: (1) the relevant professional guidelines governing the scope of practice for nursing assistants does not generally authorise them to perform such injections due to the risk of serious injury; and (2) even if an exceptionally qualified and trained nursing assistant could perform these injections, the defendant hospital granted blanket authorisation to all nursing assistants to give these injections.[286]

Outside of its own employees, the hospital must also provide for the safe organisation of treatment by physicians providing care on its premises. This includes ensuring that patients are treated by qualified physicians.[287] Unless there is an emergency situation for which no other organisational provision can be made, the hospital must ensure that treatment is carried out by sufficiently trained and experienced providers.[288] For example, the Frankfurt Higher Regional Court rejected a hospital's assertion that the patient's physician was exclusively responsible for providing medical treatment upon hospital admission for labour.[289] In this case, because the patient was not properly examined upon admission, foetal macrosomia went undetected and the risk of complications from shoulder dystocia, which the plaintiff ultimately suffered during birth, was not properly identified and managed.[290] The Court found that the hospital was negligent in failing to ensure that the patient had access to specialist obstetrics

[281] ibid.
[282] Giesen (n 5).
[283] ibid.
[284] BGH 8 May 1979 NJW 1979, 1935.
[285] ibid.
[286] ibid.
[287] BGH 27 September 1983 BGHZ 88, 248; see OLG Frankfurt am Main 11 December 2002, 13 U 199/98 ('Hospitals have organisational duty to ensure that patients have access to specialist obstetrics care upon admission either at that hospital or via transfer to another hospital.').
[288] BGH 27 September 1983 BGHZ 88, 248.
[289] OLG Frankfurt am Main 11 December 2002, 13 U 199/98.
[290] ibid.

care upon admission either at the defendant's hospital or via transfer to another hospital.[291]

Shortages in staffing cannot be used to excuse a hospital from providing patients with necessary medical care.[292] When the hospital cannot sufficiently staff a department, it cannot simply 'close its eyes' to the problems and rely on physicians to protect the patient from harm associated with understaffing; instead, it must take other actions to ensure proper staff ratios and provide protocols regarding how to handle unexpected staff shortages to protect patients.[293] For example, when a plaintiff suffered brain injury after a complication from anaesthesia monitored by a junior anaesthesiologist, the BGH noted that the hospital's failure to properly organise the anaesthesia service could not be excused by the shortage of anaesthesiologists available to fill open positions.[294]

However, similar to the situation in the US, German courts distinguish between liability for medical decision-making versus organisation of the treatment process.[295] For example, in a case in which the plaintiff suffered damages following a caesarean section, the Court found that the relevant inquiry for the organisational negligence claims did not concern the medical decision to choose between a caesarean section and vaginal delivery, but rather organisational measures that impacted the performance of the caesarean section.[296]

Hospitals in Germany must also maintain proper facilities and equipment, which includes ensuring functioning equipment[297] and hygienic facilities.[298] For example, when a patient suffered a brain injury caused by a faulty anaesthesia machine, which was likely damaged while stored in a crowded hospital corridor, the BGH noted an objective violation of the hospital's obligation to provide functioning equipment.[299] The Court further noted that while it might be impossible to prevent all damage to equipment in operation, the hospital still has an obligation to reduce the risk of patient injury by 'eliminating all recognisable sources of danger as far as possible ... [or] by increased controls'.[300] With regard to organisational errors related to hygiene, the most common source of injury results from hospital-acquired infections. In these cases, the BGH instructs:

> If it is certain that the infection must have originated in a hygienically controllable area, the hospital operator or the physician is liable for the consequences of the infection both in contract and in tort, unless he is able to exonerate himself to the effect that he is not at fault for the non-observance of the hygiene requirements, i.e.

[291] ibid.
[292] ibid.
[293] BGH 18 June 1985 NJW 1985, 2189.
[294] ibid.
[295] BGH 12 January 2021 NJW-RR 2021, 1602.
[296] ibid.
[297] BGH 11 October 1977 NJW 1978, 584.
[298] BGH 16 August 2016 VI ZR 634/15.
[299] BGH 11 October 1977 NJW 1978, 584.
[300] ibid (translation from German).

> he proves that all organisational and technical precautions against avoidable germ transmission originating from the personnel of the hospital or the physician's practice were taken.[301]

For example, in a case involving a patient's development of sepsis after receiving an infusion with contaminated fluid, the BGH found organisational liability when the hospital could not affirmatively prove that it took all reasonable measures to prevent contamination of the fluid while it was prepared and stored in the hospital.[302] On the other hand, when it is possible that the source of infection stems from an area outside of the hospital's control, the burden of proof is not reversed, and the plaintiff must prove that the hospital violated applicable hygiene standards.[303] In a case involving infection from bacteria found in all humans and which could have been carried by the plaintiff himself or visitors, the plaintiff was not entitled to a burden of proof reversal.[304] Nevertheless, the court found that the plaintiff proved a hygiene violation by showing that he was placed in the same room as another patient with an infected open knee wound.[305]

Finally, hospitals in Germany must maintain treatment records and know of their whereabouts at all times.[306] When a hospital was unable to produce X-ray images because it sent to them to the hospital where the patient was subsequently transferred, the BGH found that the hospital violated this obligation.[307] Hospitals must also ensure the accuracy of medical records, and a hospital can be liable for a transcription error that causes harm to a patient.[308] For example, when a patient's record incorrectly noted that a muscle biopsy was 'not indicated', the BGH found that this erroneous notation could be considered an organisational error if the physician's failure to order the biopsy, which led to a delayed diagnosis, was based on the transcription error.[309]

Direct organisational liability provides some movement away from a purely individual-focused liability system by recognising that healthcare organisations owe independent duties to patients. However, as currently applied, it remains limited in scope in both jurisdictions. In the US, Mello and Studdert observe that: 'Because medical malpractice doctrine does not embrace corporate liability for hospitals except in narrow circumstances, most of the system factors that contribute to medical injuries are unlikely even to be raised in malpractice litigation'.[310] Goldbach reaches a similar conclusion in Germany, noting

[301] BGH 3 March 2007 r+s 2007, 519.
[302] BGH 3 November 1981 NJW 1982, 699. See BGH 9 May 1978 NJW 1978, 1683 (contamination of alcohol used to disinfect skin was organisational error).
[303] BGH 16 August 2016 NJW-RR 2016, 1360.
[304] ibid.
[305] ibid.
[306] BGH 21 November 1995 NJW 1996, 779.
[307] ibid.
[308] BGH 7 November 2017 NJW 2018, 309.
[309] ibid.
[310] MM Mello and DM Studdert, 'Deconstructing Negligence: The Role of Individual and System Factors in Causing Medical Injuries' (2008) 96 *Georgetown Law Journal* 599.

that: 'The case law has not yet stipulated in any decision that the hospital operator must actively inform itself about uncertainties and is obliged to systematically analyse and eliminate the causes of critical and undesirable events'.[311] Despite these current limitations, the case law on direct organisational liability in both jurisdictions provides the legal fabric for doctrinal expansion. The final part of this book discusses how a duty to clinical risk management can be encompassed within the current medical liability systems as a meaningful extension of direct organisational liability.

[311] See ibid.

Part III

A Theory of Liability for Negligent Clinical Risk Management

5

A Legal Obligation to Conduct Clinical Risk Management

THE TRADITIONAL APPROACH to focusing medical liability on individual healthcare providers is outdated. It fails to consider the complexities and intricacies of modern healthcare delivery systems. It ignores the well-established role that system design defects have in causing medical injuries and the reality that 'A modern hospital can no longer do without efficient risk management.'[1] While the medical liability system cannot and is not expected to be the driving force for medical error prevention, it should ideally reinforce the accepted norms governing error prevention in modern healthcare. At the very least, the liability system should not hinder proven approaches for effective error prevention in the healthcare industry. Mello and Studdert conclude that 'a reorientation to expand corporate or enterprise liability is needed'.[2] This chapter proposes a doctrinal expansion of organisational liability to establish a theory of negligent clinical risk management.

5.1 DOCTRINAL ALIGNMENT THROUGH LIABILITY FOR NEGLIGENT RISK MANAGEMENT

The Institute of Medicine (IOM)'s 1999 report, *To Err Is Human: Building a Safer Health System*, ignited a paradigm shift that led the healthcare industry to approach medical error prevention with an organisational, rather than individual, focus. Following this shift, the healthcare industry recognised the critical role of clinical risk management for medical error prevention in modern, complex, and high-risk healthcare systems. The clinical risk management process enables healthcare organisations to detect and correct systemic deficiencies that can either induce or fail to prevent individual provider errors, and more recently, errors associated with artificial intelligence (AI)-driven medical technologies. Despite this potential for healthcare organisations to prevent medical injuries through the process of clinical risk management, individual providers remain the primary targets of medical

[1] KO Bergmann et al, 'Krankenhaushaftung un Versicherung' in KO Bergmann and HF Kienzle (eds), *Krankenhaushaftung: Organisation, Schadensverhütung und Versicherung – Leitfaden für die tägliche Praxis* (Düsseldorf, Kohlhammer Verlag, 2015).

[2] MM Mello and DM Studdert, 'Deconstructing Negligence: The Role of Individual and System Factors in Causing Medical Injuries' (2008) 96 *Georgetown Law Journal* 599.

liability for such injuries in a system that also fails to effectively integrate organisational duties to conduct clinical risk management.[3] This results in significant misalignment in the healthcare industry's approach to preventing medical errors and the legal system's approach to liability for injuries caused by medical errors. This misalignment only increases as new medical technologies are introduced and healthcare systems become more complex. Increasingly interconnected digital infrastructures and AI-driven tools create new categories of organisational risk that will likely escape meaningful attention in an individual-focused liability system.

The negligence-based medical liability system in the United States (US) and Germany seek to not only compensate victims of medical negligence but also prevent accidents by deterring substandard behaviour. The ability of the tort system to ignite change is one of its strengths; however, when the system has the wrong targets in its crosshairs, it can hinder, rather than promote, positive change. As Ofri points out, the reaction of British doctors following a highly publicised criminal conviction of a physician after a patient death was that the legal system was used as a 'weapon to scapegoat doctors for the shortcomings of the entire medical system.'[4] As long as the medical liability system serves as a public forum for scapegoating individual providers, it will not be an effective catalyst for systemic improvement. Mello and Studdert highlight that 'focusing liability on individuals may be appealing on fairness and corrective-justice grounds', but it will not effectively decrease medical errors because the deterrence signal is overly focused on both the wrong actor and the wrong behaviour.[5] Directing the liability system's deterrent signal towards individual providers for individual behaviour has negative impacts on patient safety because it decreases patient safety culture in organisations and, relatedly, conceals the most promising pathway for error prevention by ignoring system defects.

Focusing liability on individual providers decreases safety culture within healthcare organisations by discouraging individual providers from speaking about medical errors, encouraging the practice of defensive medicine, and discouraging doctors from treating complicated patients. The threat of litigation is one well-documented cause of the culture of silence – reluctance to discuss medical errors – in both the US and Germany.[6] In contrast, legal policies that encourage healthcare providers to discuss medical errors both internally and with their patients can promote safety culture, facilitate organisational learning,

[3] See Mello and Studdert (n 2); W Voit, 'Entsprechung und Abweichungen nach deutschem Arzthaftungsrecht' in P Jabornegg et al (eds), *Haftungsfragen im System der Leistungserbringung des Krankenversicherungsrechts: Beiträge zu den Deutsch-Österreichischen Sozialrechtsgesprächen 2006* (Essen, CW Haarfeld, 2006).

[4] D Ofri, *When We Do Harm: A Doctor Confronts Medical Error* (Boston, Beacon Press, 2020).

[5] Mello and Studdert (n 2).

[6] See K Loewenbrück et al, 'Disclosure of adverse outcomes in medicine: A questionnaire study on voice intention and behaviour of physicians in Germany, Japan and the USA' (2016) 30 *German Journal of Human Resources Management* 313; MM Mello and DM Studdert, 'The Medical Malpractice System: Structure and Performance' in WM Sage and R Kersh (eds), *Medical Malpractice and the U.S. Health Care System* (Cambridge, Cambridge University Press, 2009).

and decrease medical errors.[7] The practice of defensive medicine, in which providers overprescribe medical care to patients to avoid potential lawsuits, also puts patients at additional risk of harm simply because they are undergoing additional, often unnecessary, medical treatment.[8] Danielle Ofri explains how additional imaging, a common defensive medicine practice, can lead to kidney damage, cancer, and false positive diagnoses.[9] She further notes that, 'even knowing doctors win most cases doesn't assuage the terror or reduce the aggressive over-testing and overtreatment from defensive medicine'.[10] Goldbach agrees that when medical errors are equated with the personal failures of an individual physician, the physician feels attacked and assumes a defensive position.[11] Another provider response to medical malpractice lawsuits, or the mere threat thereof, that ultimately operates to the detriment of patients is reluctance to treat complicated illness.[12] Ofri recounts such a response by a psychiatrist who endured, and ultimately won, a five-year medical malpractice lawsuit that destroyed her personally and professionally after one of her patients committed suicide.[13] More than half of doctors who had been sued, and 40 per cent who only feared being sued, reported that malpractice fears affected their patient care.[14]

A medical liability system focused primarily on individual providers will also fail to act as an effective legal mechanism for creating and enforcing standards that promote systemic improvement in healthcare organisations. William Sage observed that 'patient safety has yet to improve measurably in the five years since the first IOM report, in part because medical liability and patient safety mechanisms do not yet work hand in hand'.[15] Mello and Studdert's malpractice claims analysis demonstrates a critical aspect of the problem: despite evidence that organisational factors contribute to injuries in a majority of malpractice

[7] See generally MN Duffourc, 'Filling Voice Promotion Gaps in Healthcare Through A Comparative Analysis of Error Reporting and Learning Systems and Open Communication and Disclosure Policies in the United States and Germany' (2018) 44 *American Journal of Law and Medicine* 579.

[8] Ofri (n 4) (discussing negative impact of defensive medicine on patient safety). See M Stauch, *The law of medical negligence in England and Germany: a comparative analysis* (Oxford, Hart Publishing, 2008) (regarding the widespread assumption that the practice of defensive medicine occurs in Germany and claims that malpractice litigation undermines trust and confidence in the physician–patient relationship); TL Hafemeister and JH Porter, 'The Health Care Reform Act of 2010 and Medical Malpractice Liability: Worlds in Collision or Ships Passing in the Night' (2011) 64 *Southern Methodist University Law Review* 735 (discussing the practice of defensive medicine and rising insurance premiums in the US).

[9] Ofri (n 4).

[10] ibid.

[11] C Goldbach, *Risikomanagementsysteme im Krankenhaus nach dem Patientenrechtegesetz: Sozialrechtliche Pflicht und haftungsrechtlicher Standard* (Kassel, Kassel University Press, 2014).

[12] ibid.

[13] ibid.

[14] ibid.

[15] WM Sage, 'Malpractice Reform as a Health Policy Problem' in WM Sage and R Kersh (eds), *Medical Malpractice and the U.S. Health Care System* (Cambridge, Cambridge University Press, 2009).

claims, these factors are 'unlikely even to be raised in malpractice litigation'.[16] Even when organisational factors are raised, they are often viewed through the lens of individual provider negligence, rather than viewing individual provider negligence through the lens of the organisational error. For example, when considering whether an allegation against a hospital was 'treatment-related' and within the scope of the state's medical malpractice statute, a Louisiana court noted that:

> [W]e do not find that in a case where the viability of the administrative negligence cause of action is completely dependent upon the existence of a subsequent act of malpractice by a physician, that we can consider the allegation of administrative negligence independently from, and without consideration of, the subsequent act of alleged malpractice.[17]

The result is that the medical liability system consistently focuses on the individual provider as the last link in a causal chain, while failing to recognise the role of injury-causing organisational behaviour.

To make matters worse, the organisational behaviour that evades liability exposure and assessment is precisely the type of behaviour that is most capable of preventing future errors. Mello and Studdert reiterate that 'efficient deterrence requires both accuracy in targeting the signal to the cause-in-fact of the injury and targeting it to the least-cost avoider'.[18] This aligns with Latin's observation that

> the social engineering purpose of tort liability is to induce similar actors to undertake efficient cost-minimizing behaviour in the future . . . assignment of liability will promote social engineering goals only to the extent that the class of problem-solving actors modifies precautionary decisions in response to legal rules.[19]

In the context of medical errors, healthcare organisations are precisely the types of problem-solving actors that Latin envisions: they can understand liability risks, consider the costs of engaging in risky behaviour, evaluate alternative choices, and adapt behaviour in response to risk.[20]

5.2 THE LEGAL BASIS FOR LIABILITY FOR NEGLIGENT CLINICAL RISK MANAGEMENT

A legal cause of action for negligent clinical risk management[21] under the existing medical liability system in both the US and Germany requires finding that

[16] Mello and Studdert (n 2).

[17] *Bonilla v Jefferson Parish Hospital Service District #2*, 210 So 3d 540 (La App 5 Cir 2016).

[18] Mello and Studdert (n 2).

[19] H Latin, 'Problem-Solving Behavior and Theories of Tort Liability' (1985) 73 *California Law Review* 677.

[20] See ibid.

[21] Clinical risk management focused on improving patient safety is to be distinguished from risk management focused on liability consequences that can stem from a broad range of operational

the hospital owes the patient a legal duty or obligation to prevent or minimise medical errors through the clinical risk management process. The question of whether medical liability law in both jurisdictions supports finding an affirmative duty or obligation to conduct clinical risk management must be examined in the context of the existing organisational liability law and tort law more broadly. German academics find support for an obligation to clinical risk management in organisational liability law by relying on the existing laws and regulations that require healthcare risk management. As a result, the German academic literature finding that clinical risk management is a logical extension of existing German tort law generally, and organisational negligence law specifically, serves to guide a similar finding in the US.

Ultimately, finding a duty or obligation to conduct clinical risk management can be supported in both jurisdictions as an extension of organisational liability by: (1) looking through the larger lens of negligence-based medical liability; and (2) considering liability in other legal spheres that stems from a violation of duties and obligations established to prevent harm. Here, in both jurisdictions, existing laws and regulations requiring healthcare risk management and existing product liability law provide strong support for extending organisational liability in medical negligence law to include liability for negligent clinical risk management.

5.2.1 Extending Organisational Liability to Clinical Risk Management

As a starting point, liability for negligent clinical risk management must be distinguished from the existing organisational liability already recognised by courts in both jurisdictions. As discussed in chapter four, both jurisdictions already recognise that healthcare organisations can face direct organisational liability for patient injuries. Thus far, the case law in both jurisdictions confirms that healthcare organisations are responsible for negligence in the following areas: organisation and competency of personnel; organisation of the medication administration process; provision of safe equipment and facilities; communication and medical record keeping; and the provision and qualification of specialists. Some German scholars opine that despite the lack of an explicit reference to 'risk management' clinical risk management is already required by the case law on organisational liability.[22] Indeed, the Bundesgerichtshof (BGH) has articulated a broad scope for organisational liability by obliging hospitals 'to make all reasonable efforts . . . to provide the best possible medical care to the patient and to protect the patient from inadequate and erroneous treatment

risks. See Goldbach (n 11) (explaining the difference between 'liability-based' risk management and 'medical' risk management).

[22] A Pauli, *Risikomanagement und CIRS als Gegenstand der Krankenhaushaftung* (Baden-Baden, Nomos, 2013); D Hart, 'Patientensicherheit, Fehlermanagement, Arzthaftungsrecht – zugleich ein Beitrag zur rechtlichen Bedeutung von Empfehlungen' (2012) 30 *Medizinrecht* 1.

measures'.[23] Goldbach, however, makes a convincing argument that organisational liability thus far recognised by German courts is not broad enough to encompass negligent clinical risk management.

Goldbach categorises existing organisational liability as based on 'specific obligation[s] to monitor treatment' and distinguishes clinical risk management as an 'abstract obligation to monitor treatment'.[24] According to Goldbach's view, specific treatment monitoring is concerned with the prevention of individual incidents and thus focuses solely on the last component of the risk management cycle: risk control.[25] In the current organisational negligence jurisprudence – and this is true in both jurisdictions – courts focus on specific treatment monitoring through the absence or faulty implementation of a specific organisational guideline, practice, or procedure that could have prevented the individual plaintiff's injury. Examples of specific treatment monitoring include use of a faulty piece of equipment, inadequate staffing procedures, negligent hiring of a provider, and failure to implement a specific hygienic precaution. In contrast, the clinical risk management process begins further upstream in the organisational workflow and encompasses risk identification, risk analysis, risk assessment, and risk control, a process that Goldbach labels 'abstract treatment monitoring'.[26] Examples of abstract treatment monitoring include implementation of an error reporting system and investigation of near-miss incidents. Goldbach rejects the idea that German courts have already imposed an obligation to clinical risk management: 'The case law has not yet stipulated in any decision that the hospital operator must actively inform itself about uncertainties and is obliged to systematically analyze and eliminate the causes of critical and undesirable events.'[27]

Goldbach's distinction is subtle but important: existing organisational liability asks whether a specific measure was absent; negligent clinical risk management asks whether the organisation had a process for identifying that the measure was needed. For example, in a case involving injury to an infant caused by a hot water bottle bursting in the incubator, the court assessed the sufficiency of specific risk control measures, including procedures for recording the date of purchase, instructions for nurses to inspect the water bottles prior to use, and monitoring the nursing staff.[28] By focusing on the lack of the organisational measures that led to the nurses' use of a dangerous hot water bottle, the court found direct hospital liability.[29] On the other hand, there was no consideration of organisational processes that might have led to other, potentially more

[23] BGH, 18 June 1985, NJW 1985, 2189.
[24] Goldbach (n 11).
[25] See ibid.
[26] See ibid.
[27] See ibid.
[28] BGH 1 February 1994, NJW 1994, 1594.
[29] ibid.

effective, risk control measures, for example, those that consider and account for foreseeable human errors, including, for example, errors in recording the purchase date or a nurse forgetting to inspect the bottles even if such procedures, instructions and monitoring were in place.[30]

Similarly, US courts have, thus far, also limited treatment of organisational negligence in medical malpractice cases to duties involving specific therapy monitoring. This is partially highlighted by the traditional view that medical negligence is primarily the result of an individual provider's treatment choices. In finding that an alleged negligent failure to adopt a hospital-wide patient handoff policy sounded in medical negligence, a Louisiana court noted that:

> [N]ot only is the viability of Ms. Bonilla's cause of action against the hospital administrators entirely dependent on the existence of the subsequent underlying medical malpractice by the physicians, but the complained of administrative negligence of the hospital administrators in failing to enact a handoff policy is specifically directed to instructing physicians on how to provide the very treatment to patients that Ms. Bonilla alleges her physicians negligently provided to her.[31]

In other words, the court viewed the adoption of hospital-wide policies through the lens of the individual provider's actions during patient handoff. It even went as far as to characterise a handoff policy as a type of 'supervision and training of healthcare providers' rather than as a broader, potentially independent, duty of care.[32] The court also explicitly rejected the plaintiff's argument that the adoption of a policy should have occurred prior to her admission and thus the hospital's failure to adopt such a policy was not directly related to her specific medical treatment, indicating a reluctance to assess organisational actions as part of a more comprehensive risk management process.[33] While this case only dealt with a procedural issue relating to whether the claim was subject to additional pleading requirements under the state's medical malpractice statute, it demonstrates how the court conceptualised the role of organisational behaviour (failing to adopt a handoff policy) as only secondary to the individual provider's role (negligent handoff).

The ongoing development and expansion of organisational duties in US medical liability law provides some support for incorporating liability for negligent clinical risk management. A promising indication of judicial willingness to embrace this expansion also comes from a Louisiana appellate court opinion, which referenced evidence of organisational failures relating to 'a culture of patient safety'.[34] In this case, the court noted expert testimony that 'found violations by [the hospital's] leadership of the Joint Commission and CMS [Centers for Medicare and Medicaid] Conditions for Participation standards

[30] ibid.
[31] *Bonilla*, 210 So 3d 540 (La App 5 Cir 2016).
[32] ibid.
[33] ibid.
[34] See *Dehart v Jones*, 310 So 3d 658 (La App 3rd Cir 2020).

based on their failure to implement policies, procedures, and training relative to patient safety and advocacy, as well as its own protocols and policies'. However, because the plaintiff failed to allege these claims against the hospital, they were procedurally deficient.[35] In a case involving a missed heart attack diagnosis, the Oklahoma Supreme Court reinstated previously dismissed claims against the hospital related to organisational failures in a hospital's recordkeeping process.[36] Despite settled claims against the provider for failure to diagnose the patient's heart attack, the Court confirmed the viability of an independent claim against the hospital for failing to include lab tests results and reports in the patient's physical chart. The court stressed that 'The obvious purpose of the charting requirement is to provide a record to assist the physician in properly treating the patient. Physicians depend on the reliability and trustworthiness of the chart.'[37] It also rejected an argument that the doctor's actions in missing the diagnosis automatically severed the chain of causation because 'the evidentiary material suggest[ed] that [the hospital's] failure to timely provide the test results could be determined by a jury to have been a cause or contributing factor in doctor's failure to properly diagnose and treat the heart attack'.[38] However, even these cases still concern duties comparable to what Goldbach would term 'specific treatment monitoring' in that they involve the implementation of policies and protocols as context for specific treatment errors. This is precisely the gap that Goldbach identifies in the German case law: the tendency of courts to focus on whether the specific organisational measure was absent or inadequate, not on whether the organisation had a systematic process for detecting, analysing, and managing risks upstream. Nevertheless, these cases also reflect some improvement in judicial recognition of the broader and more central role of organisational behaviour in medical negligence cases.

5.2.2 Existing Legal and Regulatory Obligations to Conduct Risk Management

In both the US and Germany, existing laws and regulations impose obligations on healthcare organisations to implement risk management and quality management systems. While these obligations differ in their degree of centralisation and specificity, they demonstrate that both legal systems already expect healthcare organisations to conduct clinical risk management and thus provide the foundation for translating this regulatory expectation into a cognisable duty of care in the medical liability system.

[35] ibid.
[36] *Johnson v Hillcrest Health Center Inc*, 70 P3d 811 (Okla 2003).
[37] ibid.
[38] ibid.

German social law, especially following the Patients' Rights Act, requires hospitals to implement quality management,[39] which, according to Goldbach, encompasses risk management.[40] German law, under § 823(2) Bürgerliches Gesetzbuch (BGB), imposes liability for a violation of protective law[41] which, considering statutes and regulations mandating the implementation of healthcare quality assurance and risk management, further support finding that organisations can be liable for negligent clinical risk management under German medical negligence law.

The passage of the Patients' Rights Act in 2013 enhanced existing social law obligations for hospitals to perform quality management and introduced the term 'risk management' into the law.[42] Prior to the Act, § 135a II Sozialgesetzbuch (SGB) V already required hospitals to implement intra-facility quality management systems, which, per Gemeinsamer Bundesausschuss (G-BA) regulations, included systems that prevented errors and enhanced patient safety.[43] The Patients' Rights Act amended § 135 SGB V to require additional and more specific quality management measures, including participation in 'cross-institutional quality assurance', and introduction and further development of intra-facility quality management, including a patient complaint system.[44] Additionally, the Patients' Rights Act included legal protection for 'Reports and data from []internal and cross-facility risk management and error reporting systems' required by the law.[45] Finally, the Patients' Rights Act delegated the task of determining, 'the basic requirements for an institution's internal quality management . . . [including] essential measures to improve patient safety and in particular lay[] down minimum standards for risk management and error reporting systems' to the G-BA.[46] The G-BA, pursuant to this legislative delegation, published guidelines to set forth 'basic requirements for a successful introduction and implementation of quality management'.[47]

The current guidelines specifically identify risk management as a method and instrument of quality management.[48] Goldbach suggests that the G-BA's quality management regulations required clinical risk management even before the Patients' Rights Act, noting that the International Organization for Standardization included the basic clinical risk management process (risk identification, analysis, and improvement) in its published standards for

[39] Though German law uses the terms 'quality management' and 'quality assurance', it does not define these terms, leading German legal scholars to find that they are synonymous. See Goldbach (n 11).

[40] Goldbach (n 11).

[41] Bürgerliches Gesetzbuch (BGB) § 823(2).

[42] Goldbach (n 11).

[43] ibid.

[44] Sozialgesetzbuch V (SGB) V § 135a(2).

[45] SGB V § 135a(3).

[46] SGB V § 136a(3); see SGB V § 137 (authorising G-BA enforcement).

[47] Gemeinsamer Bundesausschuss (G-BA), Qualitätsmanagement-Richtlinie, www.g-ba.de/richtlinien/87.

[48] ibid.

quality management.[49] However, if there was any doubt about whether the social law required clinical risk management, it dissipated with the passage of the Patients' Rights Act, which specifically identifies risk management as part of quality management.[50]

Organisational liability for negligent clinical risk management can be supported by BGB § 823(2), which imposes liability for the violation of a statute, 'intended to protect another person'.[51] Following the Patients' Rights Act, passed with the express purpose of improving patients' rights *and safety*, it is difficult to dispute that the legal obligations to quality management articulated in the social law are intended to protect patients.[52] Goldbach disagrees that sanctions for a violation of legally required quality management, which, as discussed above, includes clinical risk management, are limited to those imposed by the G-BA pursuant to §137 I 2 SGB V for two reasons.[53] First, she argues that sanctions do not provide a remedy for individual damages caused by failure to comply with the existing quality assurance regulations, leaving a need for individual patient protection in the general liability law.[54] Second, she highlights that there is no indication that the legislature sought to restrict remedies for individual damages caused by violation of the quality management regulations.[55] As a result, Goldbach takes the position that liability for negligent clinical risk management can also accrue under protective law according to § 823(2), though such a claim is ultimately judged under the same standard of reasonable care as a cause of action for general negligence under § 823(1).[56]

At the European Union (EU) level, the EU Artificial Intelligence Act (EU AI Act) imposes obligations on hospitals as deployers of AI-driven medical devices.[57] Article 4 would require hospitals that deploy AI systems in the organisation to 'take measures to ensure, to their best extent, a sufficient level of AI literacy of their staff and other persons dealing with the operation and use of AI systems on their behalf'. For AI-driven medical devices that are considered high-risk AI systems under Article 6, hospitals deploying such devices would also need to comply with Article 26 by, among other things, 'tak[ing] appropriate technical and organisational measures to ensure they use such systems in accordance with the instructions for use', ensuring competent human oversight, monitoring AI performance and use, and reporting serious incidents. The AI Act's obligations

[49] Goldbach (n 11).
[50] See ibid (the Patients' Rights Act 'should make it clear once and for all that RMS are a mandatory component of the obligation to perform internal QM').
[51] BGB § 823(2).
[52] Goldbach (n 11).
[53] ibid.
[54] ibid.
[55] ibid.
[56] ibid.
[57] Regulation (EU) 2024/1689 of the European Parliament and of the Council of 13 June 2024 laying down harmonised rules on artificial intelligence (Artificial Intelligence Act) [2024] OJ L 1689.

for deployers provide additional regulatory expressions of the organisational duties that the clinical risk management standard of care requires in the context of AI-driven technologies at the EU level.

While healthcare quality assurance laws and regulations are not as centralised in the US as they are in Germany, there are some federal laws and regulations that address healthcare quality. First, the CMS, the agency authorised to establish standards for Medicaid and Medicare providers, requires participating hospitals to establish a quality management programme, designed to, 'improve health outcomes and identify and reduce medical errors' and 'measure, analyse, and track quality indicators'.[58] Second, the Affordable Care Act seeks to improve healthcare quality through value-based healthcare purchasing programmes that consider quality of care, mandatory physician reporting of quality measures, and publication of quality reports.[59] Third, the Patient Safety and Quality Improvement Act offers legal protection for data and records, 'assembled or developed by a provider for reporting to a PSO'.[60] In terms of national uniformity, the Joint Commission, a private accreditation organisation for the healthcare industry,[61] includes an entire chapter dedicated to patient safety in its accreditation manual.[62] The chapter, 'Patient Safety Systems', is intended 'to provide health care organizations with a proactive approach to designing or redesigning a patient-centered system that aims to improve quality of care and patient safety, an approach that aligns with the Joint Commission's mission and its standards'.[63] Finally, because the individual states primarily govern healthcare quality, general negligence, and medical liability, consideration of state statutes and regulations concerning duties to healthcare risk management is essential to establishing a legal duty to conduct clinical risk management in US tort law.

Ten US jurisdictions have statutes that directly address healthcare risk management. Maryland, Massachusetts, and Alaska require implementation of hospital risk management systems as condition of licensure.[64] In Maryland, risk management encompasses 'an internal staff committee structure to conduct ongoing review and evaluation of risk management activities, a formal written programme for addressing patient complaints, a documented facility-wide risk reporting system, and ongoing risk management education programmes for all

[58] 42 CFR § 482.21.

[59] LA Reineck and JM Kahn, 'Quality measurement in the Affordable Care Act: a reaffirmed commitment to value in health care' (2013) 187 *American Journal of Respiratory and Critical Care Medicine* 1038.

[60] 42 USC § 299b-22.

[61] Although Joint Commission accreditation is not mandatory, most internships and residency programmes as well as federal support through Medicaid and Medicare require accreditation. See KA Kearney and EL McCord, 'Hospital Management Faces New Liabilities' (1992) 6 *Health Law* 1.

[62] Institute of Medicine (IOM) Committee on Quality of Health Care in America, *To Err is Human: Building a Safer Health System* (LT Kohn, JM Corrigan, MS Donaldson, eds, Washington DC, National Academies Press, 2000).

[63] ibid.

[64] Md Code Ann, Health-Gen § 19-319; Mass Gen L Ann, ch 111, § 203; Ala Stat Ann § 18.20.075.

staff'.[65] Massachusetts mandates participation in the State Board of Registration in Medicine's risk management and quality assurance programs with an exception for hospitals that 'participate in pre-existing risk management programs'.[66] Alaska's statute requires adoption of a risk management programme that 'investigate[s] the frequency and causes of incidents in hospitals that cause injury to patients; develop[s] and implement[s] measures to minimize risk of injury to patients; [and] analyze[s] patient grievances relating to patient care'.[67]

Florida, Kansas, North Carolina, and Rhode Island impose statutory requirements for healthcare organisations to conduct risk management. Notably, Florida directly imposes a legal duty to manage healthcare risks, the breach of which can lead to liability.[68] Florida's statutes generally require identification and analysis of adverse events and development of measures to prevent the same.[69] Under Florida law, preventive measures should include:

> (a) educating and training nonphysican personnel, (b) prohibiting staff members from attending to a patient in the recovery room unless authorized (except in emergencies or while under electronic/live surveillance), (c) prohibiting an unlicensed person from assisting or participating in any surgical procedures unless authorized or under immediate supervision of a licensed physician, (d) developing and implementing evaluation of procedures to accurately identify patients, planned procedures, and the correct site of the planned procedures.[70]

Kansas focuses its risk management statutes on the management of 'reportable incidents', which are defined as

> an act by a health care provider that: (1) [i]s or may be below the applicable standard of care and has a reasonable probability of causing injury to a patient; or (2) may be grounds for disciplinary action by the appropriate licensing agency.[71]

Kansas law requires 'medical care facilit[ies]' to maintain an 'internal risk management program' consisting of reporting, investigation, and analysis of 'reportable incidents' and the development of 'measures to minimize reportable incidents'.[72] North Carolina requires hospitals 'to develop a risk management program to identify, evaluate, and manage risks of injury to patients through loss reduction, prevention techniques, and quality assurance activities'.[73] Rhode Island requires hospitals and their insurance carriers to jointly establish a risk management programme that includes an internal complaint system, collection

[65] Md Code Ann, Health-Gen § 19-319.
[66] Mass Gen L Ann, ch 111, § 203.
[67] Ala Stat Ann § 18.20.075.
[68] Fla Stat Ann § 766.110.
[69] Fla Stat Ann § 395.0197.
[70] ibid.
[71] Kan Stat Ann § 65-4921.
[72] Kan Stat Ann § 65-4922.
[73] NC Gen Stat Ann § 131E-96.

of data relating to quality of care data and costs, medical assessment of quality of care, and education for hospital staff.[74]

California and Michigan delegate risk management duties to hospital administrators. In California, hospitals must appoint a Director of Risk Management to 'implement processes, tools, and systems to identify, assess, measure, and monitor risks'.[75] Michigan law tasks hospital owners, operators, and governing bodies with organising medical staff to review the quality and necessity of care provided for the purpose of reducing morbidity and mortality.[76]

New York encourages risk management in hospitals by providing grants to hospitals that integrate medical and risk management functions

> to establish quality improvement activities which will enhance all institutional processes, including clinical, managerial and support functions; support integration of management information systems to improve health care delivery; and develop an educational program on continuous quality improvement to inform staff of the institution's mission and plan for quality.[77]

Although not specifically designated as a risk management process, most states have medical error reporting systems.[78] Of these, West Virginia, Georgia, and Oregon have adopted voluntary adverse event reporting systems,[79] which, according to the IOM and World Health Organization (WHO), are valuable tools for identifying latent failures and enabling systemic learning,[80] key components of clinical risk management. Although duties and obligations for healthcare organisations to implement risk management systems are spread out between federal, state, and industry law, regulations, and guidelines, together they provide strong support for finding that healthcare organisations have legal duty to conduct clinical risk management, noting that at least one state already explicitly acknowledges a legal duty to conduct risk management.

Finally, while the US does not separate general negligence and protective law theories of tort liability, protective statutes do play an important role in determining liability in that, 'the violation of a statute or ordinance prescribing a duty for the protection and safety of persons or property is generally treated as evidence of negligence'.[81] As early as 1972, a Missouri court noted that 'modern hospitals do operate under definite rules and regulations and subject themselves to recognized accreditation standards'.[82] More recently, a Louisiana court allowed expert testimony concerning violations of hospital standards set

[74] RI Gen Law Ann § 23-17-24.
[75] Cal Health & Safety Code § 50912.5.
[76] Mich Comp Law Ann § 333.21513.
[77] NY Pub Health Law § 2807-i.
[78] Duffourc (n 7).
[79] ibid.
[80] See IOM (n 62); World Health Organization, *Patient Safety: Making Health Care Safer* (2017), iris.who.int/handle/10665/255507.
[81] Corpus Juris Secundum, Negligence, § 135, vol 65.
[82] *Gridley v Johnson* 476 SW 2d 475 (Mo 1972).

by the Joint Commission and CMS as evidence of organisational negligence.[83] Beyond serving as evidence of organisational negligence, an Oklahoma court took notice, *sua sponte*, of the state's administrative law, which 'impose[d] upon hospitals a duty to document orders, treatment, tests, and services rendered in a patient's chart'.[84] The court went on to point out that:

> Because rules and regulations enacted by administrative agencies and boards pursuant to the powers delegated to them have the force and effect of law, they are material and relevant to the issue of the applicable standard of care and its alleged breach.[85]

5.2.3 Recognition of Risk Management Obligations in Product Liability Law

Another source of the existing liability framework that supports finding a duty to conduct clinical risk management comes from product liability law. In both the US and Germany, product manufacturers have legal duties to not only produce safe products, but also to monitor and evaluate product safety after market entry. This abstract monitoring obligation in product liability law provides some analogical support for extending organisational liability to encompass a duty to clinical risk management, which requires a systematic, proactive, ongoing process of identifying, analysing, and managing risks before they manifest.

In Germany, product liability law recognises direct tort liability for manufacturers for injuries caused by unreasonable conduct under § 823(1) BGB.[86] Product liability law requires that manufacturers exercise reasonable care in organising the product manufacturing process. According to Goldbach, duties to organise the manufacturing process in product liability law correspond with the existing duties to organise the treatment process in medical liability law, as reflected in the case law as specific treatment monitoring obligations.[87] In addition to duties in the manufacturing process, German product liability case law more broadly requires manufacturers to monitor the post-market safety of products. This includes

> actively and systematically monitor[ing] and evaluat[ing] the risk and to take appropriate action, not only in the case of new products but also in the case of products that have already been introduced, and also irrespective of any damage that has already occurred.[88]

Goldbach draws a parallel between the jurisprudentially established obligation to abstract product monitoring in product liability law to the yet-to-be

[83] *Dehart v Jones* 310 So 3d 658 (La App 3 Cir 2020).
[84] *Johnson v Hillcrest Health Center Inc* 70 P 3d 811 (Okla 2003).
[85] ibid.
[86] Goldbach (n 11).
[87] ibid.
[88] ibid (translation from German).

recognised obligation to abstract treatment monitoring in organisational liability law to conclude that viewing liability in the context of a uniform legal system requires finding a legal obligation to conduct clinical risk management in the medical negligence law.[89] Pauli agrees and lays out the similarities between the two:

> The producer's liability as well as the organisational liability of the hospital operator are aimed at safety for the benefit of consumers and patients. The producer's liability and the organisational liability of the hospital operator intervene if the breach of a duty of conduct incumbent on the producer or hospital operator has caused an infringement of the consumer's or patient's rights. In both areas, the risks originate from a sphere that the consumer or the patient cannot understand or influence. Both the producer and the hospital operator are obliged to organise their company in such a way that identifiable risks are excluded. For this purpose, the goods manufacturer is obliged, among other things, to take suitable measures to identify and exclude risks. Taking into account the above, there are no reasons why the obligation to identify and prevent or minimise risks should not apply analogously to the hospital operator, as it undoubtedly aims to increase patient safety and protect the legal interests of life, body and health.[90]

Once an obligation to conduct abstract treatment monitoring, and thus clinical risk management, is justified through comparison to the abstract product monitoring obligations recognised in product liability law, the obligations to clinical risk management set forth in social law form a legal basis for tort liability under BGB § 823(1), because as Goldbach points out, 'solutions to problems under social law cannot be irrelevant to liability law'.[91]

As in Germany, existing duties in US product liability law further support expanding current theories of organisational liability in medical negligence law to include liability for negligent clinical risk management. Although, an abstract duty to monitor products for safety is not the general rule, similar abstract duties exist in the form of pre-market testing for all manufacturers and post-market monitoring for drug and medical device manufacturers. Regarding pre-market testing, manufacturers must perform reasonable testing to discover risks as well as undertake responsive 'risk-avoidance measures'.[92] Additionally, drug and medical device manufacturers have post-market duties to monitor product safety.[93] Federal district courts in New York describe a drug manufacturer's continuous duty to monitor as two-fold, requiring

> the manufacturer to keep abreast of the current state of knowledge of its products as gained through research, adverse reaction reports, scientific literature, and other

[89] ibid.
[90] Pauli (n 22) (translation from German).
[91] Goldbach (n 11).
[92] Restatement (Third) of Torts § 2 comment m (American Law Institute 1998).
[93] 'Litigation of Continuing or Post-Sale Duty to Warn, Retrofit, or Recall in Products Liability Actions' in *American Jurisprudence Trials*, vol 157 § 5 (Thomson Reuters Westlaw).

> available methods, and to take reasonably necessary steps to bring that knowledge to the attention of the medical profession.[94]

A federal district court in Pennsylvania explicitly recognised a legally cognisable claim against a drug company for negligent risk management under state law based on an allegation that:

> Bayer is liable for breaching a 'duty to have in place a reasonable risk management procedure' that ensured that non-conforming products (a female birth control device which did not work as intended) could be tracked appropriately, and that adverse reports were considered in its risk analysis.[95]

As in Germany, the existing legal obligations to conduct risk management activities as well as the imposition of liability for the breach of similar risk management obligations under product liability law support expanding organisational negligence in medical liability law to encompass a legal duty to clinical risk management.

The analogy to duties in product liability law is reinforced by the increased focus on risk management obligations for AI-driven technologies and growing integration of those technologies into healthcare delivery. The EU AI Act's risk-based approach to AI governance emphasises the importance of risk management for manufacturers of high-risk AI systems. For AI-driven medical devices, which will generally trigger high-risk classification under Article 6(1) of the AI Act, Article 9 requires the establishment and implementation of a risk management system, which it describes as a 'continuous iterative process planned and run throughout the entire lifecycle of a high-risk AI system, requiring regular systematic review and updating'.[96] The risk management system for high-risk AI systems includes – like clinical risk management – identification, analysis, and evaluation of 'known and the reasonably foreseeable risks that the high-risk AI system can pose to health, safety or fundamental rights' followed by appropriate risk control measures to eliminate or mitigate those risks.[97]

In the US, there is no federal law comparable to the EU's AI Act; however, some US states have passed state laws to regulate AI-driven technologies. California's Transparency in Frontier Artificial Intelligence Act[98] requires developers of large AI models to develop and implement a 'Frontier AI framework',[99] which the Act defines as 'documented technical and organizational protocols to

[94] ibid (citing *Rosen v Saint Jude Medical Inc* 41 F Supp 3d 170 (Northern District of New York, 2014); *Baker v Saint Agnes Hospital* 70 AD2d 400 (New York Appellate Division Second Department, 1979)).

[95] *McLaughlin v Bayer Corp* 172 F Supp 3d 804 (Eastern District of Pennsylvania, 2016) (ultimately finding that the plaintiff failed to prove causation and therefore could not sustain a claim for negligent risk management).

[96] AI Act, Art 9(2).

[97] ibid.

[98] Transparency in Frontier Artificial Intelligence Act, Cal Bus Prof Code §§ 22757.10–22757.16.

[99] Cal Bus Prof Code § 22757.12.

manage, assess, and mitigate catastrophic risks'.[100] New York's Responsible AI Safety and Education Act[101] similarly requires developers of large AI models to 'implement a written safety and security protocol' and 'implement appropriate safeguards to prevent unreasonable risk of critical harm'.[102] Colorado's AI Act requires providers of "automated decision-making technology" to provide deployers with documentation describing, among other things, the AI's limitations and risks and notification of post-market changes and risk mitigation for the system.[103] In addition to informing consumers about the use of AI to make consequential decisions, including those in the healthcare domain, deployers of these systems must also retain records relating to AI-decision making and "material mitigation changes".[104]

Recent regulatory activity focused on the risks of AI-driven technologies generally also reinforces the regulatory focus on risk management for medical devices in both jurisdictions. In the EU, the Medical Device Regulation (MDR) also requires medical device manufacturers to engage in risk management, which the MDR similarly describes as a 'continuous iterative process throughout the entire lifecycle of a device, requiring regular systematic updating'.[105] This is also consistent with the US FDA's and the International Medical Device Regulators Forum (IMDRF)'s approach to life-cycle risk management for medical devices that relies on established international risk management standards.[106]

In the EU, a manufacturer's failure to comply with risk management obligations under the AI Act, MDR, or national law can also impact whether the medical device is considered defective under the EU Product Liability Directive.[107] Although the product liability directive imposes strict, rather than fault-based liability, on manufacturers whose defective products cause patient injuries, the connection between risk management obligations in safety regulations and liability for injuries caused by dangerous products shows the inherent relationship between *ex ante* safety law and ex post liability law. In the US, a violation of

[100] Cal Bus Prof Code § 22757.11(g).

[101] Responsible AI Safety and Education (RAISE) Act, New York General Business Law Art 44-B §§1420–1425.

[102] RAISE Act § 1421.

[103] Co Rev Stat § 6-1-1701(2).

[104] ibid § 6-1-1703(1),(3),(4).

[105] Regulation (EU) 2017/745 of the European Parliament and of the Council of 5 April 2017 on medical devices, amending Directive 2001/83/EC, Regulation (EC) No 178/2002 and Regulation (EC) No 1223/2009 and repealing Council Directives 90/385/EEC and 93/42/EEC (Text with EEA relevance) (MDR) [2017] OJ L 117, Art 10(9)–(10), Annex I §3.

[106] International Medical Device Regulators Forum, MDRF/GRRP WG/N47 FINAL:2024 (Edition 2), Essential Principles of Safety and Performance of Medical Devices and IVD Medical Devices (2024). See, eg ISO 14971:2019 Medical Devices; IEC 80002-1:2009 Medical device software; Food and Drug Administration, Artificial Intelligence-Enabled Device Software Functions: Lifecycle Management and Marketing Submission Recommendations, Draft Guidance for Industry and 6 Food and Drug Administration Staff (issues on 7 January 2025).

[107] Directive (EU) 2024/2853 of the European Parliament and of the Council of 23 October 2024 on liability for defective products and repealing Council Directive 85/374/EEC (Text with EEA relevance) (PLD) [2024], Art 7.

the Food and Drug Administration's continuing reporting requirements, which require medical device manufacturers to both monitor and report adverse health consequences, can form the basis of a product liability claim under either state or federal tort law.[108]

Returning to support for a fault-based theory of negligent clinical risk management in medical liability law, an analogy can be made between the decisions that healthcare organisations make about AI system selection, implementation, validation, monitoring, and governance, and the lifecycle risk management and product-monitoring decisions that manufacturers make after bringing a product to market. In both cases, the organisation deploys a complex system whose risks are not fully ascertainable at the time of deployment and must be actively managed through ongoing monitoring and evaluation. The product liability consequences of failing to properly conduct risk management exists precisely because the risks of deployed products can manifest in unpredictable ways; the same logic applies to the risks of deployed AI systems in healthcare organisations.

[108] *McConologue v Smith & Nephew*, 8 F Supp 3d 93 (D Conn 2014).

6

Establishing Liability for Negligent Clinical Risk Management

Chapter five established that liability for negligent clinical risk management is supported in both jurisdictions by the existing fault-based liability law, including case law recognising direct organisational liability for medical injuries, and existing legal duties and obligations to conduct clinical risk management found in other legal and regulatory spheres. A duty or obligation to conduct clinical risk management is further supported by similar duties and obligations in product liability law that require product manufacturers to identify and control risks.

This chapter aims to provide rules that achieve the dual goals of compensating plaintiffs for damages caused by negligent clinical risk management and deterring future error-causing organisational behaviour. To achieve this aim, it provides a framework to support a cause of action for negligent clinical risk management. It sets forth methods for setting standards of care that follow the generally accepted clinical risk management process and illustrates how those standards can be applied and measured in practice. It also provides legal proof rules that balance the level of confidentiality necessary for successful clinical risk management with the transparency needed for patients to succeed on valid negligence claims. Finally, it concludes by situating the cause of action for negligent clinical risk management within the larger medical liability system, demonstrating how it operates concurrently with existing individual and organisational liability theories to advance the patient safety goals that this book identifies throughout.

6.1 LEGAL STANDARDS OF CARE FOR CLINICAL RISK MANAGEMENT

Florence Nightingale lamented in 1859 about the lack of attention to governing standards in the management of healthcare systems:

> If you look into the reports of trials or accidents, and especially of suicides, or into the medical history of fatal cases, it is almost incredible how often the whole thing turns upon something which has happened because "he,' or still oftener 'she,' 'was

> not there.' But it is still more incredible how often, how almost always this is accepted as a sufficient reason, a justification; why, the very fact of the thing having happened is the proof of its not being a justification. The person in charge was quite right not to be '*there*,' he was called away for quite sufficient reason, or he was away for a daily recurring and unavoidable cause: yet no provision was made to supply his absence. The fault was not in his 'being away,' but in there being no management to supplement his 'being away.' When the sun is under a total eclipse or during his nightly absence, we light candles. But it would seem as if it did not occur to us that we must also supplement the person in charge of sick or of children, whether under an occasional eclipse or during a regular absence.[1]

Nightingale describes 'fatal accidents' in military hospitals in which patients were overseen by (often drunk) medical officers, and despite her contempt for the abhorrent behaviour of the officers involved, she concludes that 'The fault lies in there being no organized system of attendance.'[2] Nightingale might be delighted to learn that modern healthcare systems have substantially progressed to recognise that 'Patient safety is a management issue.'[3] But she would almost certainly still criticise the lack of attention to healthcare management standards in liability cases involving patient injuries.

Once a healthcare organisation is legally obliged to conduct clinical risk management, the question remains: what are the standards of care that govern this obligation? The modern healthcare industry is seeing an explosion of internal and external regulations and policies governing clinical risk management, all of which create new potential standards of care for healthcare organisations. Weit notes that in the United States (US) courts have been able to rely upon a 'virtually limitless evidentiary base' of regulations for finding direct negligence against the hospital.[4] In Germany, Goldbach observes, the lack of 'uniform criteria' to guide the judicial development of organisational standards of care.[5] Additionally, Chiozza and Ponzetti highlight that 'increasingly complex and innovative health care processes redefines the competences' needed at the organisational level to coordinate clinical risk management activities.[6] Although legal, regulatory, and institutional standards should reflect the industry's best practices and provide flexibility, holding healthcare organisations to such vast and vague standards of care in liability cases may jeopardise the very safety culture that new risk management standards are meant to create. According to Shuman:

[1] F Nightingale, *Notes on Nursing: What it is, and What it is not* (Philadelphia, JB Lippincott Company, 1946).

[2] ibid.

[3] ML Chiozza and C Ponzetti, 'FMEA: A Model for Reducing Medical Errors' (2009) 404 *Clinica Chimica Acta* 75.

[4] MJ Weit, 'Darling v. Charleston Community Memorial Hospital and Its Legacy' (2005) 14 *Annals of Health Law* 399.

[5] C Goldbach, *Risikomanagementsysteme im Krankenhaus nach dem Patientenrechtegesetz: Sozialrechtliche Pflicht und haftungsrechtlicher Standard* (Kassel, Kassel University Press 2014).

[6] Chiozza and Ponzetti (n 3).

> Because of the importance of certainty in deterrence theory, tort law should articulate a clear, understandable standard of behaviour that is communicated to decision makers who can then modify their behaviour to avoid the tort sanctions that would otherwise accrue.[7]

Goldbach agrees that 'it is incumbent on the judiciary to review the behavioural requirements established in fact for their normative suitability and, if necessary, to concretise them through judicial law'.[8]

Generally, healthcare industry standards for preventing injuries through clinical risk management will be similar in the US and Germany because they are derived from internationally accepted concepts in medical and error prevention science.[9] German legal scholars, drawing from these concepts, have suggested that the jurisprudential development of legal standards of care can be organised in accordance with the core clinical risk management process.[10] Pursuant to this process, clinical risk management occurs in four phases: (1) risk identification; (2) risk analysis; (3) risk assessment; and (4) risk control.[11] All phases require the hospital to employ adequate personnel and resources to carry out the iterative clinical risk management process.[12] This includes retention of risk management specialists, who ensure the proper functioning and continued development of the clinical risk management process, as well as provision of physical and technical components needed for the process to function.[13]

6.1.1 Anchoring Standards in the Clinical Risk Management Process

The first phase of the clinical risk management process is identifying the existence of risks that can lead to patient injuries. According to Pauli, the hospital must organise the treatment process to incorporate methods of collecting

[7] D Shuman, 'The Psychology of Deterrence in Tort Law' (1993) 42 *University of Kansas Law Review* 115.

[8] Goldbach (n 5).

[9] See ibid (regarding acceptance of risk management as an essential component of healthcare in the German healthcare industry); NEJM Catalyst, 'What Is Risk Management in Healthcare?' (2018), catalyst.nejm.org/doi/full/10.1056/CAT.18.0197 (regarding acceptance of proactive risk management in the US healthcare industry).

[10] See generally A Pauli, *Risikomanagement und CIRS als Gegenstand der Krankenhaushaftung* (Baden-Baden, Nomos, 2013); Goldbach (n 5); D Hart, 'Patientensicherheit nach dem Patientenrechtegesetz' (2013) 31 *Medizinrecht* 159.

[11] Pauli (n 10). See also Aktionsbündnis Patientensicherheit (APS), 'Requirements on Clinical Risk Management Systems in Hospitals' (February 2017), www.aps-ev.de/hempfehlungen/requirements-on-clinical-risk-management-systems-in-hospitals; see International Organization for Standardization, *ISO 31000:2018: Risk Management* (2018) (the risk management process includes identifying, analysing, evaluating, and where required, treating risks).

[12] See APS (n 11); NEJM Catalyst (n 9) (describing the various components required for risk management in healthcare).

[13] Pauli (n 10) (comparing risk management to a medical specialty, which requires continuous training to remain up to date with current medical standards). See NEJM Catalyst (n 9).

information that can identify potential risks to patient safety.[14] Goldbach agrees that healthcare organisations are legally required to 'do everything reasonable to ensure that the greatest possible information is obtained about possible risks of damage'.[15] Sources of risk information can include internal sources like patient complaint systems, error reporting systems, and claims information, as well has external sources that discuss near-misses, errors, claims, and medical liability judgments occurring outside of the hospital.[16] Although the size and scope of tools used to collect information about organisational risks may vary with the healthcare organisation, the obligation to conduct clinical risk management should require hospitals to take an active role in collecting risk-identifying information. In addition to collecting risk information, the standard of care for risk identification includes a 'continuous duty to ensure up-to-date sources of information and effectiveness of current information sources'.[17]

The second phase of the clinical risk management process is the risk analysis stage, during which risk management specialists analyse information from risk identification sources to determine the causes and effects of and relationships between identified risks.[18] Implementing systems designed to identify patient safety risks is pointless if the risk information collected from those systems does not become a catalyst for minimising or preventing potential harm. As Goldbach points out, 'the hospital operator is also obligated to respond to the risk information obtained by doing everything reasonable to eliminate avoidable hazards'.[19] This includes the provision of adequate personnel, technology, equipment, and procedures for carrying out risk analysis.[20] To properly conduct clinical risk management at the risk analysis stage, healthcare organisations might meet the standard of care for analysing risks using a combination of accepted methods for risk analysis in healthcare. This can include reactive risk management tools like root cause analysis (RCA) and blunt end analysis of errors captured from an incident reporting system,[21] or proactive tools like failure modes effect analysis (FMEA) and sociotechnical probabilistic risk assessment (ST-PRA).[22,23] Regardless of the chosen method, the hospital should maintain clear policies

[14] Pauli (n 10).

[15] Goldbach (n 5).

[16] Pauli (n 10). See NEJM Catalyst (n 9) (describing the need to identify risks using data, institutional and industry knowledge and engaging all actors in the healthcare system).

[17] See sources cited (n 16).

[18] See sources cited (n 16); APS (n 11).

[19] Goldbach (n 5).

[20] Pauli (n 10).

[21] P Leroy 'Medical errors: the importance of the bullet's blunt end.' (2011) 170 *European Journal of Pediatrics* 251.

[22] D Marx and A Slonim, 'Assessing patient safety risk before the injury occurs: an introduction to sociotechnical probabilistic risk modelling in health care' (2003) 12 (Suppl 2) *BMJ Quality & Safety* ii33.

[23] See Pauli (n 10) (identifying RCA, Ishikawa diagram, and FTA as acceptable methods of risk analysis); NEJM Catalyst (n 9) (identifying Blunt End/Sharp End Evaluation, RCA, and FMEA as acceptable methods of risk analysis).

and procedures for carrying out risk analysis using its chosen methods, as well as records showing that risk analysis is a continuous functioning process as evidence of compliance with the standard of care for clinical risk management.

Once risks are identified and analysed, the third phase in the clinical risk management process requires them to be assessed to determine the likelihood and degree of severity of potential harm posed by each risk.[24] Proper assessment of risks allows the healthcare organisation to prioritise risks so that they can be managed accordingly in the risk control phase.[25] As with risk analysis, healthcare organisations should be free to choose a method of risk assessment as long as the chosen method produces a reasoned, documented, and defensible prioritisation of identified risks. This process might integrate one or more of the following methods for risk assessment: risk matrix or map method; Fuzzy Analytic Hierarchy Process; Sequential Updating Approach; and Pareto Analysis.[26] Again, as with risk analysis, regardless of the risk assessment method chosen, healthcare organisations must implement and maintain a functioning risk assessment strategy. The standard of care is not compliance with a particular formula or use of a specific tool but, instead, the exercise of reasonable organisational judgement, guided by recognised methodologies, about which risks are most urgent and how resources should be allocated to address them.

The fourth phase of the clinical risk management process is risk control, which involves the development of measures that eliminate or minimise identified, analysed, and assessed risks.[27] In this phase of risk management, healthcare organisations are 'obligated to respond to the risk information obtained by doing everything reasonable to eliminate avoidable hazards'.[28] Depending on the type and severity of the risk, risk control can manifest in a variety of ways including risk avoidance by eliminating the risk-producing activity, risk reduction through preventive measures, risk reduction through transferring the risk, or risk acceptance with or without additional supervision.[29] According to Pauli, the standard of care as it relates to the risk control process allows healthcare organisations to consider the financial and time expenditures involved with risk control measures that equally maximise patient safety to determine which measure to employ.[30]

The specific risk control measures required vary widely and can include, but are not limited to: changes to the physical treatment environment (ie lighting, placement of equipment); staffing protocols (ie scheduling, training, supervision); guidelines (ie checklists, instructions); changes in equipment and apparatus (ie medical device repairs, provision of surgical instruments); and improved

[24] Pauli (n 10); APS (n 11).

[25] G Pascarella et al, 'Risk Analysis in Healthcare Organizations: Methodological Framework and Critical Variables' (2021) 14 *Risk Management and Healthcare Policy* 2897.

[26] Pascarella et al (n 25); Pauli (n 10).

[27] Pauli (n 10).

[28] Goldbach (n 5).

[29] APS (n 11).

[30] Pauli (n 10).

communication (continuity of care guidelines, protocols for patient communication).[31] As discussed in chapter four, although the process of deriving risk control measures through a more comprehensive clinical risk management process is not explicitly recognised as an organisational duty, the failure to implement specific risk control measures can already be a basis for organisational liability under the existing case law. As such, jurisprudential precedents already exist in both jurisdictions to guide a determination of whether implementation of or failure to implement a specific risk control measure falls below the standard of care.

However, risk control does not end upon selection and implementation of a specific risk control measure. Instead, once risk control measures are identified and implemented, they must be properly communicated to necessary personnel and their effectiveness monitored and evaluated.[32] According to Pauli, 'Risk communication means providing the right information and evaluations to the right recipients at the right time and in the right way.'[33] Proper communication ensures that predicted damage from identified risks is prevented or minimised within a reasonable time.[34] To meet the standard of proper risk communication, healthcare organisations must identify the proper means and modes of communication, which, depending on the nature of the risk, can range from communication via email, to alerts on an intranet, to discussion at employee meetings, to publication in a staff newsletter.[35] Once properly implemented and communicated, specific risk control measures must be monitored and evaluated to determine compliance, effectiveness, and sustainability.[36] Risk monitoring and evaluation can lead to further duties to reanalyse and reassess identified risks, and to reconsider risk control measures.[37] Like all other stages of the risk management process, proper documentation of actions taken during the risk control phase is crucial to showing compliance with the standard of care. As Pauli points out, 'In the event of liability, proper documentation can make it easier for the hospital operator to prove that it has done what was necessary and reasonable to avoid the risk.'[38]

6.1.2 Operationalising Standards: Recognised Approaches to Clinical Risk Management

It is helpful to supplement the general clinical risk management process, within which legal standards of care can be developed and applied, to provide more

[31] See D Hart, 'Patientensicherheit, Fehlermanagement, Arzthaftungsrecht – zugleich ein Beitrag zur rechtlichen Bedeutung von Empfehlungen' (2012) 30 *Medizinrecht* 1.

[32] Pauli (n 10). See also APS (n 11) (listing risk evaluation as a separate phase of clinical risk management).

[33] Pauli (n 10).

[34] ibid.

[35] ibid.

[36] ibid.

[37] ibid.

[38] ibid.

concrete examples of how clinical risk management activities might manifest in practice. While it is not possible to describe all clinical risk management methods available to healthcare organisations, this section illustrates how the process, when properly conducted, can demonstrably improve patient safety in modern healthcare organisations.

Standards of care relating to risk identification in the clinical risk management process require organisations to maintain active, functioning systems for collecting risk information from both internal and external sources. Error-reporting and complaint systems can provide a method of risk identification in healthcare organisations. In Germany, Goldbach opines that the implementation of internal patient complaint and error-reporting systems already required by federal regulations, as well as participation in and monitoring alerts from external reporting systems are required to satisfy a legal duty to conduct clinical risk management.[39] Goldbach notes that although more than 95 per cent of German hospitals have patient complaint systems, risk management requires incorporation of patient complaint systems into the risk identification phase.[40] Regarding internal error-reporting, implementation of Germany's anonymous critical incident reporting system (CIRS), 'represent[s] the standard of good organization in the hospital.'[41] Regarding participation in external error-reporting, Goldbach opines that some level of participation in freely accessible external supra-regional reporting systems, like Krankenhaus-CIRS-Netz-D, should be required under the legal standard of care.[42] This includes 'systematic observation and analysis of at least the most significant cases.'[43]

In the US, the lack of centralised regulations concerning complaint and error reporting systems highlights the need for a uniform legal standard of care for risk identification under a duty to conduct clinical risk management. As in Germany, US healthcare organisations should, at a minimum, implement and integrate internal patient complaint and error reporting systems into the clinical risk management process as well as monitor risk information from external sources. To accomplish error prevention goals, internal error-reporting systems, like Germany's CIRS, should focus on near-misses and be voluntary, anonymous, and sanction-free.[44] Examples of external risk information sources in the US include reports and recommendations from the Agency for Healthcare

[39] Goldbach (n 5).
[40] ibid.
[41] ibid.
[42] ibid.
[43] ibid.
[44] See MN Duffourc, 'Filling Voice Promotion Gaps in Healthcare Through A Comparative Analysis of Error Reporting and Learning Systems and Open Communication and Disclosure Policies in the United States and Germany' (2018) 44 *American Journal of Law and Medicine* 579; see also Institute of Medicine (IOM) Committee on Quality of Health Care in America, *To Err is Human: Building a Safer Health System* (LT Kohn, JM Corrigan, MS Donaldson, eds, Washington DC, National Academies Press, 2000).

Research and Quality (AHRQ)'s Patient Safety Network Web Morbidity and Mortality (WebM&M) programme,[45] and risk reduction information gleaned from the Joint Commission's Sentinel Event Policy.[46]

The risk identification standard of care also encompasses the proactive identification of risks caused by latent errors in a healthcare system's design. FMEA, discussed further below in the context of risk analysis, enables organisations to review existing processes and identify latent defects that might create patient safety risks. This type of proactive risk identification can supplement retroactive approaches, like error reporting, to improve risk identification. Devario et al conducted a four-year prospective observational study in a paediatric intensive care unit at a hospital in Padua, Italy to determine whether introducing FMEA protocols alongside the existing voluntary error-reporting system impacted error identification in the unit.[47] They found that after the introduction of FMEA, the rate of reported errors increased by 165 per cent compared with the error-reporting system alone.[48] Reports of near-miss errors increased (from eight per cent to 21 per cent) and reports of errors that did not lead to patient harm increased from (from 38 per cent to 65 per cent), a result that the authors attributed to the changed 'mentality of [the] clinical staff' and 'increased the awareness that a problem exists and the need to do something to correct it'.[49]

Standards of care relating to risk analysis in the clinical risk management process require organisations to process information about identified risks to determine their causes and effects. Reactive methods, such as root cause analysis (RCA) and blunt end analysis of errors captured from an error-reporting system, are valuable for learning from specific incidents and identifying the organisational conditions that contributed to them.[50] Organisations should complement these reactive methods of risk analysis with proactive methods, like FMEA and ST-PRA, to meet the standard of care. Notably, the Joint Commission 'now requires the incorporation of prospective process analysis methods into organizational patient safety plans'.[51]

FMEA is used to proactively examine organisational processes from start to finish without a triggering adverse event to anticipate where and how failures may occur. According to Chiozza and Ponzetti, 'FMEA places the primary burden of error prevention, not on individuals, but on the designers of the

[45] Agency for Healthcare Research and Quality (AHRQ), 'Patient Safety Network: Submit a Case to WebM&M', psnet.ahrq.gov/webmm/submit-case.

[46] The Joint Commission, 'Sentinel Event Policy and Procedures', www.jointcommission.org/sentinel_event_policy_and_procedures.

[47] M Daverio et al, 'Failure mode and effective analysis ameliorate awareness of medical errors: a 4-year prospective observational study in critically ill children' (2015) 25 *Paediatric Anaesthesia* 1227.

[48] ibid.

[49] ibid.

[50] Leroy (n 21).

[51] Marx and Slonim (n 22).

systems in which they work.'[52] They stress the value of FMEA in laboratory medicine, noting the substantial impact that even a small incidence of errors across 'billions of tests performed every day worldwide' will have on the reliability of diagnosis and accuracy of treatments.[53] The International Organization for Standardization's ISO/TS 22367 for medical laboratories expressly recognises FMEA as the method of choice for 'prospective risk analysis of high-risk processes to identify needed improvements that will reduce the chance of unintended adverse events'.[54] Beyond the standard recommendation, Chiozza and Ponzetti highlight empirical evidence that FMEA reduces risks in clinical laboratories: a study that used FMEA to redesign the blood cross-matching process resulted in both a decrease in errors and an increase in the likelihood of detecting errors; a study applying FMEA to common laboratory tests (glucose, cholesterol, and bilirubin) reduced the probability of risks relating to storage temperature and contaminated reagents and calibrators; and a study applying FMEA to point-of-care testing reduced error rates relating to identification.[55]

Standards of care relating to risk assessment in the clinical risk management process require organisations to consider the likelihood that the risk will manifest and the severity of potential harm. In practice, risk analysis and risk assessment are often integrated within a single methodological framework. FMEA exemplifies this integration: its risk analysis framework includes assessing risk levels and ranking risk priorities by assigning each risk a priority number.[56]

Digitisation in healthcare systems introduces new types of risks and failure modes that require robust and proactive risk management. Recognising that 'digital transformation of healthcare has resulted in a substantial increase in the volume and diversity of data types', Wassem et al used a data-driven FMEA approach to identify and evaluate risks in digital health systems.[57] They identified critical failure modes across clinical, operational, and patient-reported data categories, as well as across text, image, tabular, audio, and video data modalities.[58] For clinical data, 'encompass[ing] patient medical records, diagnostics, lab results, and treatment histories', the clinical risk consequences included treatment and diagnostic inaccuracies, which had a range of potential causes, including system and human errors, system/network incompatibility, and cybersecurity issues.[59] For operational data, 'includ[ing] staffing schedules, resource allocation details, compliance management, and supply chain data, each essential for the effective delivery of healthcare services', they identified

[52] Chiozza and Ponzetti (n 3).
[53] ibid.
[54] ibid.
[55] ibid.
[56] B Streimelweger et al, 'Improving Patient Safety through Human-factor-based Risk Management' (2015) 64 *Procedia Computer Science* 69.
[57] HM Waseem et al, 'Data-driven FMEA approach for hazard identification and risk evaluation in digital health' (2025) 15 *Scientific Reports* 52856.
[58] ibid.
[59] ibid.

the potential for operational disruption and inefficiency and delayed care caused by high workloads, inadequate testing, poor synchronisation, manual entry errors, and system failures.[60] For patient-reported data, 'encompass[ing] health information provided directly by patients', they identified risks with potential safety consequences, including inappropriate diagnosis and treatments, clinical misinterpretations, and analytical errors caused by poor protocols, lack of standardisation, and patient non-compliance.[61] This study exemplifies the need for 'proactive risk assessment that can support safer and more efficient digital healthcare operations'.[62]

Because FMEA is not designed to consider risk combinations, including those stemming from human error, in complex healthcare system processes, FMEA can be modified or supplemented to improve risk assessment.[63] Streimelweger et al proposed an FMEA method for assessing clinical risks that considers 'the dependency between different risk factors expressed by human factors'.[64] They evaluated this proposed method using risk information from an anonymous voluntary CIRS available in Germany and Austria, and concluded that CIRS data could be used to improve risk assessment with a modified approach that considers human factors.[65] Liu et al considered a modified FMEA approach for assessing failure modes stemming from the use of medical devices in healthcare settings. They highlight that insufficient risk information about medical device failures increased subjectivity in risk analysis and assessment, and proposed a more rigorous mathematical framework – based on Fuzzy Mathematics and Grey Relational Analysis to facilitate a more objective and quantitatively rigorous basis for risk assessment. When applying this modified FMEA methodology to analyse and assess use-related risks of a C-arm X-ray machine, they identified inadequate radiation protection caused by limited protective conditions, improper protection systems and device fatigue/overuse caused by lack of devices and conflicts in arrangements for device use as the high-priority failure modes.[66]

A complementary proactive approach for organisations facing highly complex, multi-system risk environments is probabilistic risk assessment (PRA). Marx and Slonim describe PRA as 'a process for modelling the combinations of multiple failures leading to a specific undesirable outcome'. They propose that ST-PRA is valuable for assessing risks in healthcare systems due to its ability to consider human behaviours in modelling system failures.[67] While FMEA begins by analysing a process to investigate possible failure modes, PRA

[60] ibid.
[61] ibid.
[62] ibid.
[63] See Waseem et al (n 57); Marx and Slonim (n 22).
[64] Streimelweger et al (n 56).
[65] ibid.
[66] ibid.
[67] Marx and Slonim (n 22).

begins by analysing an undesirable outcome to investigate the possible combinations of process failures that can cause the undesirable outcome.[68] Marx and Slonim highlight this 'top-down' approach as a strength of PRA, considering the complexity of 'interactions between patients, providers, and technology'.[69] Iper et al reported the results of combining FMEA with ST-PRA to manage risks related to nearby demolition and construction work that impacted operations in a Turkish hospital.[70] To prevent risks related to the 'probable interruption to services and more importantly, the potential to severely harm patients', the hospital used ST-PRA to quantitively assess risks and FMEA to prioritise risks and interventions.[71] This approach resulted in 'zero error – zero collateral effect' with Iper et al reporting:

> No incidences of hospital-related infections were observed in patients that underwent surgery, or that were being treated in the intensive care or oncology units during this period; and no interruptions, errors or harm to patients were found in the aforementioned processes during the monitoring period of 6 months.[72]

The success of the hybrid approach taken by the hospital in this case demonstrates both the feasibility and efficacy of risk management for error prevention in complex healthcare organisations.

The risk control phase requires organisations to develop and implement measures that eliminate or minimise the risks identified, analysed, and assessed in the preceding phases of the clinical risk management process. Chiozza and Ponzetti describe the practical expectations for risk control:

> Once the root causes of critical failures have been identified, the team's goal is to eliminate the risk of failures, reduce the likelihood of failure or mitigate the effects of failure should it affect the patient. A search of the literature should be made, and benchmarking procedures used to identify the ways in which other organisations have made similar processes safer for patients.[73]

As discussed in chapters four and five, while courts do not yet focus on the comprehensive upstream risk identification, analysis, and assessment behaviours in an organisation's clinical risk management process, the failure to implement specific risk control measures has already been the subject of organisational liability claims. This means that organisational failures relating to adequate staffing protocols, equipment maintenance, and hygienic facilities can already constitute direct organisational liability, as discussed in chapter four.

[68] ibid.
[69] ibid.
[70] HST Iper et al, 'ST-PRA+FMEA Hybrid Risk Analysis Application for Catastrophic Events at Hospitals' (2022) 41 *European Journal of Science and Technology* 221.
[71] ibid.
[72] ibid.
[73] Chiozza and Ponzetti (n 3).

It is worth highlighting here the relationship between organisational risk control obligations in the context of medical technology. In *Ambrose v Saint Joseph's Hospital of Atlanta*, a patient underwent surgery that involved the use of 'a technologically advanced system that, among other things, integrates a surgical microscope and lighting system with digital video recording and the hospital's information infrastructure'.[74] The patient suffered burns from the system's ultraviolet light, and alleged that the hospital's failure to update the system's software caused his injury and violated the hospital's duty to provide safe equipment.[75] Although the court did not decide the case on the merits, it determined that the patient had alleged a valid claim of negligence against the hospital.[76] The *Ambrose* case demonstrates that clinical risk management requires technology-aware risk control procedures that reflect the iterative and dynamic nature of new medical technologies and the clinical environments in which they are deployed. AI-driven technologies, especially, can present patient safety risks that are either not ascertainable at the time of deployment or that develop post deployment.

6.2 PROVING NEGLIGENT CLINICAL RISK MANAGEMENT: BALANCING CONFIDENTIALITY AND ACCOUNTABILITY

In addition to identifying a framework for developing legal standards of care, a theory of liability for negligent clinical risk management also requires the development of proof rules that balance the plaintiff's ability to recover damages caused by negligent clinical risk management with the defendant's ability to implement and maintain a patient safety culture that enables successful clinical risk management. Safety culture is central to the success of a clinical risk management system. The Aktionsbündnis Patientensicherheit (APS) describes safety culture in the clinical risk management process as

> the manner in which safety is organised in the context of patient care and thus reflects the attitudes, convictions, perceptions, values and conduct of management and other staff with respect to the safety of patients, staff and the organisation itself.[77]

The Joint Commission similarly defines safety culture as, 'the product of individual and group beliefs, values, attitudes, perceptions, competencies, and patterns of behaviour that determine the organization's commitment to quality and patient safety'.[78] The successful development of safety culture in healthcare

[74] *Ambrose v Saint Joseph's Hospital of Atlanta Inc* 325 Ga App 557 (Ga Ct App 2014).
[75] ibid.
[76] ibid.
[77] APS (n 11).
[78] The Joint Commission, 'Sentinel Event Alert 57: The Essential Role of Leadership in Developing a Safety Culture' (2017), www.jointcommission.org/en-us/knowledge-library/newsletters/sentinel-event-alert/issue-57.

organisations requires a delicate balance of confidentiality and accountability.[79] On one hand, healthcare providers should be 'afforded a certain level of confidentiality necessary to promote open discussion of medical errors'.[80] On the other hand, patients should be able to hold healthcare providers accountable for damages caused by negligent clinical risk management.[81] To support the development and maintenance of safety culture, a legal cause of action against healthcare organisations for negligent clinical risk management should aim to strike a balance between providing confidentiality for some clinical risk management activities through evidentiary protections while also giving patients a viable path to recovering damages caused by negligent clinical risk management through burden-shifting mechanisms.

6.2.1 Rules for Obtaining Evidence

Evidentiary protections that maintain confidentiality of systems used in the risk identification phase of clinical risk management, like voluntary error reporting, are necessary for safety culture. The Joint Commission describes non-punitive error reporting and learning as 'absolutely crucial' to safety culture. Germany too has embraced sanction-free error reporting as an indispensable element of a 'trustworthy learning and safety culture'.[82] The WHO also agrees that implementation of non-punitive error reporting and learning systems are necessary to detect, and ultimately prevent, systemic errors.[83] To ensure that participation in voluntary error reporting systems are non-punitive and sanction-free, error reports made within these systems should not lead to liability for individual healthcare providers who either report or are implicated in reports.[84] Phillips et al note that 'voluntary reporting systems can measurably improve safety if reporting is protected against discovery and provides reporters with useful information from expert analysis'.[85] As such, voluntary error reports made during the risk identification phase should neither be discoverable nor admissible as evidence in claims against healthcare organisations for negligent clinical risk management.

[79] Duffourc (n 44).

[80] ibid.

[81] ibid.

[82] See S Barth, 'Aus Fehlern lernen –Schwachstellen im System rechtzeitig erkennen' (2009) I *Berliner Ärzte* 14; G Jonitz and S Barth, 'Etablierung von Patientensicherheit – national und international' (2013) 15 *Trauma Berufskrankh* 154.

[83] World Health Organization, 'WHO Draft Guidelines for Adverse Event Reporting and Learning Systems: From Information to Action' (2005), www.who.int/publications/i/item/WHO-EIP-SPO-QPS-05.3.

[84] See IOM (n 44).

[85] RL Phillips et al, 'The AAFP Patient Safety Reporting System: Development and Legal Issues Pertinent to Medical Error Tracking and Analysis' in K Henriksen, et al (eds), *Advances in Patient Safety: From Research to Implementation, Volume 3: Implementation Issues* (Agency for Healthcare Research and Quality, 2005), www.ncbi.nlm.nih.gov/books/NBK20535.

Both jurisdictions have made some efforts toward providing legal protection for voluntary error reports, but neither has offered a comprehensive privilege sufficient to ensure the requisite freedom from sanctions. Pursuant to the Patients' Rights Act in Germany, data from voluntary error reporting systems cannot be used against the reporter in legal proceedings.[86] While this legal protection is primarily aimed at protecting whistleblowers and not individual healthcare providers more broadly, data from Germany's CIRS system has thus far not been used against healthcare providers in medical malpractice litigation, leaving the question of admissibility of CIRS data in civil litigation unanswered in the case law.[87] Pauli opines that a patient has no right of access to the documentation or data from clinical risk management and internal hospital CIRS systems.[88] Goldbach is less sure and considers the circumstances under which CIRS reports can be used in civil litigation to be unclear.[89] Regardless of how German courts resolve the question of admissibility, anonymisation of CIRS data and Germany's conservative discovery rules are likely to prevent voluntary error reports from being used as evidence against healthcare providers.[90]

In the US, peer review and Patient Safety Work Product discovery privileges, as discussed in chapter four, provide some protection for data in voluntary error reporting systems, but the case law applying these privileges to voluntary medical error reports is inconsistent.[91] Additionally, liberal discovery practices in the US threaten the confidentiality of voluntary error reports, and therefore, also threaten the establishment of safety culture required for successful clinical risk management.[92]

To date, both jurisdictions are still lacking clear and comprehensive evidentiary protections for voluntary error reports used for risk identification in the clinical risk management process. As such, liability for negligent clinical risk management should also incorporate legal rules excluding data relating to individual voluntary error reports from discovery and evidence in litigation.

To ensure access to evidence regarding the reasonableness of an organisation's clinical risk management activities in civil litigation, there must be limits to the confidentiality provided by evidentiary protections for the sake of transparency and accountability. To accomplish this goal, documents that relate to the organisational safety commitments, including those made to obtain accreditation, should be discoverable. The North Carolina Supreme Court observed

[86] Sozialgesetzbuch V (Social Code, Book V) § 135a(3).

[87] See BT-Drucks 18/10203, dip21.bundestag.de/dip21/btd/18/102/1810203.pdf.

[88] Pauli (n 10).

[89] J Thüß, *Rechtsfragen des Critical Incident Reportings in der Medizin* (Christian Katzenmeier ed, Heidelberg, Springer-Verlag Berlin, 2012).

[90] Duffourc (n 44).

[91] See CJ Dollar, 'Promoting Better Healthcare: Policy Arguments for Concurrent Quality Assurance and Attorney-Client Hospital Incident Report Privileges' (1993) 3 *Health Matrix* 259.

[92] See Duffourc (n 44).

the inherent relevance of such documents in a claim of administrative negligence against a hospital:

> This evidence included documents defendant had previously submitted as part of an application to gain accreditation as a Chest Pain Center. Plaintiff also offered expert testimony that the policies and protocols within the Chest Pain Center application documents were consistent with the standard of care applicable to Mr. Savino's clinical care in defendant's emergency department. To the extent plaintiff argued that the hospital violated the applicable standard of care by failing to implement or follow appropriate health care policies and protocols as outlined in these documents, we agree with the Court of Appeals that this argument was directly relevant to the medical negligence claim.[93]

At the most basic level, healthcare organisations cannot benefit from accreditation based on their commitments to safety practices, but remain insulated from liability for failing to follow these practices. Other organisational information that relates to the establishment and execution of risk management activities should also be discoverable. For example, plaintiffs should be able to access documents relating to the existence of an error-reporting system, including guidelines and protocols for implementation and maintenance of the system, statistics regarding the number and types of reported errors, and documents that show a final organisational response to reported errors through the risk control process. General information about compliance with clinical risk management standards is required to hold organisations accountable for negligent clinical risk management or, as Pauli points out, exonerate organisations that meet the applicable standards of care.[94]

To ensure a sufficient level of confidentiality, voluntary error reports identifying and discussing individual events as well as the analysis and assessment of those individual events should be protected from discovery. Additionally, even discoverable information and documents regarding the general operation and maintenance of clinical risk management should only be admissible to prove claims of organisational negligence against the healthcare organisation. As Goldbach points out, 'the organisational measures required by [risk management] do not interfere with individual medical treatment, but rather set an external framework with general requirements without affecting medical treatment decisions'.[95] For a legal duty to conduct clinical risk management to incentivise organisational improvements, courts that recognise a liability for negligent clinical risk management must resist the common urge to associate medical damages with 'bad doctors' and 'bad nurses'. This requires focusing on evidence relating to the organisation's clinical risk management activities. Carefully developed evidentiary rules can help maintain this organisational focus.

[93] *Estate of Savino v Charlotte-Mecklenburg Hospital Authority* 375 NC 288 (NC Sup Ct 2020).
[94] See Pauli (n 10).
[95] Goldbach (n 5).

6.2.2 Rules that Modify the Burden of Proof

Proving organisational negligence based on a failure to conduct clinical risk management is difficult for several reasons. First, because patients' primary contact with the healthcare system is through individual providers, they generally 'equate[] medical errors with a personal failure on the part of the physician', leaving them unaware of possible negligent organisational behaviour.[96] Second, even if they suspect an organisational error, patients neither have insight into the inner workings of the healthcare organisation nor are they expected to be experts on the process of clinical risk management.[97] Third, the evidentiary protections recommended above impose limitations on a patient's ability to obtain information and documents about the organisation's clinical risk management process. As a result, for a claim of negligent clinical risk management to function in practice, there must be an appropriate modification of the burden of proof rules.[98]

Goldbach proposes burden of proof modifications for claims of negligent clinical risk management that are grounded in the burden-shifting mechanisms found in the German Patients' Rights Act. Of course, American courts can impose similar burden-shifting rules or legal presumptions for claims of negligent clinical risk management that make such claims practically viable from a proof standpoint. According to Goldbach, because the entire process of clinical risk management is controlled by the healthcare organisation, plaintiffs who claim negligent clinical risk management are initially relieved from proving a breach of the standard of care under the legal rule that shifts the burden of proof for negligence in cases involving 'fully controllable' risks.[99] However, in order to take advantage of this burden-shifting mechanism, a plaintiff must 'first demonstrate that the risk actually originates from this fully controllable area' by providing some 'evidence that suggests that a breach of the [risk management] obligation is probable'.[100] The defendant can then rebut the presumption of negligence by showing that either: (1) the injury that the plaintiff sustained could not have been prevented through risk management; or (2) reasonable risk management measures to prevent the injury were in place.[101] Shifting the burden of proving a breach of the standard of care in negligent clinical risk management claims in the US could similarly manifest as follows.

First, the plaintiff would be required to make a prima facie case of negligence by putting forth some evidence that: (1) they sustained an injury that (2) was within the scope of risks that could be controlled by proper clinical risk

[96] ibid.

[97] ibid.

[98] See Goldbach (n 5) (noting that if plaintiffs cannot prove negligent risk management recognising a duty to negligent risk management has no 'practical relevance').

[99] See Goldbach (n 5); Bürgerliches Gesetzbuch (BGB) § 630h(1).

[100] Goldbach (n 5).

[101] ibid.

management. Upon making a prima facie case, a rebuttable legal presumption of negligence would arise.

Second, the defendant could rebut this presumption of negligence by producing evidence that the kind of risk that materialised to cause the plaintiff's injury is outside of the scope of risks prevented by compliance with clinical risk management and/or that it reasonably complied with the applicable standards of care to prevent the risk that allegedly led to the plaintiff's injury. As Chiozza and Ponzetti point out:

> No prospective risk assessment method, not even FMEA, can guarantee the absolute safety of health care processes, but risk assessment can help reduce the occurrence of adverse events when an analytic technique is used systematically in order to identify and address failure modes in high-risk processes.[102]

In other words, there is no liability for risks that could not have been reasonably prevented through a reasonably functioning clinical risk management system.

The burden of proving that negligent clinical risk management caused a patient's injury could also be subject to burden of proof modifications. In Germany, the Patients' Rights Act codified the previous case law that shifted the burden of proof on causation for 'gross errors'.[103] According to Goldbach, this burden-shifting mechanism would apply to causes of action for negligent clinical risk management if, judged under the facts of the case, the degree of deviation from the organisational standard was objectively 'so serious as to justify the application of the reversal of the burden of proof'.[104] For example, she opines that insufficient implementation of a clinical risk management process might not be considered a gross error, while an absolute failure to analyse, assess, and control risks that were previously identified in the clinical risk management process would be considered a gross error, thereby reversing the burden of proof on causation.[105] Goldbach provides a caveat that 'the risk whose non-observance makes the breach of duty appear gross would also have to have materialized', making the damage foreseeable.[106] Such would be the case in a situation in which several near-miss errors concerning the administration of medication that did not lead to patient damage were reported to the healthcare organisation in the risk identification phase, and because the hospital did nothing to subsequently analyse, assess, and control the risk, the plaintiff suffered damages from a same or similar medication administration error.

The concept of gross negligence is recognised in US tort law as 'an act or omission involving subjective awareness of an extreme degree of risk, indicating

[102] Chiozza and Ponzetti (n 3).
[103] BGB § 630h(5).
[104] Goldbach (n 5).
[105] ibid.
[106] ibid.

conscious indifference to the rights, safety, or welfare of others'.[107] While there are legal consequences for tortfeasors who commit gross negligence,[108] they do not include reversing the burden of proof on causation for tort law causes of action. However, Germany's approach to shifting the burden of proof on causation will likely prove essential to the development of a cause of action for negligent clinical risk management in US medical negligence law. As such, US courts can, and should, develop a comparable burden-shifting framework either through: (1) a complete shifting of the burden of proof on the element of causation in the case of gross negligence, thereby requiring the defendant to prove by a preponderance of the evidence that the plaintiff's injury was not caused by the grossly negligent practice at issue; or (2) the application of a legal presumption, which can be rebutted using a relaxed standard of proof, whereby the defendant must produce some evidence (less than a preponderance) refuting causation to shift ultimate burden of proving causation back to the plaintiff.

6.3 NEGLIGENT CLINICAL RISK MANAGEMENT IN THE LARGER MEDICAL LIABILITY SYSTEM

Recognising a cause of action for negligent clinical risk management does not displace existing theories of individual provider liability or organisational liability. Rather, it adds a direct claim against the healthcare organisation that runs parallel to existing theories of liability. This reflects the reality that most medical injuries involve both individual and organisational contributing factors. Understanding how these concurrent claims operate and how liability is allocated among multiple defendants is essential to demonstrating that a theory of liability for negligent clinical risk management is workable within the existing legal frameworks of both jurisdictions.

In the typical liability claim involving a medical injury caused by a combination of organisational and individual behaviours, the plaintiff could have three concurrent claims: a medical negligence claim against the individual provider; a vicarious liability claim against the healthcare organisation for the individual provider's negligence; and a direct claim against the healthcare organisation for organisational negligence. A theory of negligent clinical risk management operates within the latter, to support a direct claim against the organisation for failing to identify, analyse, assess, or control the systemic risk that induced or failed to prevent the individual provider's error.

[107] SM Speiser et al, 3 *American Law of Torts* § 10:15 Thomson Reuters Westlaw (database updated February 2026).

[108] See *Myers v Lashley* 44 P 3d 553 (Okla Sup Ct 2002) as amended (20 March 2002) (contributory negligence is not a defence against gross negligence); *Cooper v Rodriguez* 118 A 3d 829 (Md Ct App 2015) (finding that corrections officer was grossly negligent and, thus, was not entitled to immunity).

Unlike claims against individual providers or vicarious liability claims that target active failures at the end of the error process chain, a claim of negligent risk management addresses the latent failures that Reason's Swiss Cheese Model would point to as the more fundamental causes of most medical injuries. As Chiozza and Ponzetti observe 'human errors are often the result of processes beyond the conscious control of the very professionals who make errors'.[109] A claim for negligent clinical risk management is also distinct from existing claims of organisational liability which limit their focus to specific risk control measures. A negligent clinical risk management claim would focus instead on whether the organisation had in place the systematic processes needed to identify and correct those conditions before they combined to cause harm. If the organisation cannot demonstrate that such a process was in place and functioning, a presumption arises that it was not and that, had it been, the organisational conditions enabling the individual provider's error would have been identified and addressed. This approach mirrors the burden-shifting mechanisms already recognised in both jurisdictions for specific organisational failures and extends them logically to duties related to abstract treatment monitoring.

Finally, it is worth noting that the medical liability system in both the US and Germany allows for the allocation of liability in cases involving multiple negligent actors. Both jurisdictions recognise that the behaviour of multiple actors can independently or jointly cause injuries. Where an organisation's clinical risk management failure and an individual provider's negligence jointly caused the plaintiff's injury, the factual and legal causation frameworks discussed in chapter four already provide the framework needed to determine how liability should be apportioned. The 'substantial factor' test in the US and the concurrent causation framework in Germany both recognise the possibility that multiple causes can contribute to an injury without requiring any single cause to be sufficient on its own. Considering that organisational factors play a prominent role in medical injuries, a claim of negligent clinical risk management can help reflect this causal reality and improve the liability system's role in error prevention.

[109] Chiozza and Ponzetti (n 3).

Conclusion

MODERN MEDICINE, WHICH seeks to provide patients with scientifically reliable and therapeutically beneficial treatment, did not begin to develop until the late nineteenth century. As medical practice gained success and acceptance as a central societal institution, hospitals also transformed from houses for the sick and dying to institutions for teaching, research, and healing. Despite the advancements of medical science and the modern organisation of healthcare delivery, patients continued – and still continue – to suffer harm as a result of medical treatment, and medical errors became a recognised threat to patient safety. Medical errors remain a significant and preventable source of patient injuries in the US and Germany.

When medical errors cause harm, the medical liability system provides patients with a legal mechanism for compensation. Within this system, individual healthcare providers have been targeted as the primary persons responsible for medical errors. Many legal and medical scholars have highlighted that focusing liability for injuries caused by medical errors on individual healthcare providers is outdated and fails to consider the complexities of modern healthcare delivery systems. Joining that chorus, this book has discussed the well-established role that system design defects play in medical errors to focus more intently on the ability of clinical risk management to detect and correct those defects. It has argued that liability for negligent clinical risk management would help align the medical liability system with the systems-focused error prevention efforts of the healthcare industry and, in doing so, can have a positive impact on patient safety.

Modern hospitals have considerable influence over how and where patients receive medical treatment. They also control the organisation of the treatment process within the hospital and can directly affect the rate of medical errors through the process of clinical risk management. Clinical risk management can reduce patient safety risks by identifying, evaluating, and correcting deficiencies in the organisational processes that impact nearly every aspect of patient care. Effective clinical risk management turns a healthcare institution into a self-learning system that constantly improves the safety and quality of the medical treatment process. The idea that medical errors were primarily caused, and could be better prevented, by focusing on the healthcare organisation rather than on individual doctors and nurses was popularised by the Institute of Medicine (IOM)'s 1999 report, *To Err Is Human: Building a Safer Health System*. In that report, the IOM relied on the organisational and error research of sociologist

Charles Perrow and psychologist James Reason to explain that medical errors primarily occur in modern healthcare – a complex, tightly coupled, high-risk system – because of systemic, rather than individual provider, failures. It identified the prevailing culture of individual blame and shame as a barrier to systemic improvement.

The IOM's report attracted the attention of healthcare systems worldwide, which responded with efforts to decrease medical errors through organisational improvement. The World Health Organization (WHO) has since encouraged its Member States to collaborate to advance national and international patient safety efforts. Drawing from the IOM's report, the WHO focuses these efforts on systemic improvement and discourages individual blame. It identified voluntary, anonymous, and sanction-free error reporting systems as a critical tool for organisational learning. The Organisation for Economic Co-operation and Development (OECD) also acknowledged the global cost of medical errors and urged healthcare systems to focus on prevention by creating a patient safety culture designed to expose and remedy systemic defects. Meanwhile, the European Union (EU) prioritised patient safety and initiated several international and national efforts to decrease medical errors, including recommendations designed to empower and inform patients, improve training and working conditions for healthcare workers, implement effective clinical risk management strategies, facilitate error reporting and learning, and encourage international collaboration through research to develop systems-based patient safety strategies.

In Germany, patient safety was being addressed both through the EU's patient safety strategy and through national initiatives. In 2001, the Federal Health Monitoring Report quantified the problem of medical errors in Germany and focused its preventive call to action on curing organisational deficits. Progress toward establishing patient safety culture in Germany to prevent medical errors continued in 2002 as the German Medical Centre for Quality in Medicine's (ÄZQ) newly established Patient Safety Expert Group sought to develop a common strategy for error reporting and analysis. In 2003, the German Advisory Council for Concerted Action in Healthcare's biannual report discussed the systemic causes of medical errors and encouraged systems-based solutions, including the use of error reporting and analysis. 2005 was a landmark year for patient safety in Germany. That year, the German Coalition for Patient Safety (APS) was founded to encourage an interdisciplinary 'bottom-up' practical approach to solving the problem of medical errors in Germany. Through the APS's efforts, German healthcare organisations began participating in international and national patient safety campaigns to reduce healthcare-related patient injuries. The year 2005 also saw the birth of Germany's Critical Incident Reporting System, a national anonymous error reporting and learning system designed to identify and correct organisational deficiencies. In 2009, APS established the Institute for Patient Safety (IfPS), which conducts academic research surrounding the issue of patient safety and provides recommendations and training aimed at preventing medical errors. In 2013, Germany's Patients' Rights

Act sought to both improve patient safety and strengthen patients' rights. The Patients' Rights Act mandated the implementation of risk and quality management as well as patient complaint and error-reporting systems in healthcare organisations, prompting a drastic increase in the uptake of error reporting as a preventive strategy in Germany's hospitals.

In the United States (US), Congress passed the Healthcare Research and Quality Act of 1999, which tasked the new Agency for Healthcare Research and Quality (AHRQ) with identifying and remedying causes of medical errors. The AHRQ funded projects designed to improve patient safety culture, reduce medical errors, and resolve medical malpractice claims out of court. In 2005, Congress passed the Patient Safety and Quality Improvement Act (PSQIA) to improve patient safety and the quality of healthcare. The PSQIA encouraged the development and use of patient safety organizations (PSOs) that analyse organisational performance to improve patient safety. In the private sphere, shortly after the IOM's 1999 report, the Joint Commission, which accredits hospitals, also began to focus its regulatory efforts on patient safety and organisational performance. By 2008, the Joint Commission advocated for a 'zero harm' strategy by using a systems approach to medical error prevention based on high reliability science. In 2015, Congress passed the Patient Protection and Affordable Care Act (PPACA), which prioritised quality of care in its new funding and payment systems. In 2015, the Joint Commission began including patient safety chapters in its accreditation manuals for hospitals and other healthcare organisations. These chapters are designed to provide organisations with a strategy for reaching the ultimate goal of 'zero harm' through systems improvement, and particularly the implementation of 'a fair and just safety culture'.

The rapid integration of artificial intelligence (AI)-driven technologies into healthcare delivery has further magnified the importance of organisational approaches to medical error prevention. AI-driven medical technologies amplify both the complexity and the tight-coupling of modern healthcare systems, which are the very characteristics that Perrow's normal accident theory identifies as preconditions for error-prone environments. Additionally, system design flaws that lead to poor interoperability, inadequate staff training, insufficient human oversight, and the absence of clear accountability structures for AI system use are organisational failures that create latent conditions, which are the very conditions that Reason's Swiss Cheese Model identifies as the more fundamental causes of most errors. These latent conditions cannot be attributed to any individual provider and, more importantly, cannot be corrected by targeting individual behaviour. They require the kind of systematic, proactive, ongoing organisational response that a functioning clinical risk management process provides.

While the IOM's report identified external factors, including the legal system, as affecting patient safety within healthcare organisations, it underestimated the ability of the medical liability system to hinder the industry's patient safety efforts. The legal system can encourage organisational investment in preventing medical errors through a systems approach by making errors 'costly', but a crucial question is: by whom is this cost being absorbed? Because both the US and German medical liability systems target primarily the actions of individual healthcare providers rather than organisations, there is a growing disconnect between the entities responsible for and capable of preventing medical errors through systems design (healthcare organisations) and the persons deemed responsible for medical errors (individual providers).

The US and Germany both have negligence-based medical liability systems, despite operating within distinct common law and civil law traditions respectively. Medical negligence law in both jurisdictions is primarily judge-made law, though Germany's Patients' Rights Act has codified some of the existing medical malpractice case law. A second distinction between the two jurisdictions is the primacy of tort law in the US versus contract law in Germany as a basis for medical liability claims. Nevertheless, both jurisdictions apply similar legal standards for deciding medical malpractice cases. This convergence can be attributed broadly to Taekema's theory of pragmatist interactionism, or more concretely to the fact that the principles of negligence govern both tortious and contractual causes of action for medical malpractice in both countries.

Negligence-based systems impose liability on actors who exhibit substandard conduct. As a result, the medical liability system in the US and Germany aims to provide compensation for injuries caused by substandard conduct and to deter actors from engaging in such conduct. In Germany, the compensatory role of the medical liability system is tempered by the support malpractice victims receive from Germany's strong social insurance system. In the US, the liability system's compensatory role is criticised for being unreliable, ineffective, and inefficient.

Regarding the medical liability system's role in deterring undesirable or substandard conduct, both jurisdictions recognise deterrence as a legitimate goal. In the US, tort law generally seeks to deter negligent conduct and reduce accidents, and as a subset of tort law, medical negligence law also seeks to prevent medical errors by deterring healthcare providers from engaging in behaviour that falls below acceptable standards of care. In Germany, the merging of contract with tort law to evaluate medical liability using the negligence standard implicitly encompasses a goal of deterrence. Additionally, both the German Medical Law Association and German legislators have explicitly recognised deterrence and error prevention as driving forces behind Germany's medical liability system.

Whether fault-based liability effectively deters substandard conduct and prevents accidents has long been the subject of interdisciplinary debate. The economic theory of US tort law and the economic efficiency model of German tort law both support the conclusion that imposing liability for negligent conduct that causes injuries will deter others from engaging in that same conduct. According to the economic theory of tort law, rational actors will avoid liability-inducing behaviour for their own economic benefit. German tort law operates under a similar theory, positing that courts organically create standards of care by weighing the social gain of an activity against the cost of preventive measures and that actors will correspondingly adjust their behaviour to comply with evolving standards of care.

Legal realists contend that factors external to the tort system are responsible for non-negligent behaviour and accident prevention. Other legal scholars accept the tort system's capacity for deterrence, but argue that its current organisation frustrates its ability to change conduct. Priest attributes this failing partly to the system's reliance on strict liability, which holds actors legally responsible for harm regardless of their ability to prevent it. Latin argues that the tort system fails to target 'problem-solving actors' who have the greatest ability to prevent accidents. Shuman's psychological approach to tort law maintains that behaviour will not change in response to the current tort system because not all actors are rational decision-makers, and that even if they were, the requisite certainty of punishment for substandard behaviour through the tort system is lacking.

The current medical liability system in the US and Germany, while recognising deterrence as a goal, have had limited success in preventing medical errors. The relationship between individual healthcare providers and their patients distinguishes medical malpractice defendants from tortfeasors generally, making potential economic motivations for behavioural change less impactful. Since individual healthcare providers generally prioritise their patients' wellbeing regardless of the potential for liability, the emotional and professional consequences of being named defendants in a medical malpractice lawsuit often lead not to better, safer behaviour, but rather to the practice of defensive medicine. Defensive medicine, at best, has no impact on patient safety and, at worst, increases the rate of medical errors. Because defensive medicine is a behavioural change in response to tort liability, Mello and Studdert aptly label it 'mutant deterrence'.

The medical liability system also fails to reliably identify medical malpractice, making it a poor source of information about why medical errors occur and how they can be prevented. As a result, the medical liability system is often perceived by individual healthcare providers as arbitrary and therefore lacking the certainty required to trigger a deterrent effect. However, even if individual acts of negligence were successfully deterred by the medical liability system, the effect on the medical error rate would likely be negligible: targeting preventive efforts toward active errors by individuals at the end of the process chain will not cure the organisational deficiencies that induced the injury-causing error in the first place. Those unaddressed organisational deficiencies will continue to induce similar injuries in the future. The problem is compounded by providers reluctance to report and discuss the systemic causes of medical errors for fear of legal repercussions – a dynamic that Mehlman identifies as 'cloaking behaviour'. Again, the integration of AI-driven technologies into healthcare delivery only exacerbates these problems. As AI systems introduce new risks into clinical practice, a liability system focused on individual providers will be even less capable of identifying the upstream organisational failures that enable AI-related medical errors.

The medical liability system must also be perceived as fair. Thus far, both the US and Germany have rejected the proposed adoption of no-fault medical liability, opting instead to retain negligence-based systems. Reform efforts in both countries have addressed issues such as out-of-court dispute resolution, screening panels, and damages caps to curb rising malpractice insurance premiums, the deterioration of the doctor–patient relationship, and reluctance among doctors to practise in high-risk specialties. These reforms have attempted to address the perception, whether accurate or not, that the medical liability system is unfair. To achieve effective medical liability reform within a negligence-based system, however, reform efforts should also attempt to trigger a paradigm shift that aligns the medical liability system with the systems-based approach to medical errors used in the healthcare industry. Shifting liability from individual providers to healthcare organisations holds more promise for achieving the medical liability system's goal of deterrence while simultaneously removing barriers to the industry's error prevention efforts.

Both jurisdictions evaluate civil liability for medical and organisational errors under a negligence-based regime that seeks to deter unreasonable conduct and compensate injured patients. Medical negligence occurs when the violation of an established legal duty or obligation causes a patient injury. In the US, that duty arises from the doctor–patient relationship. In Germany, providers are obliged both specifically under the treatment contract and broadly under German tort law to provide non-negligent treatment to patients. Accordingly, US courts look primarily to duties owed in tort, while German courts focus primarily on the relationships established by the treatment contract. Nevertheless, both jurisdictions examine the behaviour of individual providers to determine whether treatment malpractice occurred, and both recognise theories of vicarious liability for healthcare organisations that oversee or employ negligent providers. Both jurisdictions also recognise that healthcare organisations can commit organisational errors by directly and independently causing patient harm.

Reasonable conduct in the context of medical treatment by an individual provider incorporates standards established by the medical profession. Both jurisdictions apply objective standards of care guided by the state of medical science at the time of the alleged malpractice, while remaining flexible enough to consider the circumstances of each individual case. Both jurisdictions hold physicians to an objective competence-based standard of care set by the current state of medical science, but adjust that standard based upon the resources available to the physician in question. Establishing a breach of the applicable standard of care generally requires the opinion of an expert witness in both jurisdictions. While US courts may dispense with the requirement of expert testimony to establish the standard of care in certain cases, German courts will require expert testimony but may disregard the expert's opinion regarding the applicable legal standard of care where the socially required care was not observed.

To determine whether a breach of the standard of care sufficiently caused a medical injury, both jurisdictions consider whether the breach was a but-for cause of the injury, and whether it is sufficiently connected to the resulting harm to render the imposition of liability fair and just. In the US, the injury must be a reasonably foreseeable consequence of the breach. In Germany, the breach must be 'generally apt' to bring about the patient's injury, and the injury must fall within the protective purpose of the norm governing the negligent conduct. Neither jurisdiction requires that negligent conduct be the sole cause of an injury, and a tortfeasor will generally not be relieved of liability in the case of concurrent or successive causes.

When a breach of the standard of care causes a patient injury, compensable damages include both economic damages (such as medical expenses and lost wages) and non-economic damages (such as pain and suffering and loss of enjoyment of life). The jurisdictions diverge on several aspects of damages. Loss of a chance of a better outcome is recoverable in the US but not in Germany. Non-economic damages in Germany are substantially lower than the pain and suffering awards in the US, though medical malpractice caps impose limits in some US jurisdictions. US courts generally award lump sums for future economic damages, while Germany provides for quarterly pensions. At a policy level, Germany's strong social insurance system provides a level of protection for basic human needs that decreases reliance on damages awarded through the legal system as a form of social insurance, as seen in the US.

The same negligence framework governs liability for organisational errors; however, since the healthcare organisation does not technically practise medicine, organisational errors are assessed under different norms for legal duties and standards of care. Both jurisdictions recognise that modern hospitals have independent responsibilities to patients to organise medical treatment rendered in the hospital. In the US, an organisation can be directly liable for failure to select and retain competent physicians, maintain appropriate facilities and equipment, train and supervise employees, and implement appropriate protocols and procedures. In Germany, the law has recognised similar organisational duties, including those relating to personnel scheduling, supervision and guidance and processes for patient intake, consent, documentation, hygiene and sedation. The standard of care applicable to healthcare organisations in the US is primarily derived from a combination of state regulatory licensing standards, accreditation standards, and the organisation's own policies and regulations. In Germany, the organisational standard of care requires reasonable efforts to ensure quality medical care and the elimination of errors according to accepted standards in medicine. Despite the expanding legal framework for organisational negligence in both jurisdictions, the law in this area has not thus far focused on the healthcare organisation's responsibility to prevent medical errors through clinical risk management.

In both jurisdictions, the default proof rules require plaintiffs to establish the elements necessary to prove their claims. One distinction lies in the standard used to determine whether an element is proven (standard of proof): the US employs a 'reasonable degree of medical certainty' standard, while Germany uses a stricter 'full judicial conviction' standard. There are circumstances in which the plaintiff's burden of proving that the defendant breached the standard of care is lessened or eliminated. In the US, the doctrine of *res ipsa loquitur* provides the plaintiff with a rebuttable presumption of negligence. In Germany, the concept of 'fully masterable risks' shifts the burden of proving negligence to the defendant. German law also shifts the burden of proving causation in cases of beginners' errors or gross errors.

The primary source of proof in medical malpractice cases is the patient's medical treatment records. Both jurisdictions provide patients with a legal right to obtain their own medical records directly from the defendant provider. Germany additionally provides patients who suspect a medical error with a legal right to assistance from their health insurer, which can include assistance in obtaining medical records. Both jurisdictions also allow parties to request records from one another in the course of litigation, though Germany's pre-trial discovery rules are more conservative than those in the US and impose greater restrictions on access to documents. Both jurisdictions provide some level of confidentiality to documents and information used to improve the quality of care by exempting them from discovery; however, more reliable protection of an organisation's efforts to improve patient safety is crucial to establishing a legal duty for organisations to manage healthcare risks.

Before healthcare organisations can be liable for negligent clinical risk management in either jurisdiction, they must have a legal duty or obligation to conduct clinical risk management in the first place. German legal scholars have argued that this legal obligation, though not explicitly recognised by the case law, can be found as an extension of the existing organisational obligations under the general law of negligence, case law, and by analogy to the obligations of product manufacturers to identify and control risks under product liability law. Applying the German analytical framework to the US, this book concludes that liability for negligent clinical risk management is equally supported in the US because both jurisdictions operate using similar negligence-based principles, the case law in both jurisdictions recognises comparable organisational duties, and the product liability law of both jurisdictions imposes analogous risk management obligations on manufacturers. Existing legal and regulatory obligations to conduct risk management in both jurisdictions further supports finding a duty to conduct clinical risk management.

Regulatory developments governing AI-driven technologies reflect the importance of risks management for harm prevention. In the EU, the AI Act's risk-based approach to AI governance requires manufacturers of high-risk AI systems – a classification that will generally apply to AI-driven medical devices – to establish and maintain a continuous, iterative risk management system throughout the product's lifecycle. The AI Act also imposes obligations on deployers of high-risk AI systems, including hospitals, to ensure AI literacy, human oversight, performance monitoring, and incident reporting. In the

US, state-level AI legislation in California, Colorado, and New York similarly requires developers and deployers of high-risk AI systems to implement risk management frameworks. These regulatory developments reflect a growing legal consensus that the risks of AI-driven technologies cannot be managed at the point of individual use but must be governed through systematic, ongoing organisational processes, which are precisely the kind of processes that clinical risk management is designed to provide.

Once healthcare organisations are found to be legally obliged to conduct clinical risk management, there must be standards of care by which this obligation is judged. To effectively deter negligent conduct, those standards must be both reasonable and predictable. This book proposes that standards of care for clinical risk management be anchored in the internationally accepted clinical risk management process, organised into four phases: risk identification; risk analysis; risk assessment; and risk control. Risk identification requires healthcare organisations to implement systems designed to discover systemic deficiencies. Voluntary error-reporting and learning systems are a critical tool in this phase, and their effective operation depends upon the creation and maintenance of a genuine organisational safety culture. Risk analysis is used to determine the causes and effects of identified risks in order to better understand why risks manifest and how they can be prevented or minimised. Reactive methods, such as root cause analysis and blunt end analysis, should be complemented by proactive tools, including Failure Modes and Effect Analysis (FMEA) and Sociotechnical Probabilistic Risk Assessment (ST-PRA), which enable organisations to identify latent failure modes before they cause harm. Risk assessment determines the probability and severity of each identified risk so that risks can be prioritised for the risk control process. Risk control requires healthcare organisations to develop, implement, communicate, and monitor risk prevention measures. The selection of appropriate methods for each phase of the clinical risk management process may vary with the size, resources, and risk profile of the healthcare organisation, but the obligation to maintain a functioning, iterative, and documented clinical risk management system is uniform.

In the context of AI, the clinical risk management process is essential for safe integration of AI-driven technologies. The risks of AI-driven medical devices may not be fully known at the time of deployment, because they can evolve as the technology is used in clinical practice. These new technologies may interact with existing organisational systems and human workflows to create new risks. The risk identification phase must therefore incorporate mechanisms for monitoring AI system performance and detecting novel failure modes as they emerge in clinical practice. The risk analysis and assessment phases must be capable of evaluating both the technical performance of AI systems and the human and organisational factors that might amplify or mitigate these risks. The risk control phase must include not only technical safeguards but also organisational governance structures, oversight protocols, and clear accountability mechanisms for AI system selection, deployment and use. A theory of negligent clinical risk management provides the doctrinal framework for medical liability that can be responsive to the patient safety risks created by new AI-driven technologies.

A legal thoery of negligent clinical risk management must also balance the confidentiality needed to establish safety culture in healthcare organisations – which is crucial to the success of clinical risk management – with the transparency required to ensure that healthcare organisations can be held accountable for negligent practices. To facilitate the level of confidentiality required for safety culture, courts should provide discovery and evidentiary protections for documents and information developed within the clinical risk management system that relate to individual incidents and identify individual providers. Voluntary error reports, in particular, should neither be discoverable nor admissible as evidence in claims of negligent clinical risk management. At the same time, documents relating to the establishment and execution of an organisation's clinical risk management activities, including its safety commitments made to obtain accreditation, its error-reporting system policies and protocols, and its documented responses to identified risks, should remain discoverable and admissible to prove claims of organisational negligence.

To ensure that patients have a viable claim for negligent clinical risk management, courts should adopt burden-shifting mechanisms informed by Germany's Patients' Rights Act and the existing case law on organisational liability in both jurisdictions. Specifically, because the entire clinical risk management process is controlled by the healthcare organisation, a rebuttable presumption of negligence should arise when the plaintiff establishes that their injury arose from a risk that was fully within the organisation's control. The healthcare organisation should then be required to rebut that presumption by producing evidence either that the kind of risk that materialised was outside the scope of risks addressed by a functioning clinical risk management system, or that it reasonably complied with clinical risk management standards of care to prevent that risk. Where the deviation from clinical risk management standards is sufficiently serious and amounts to a gross error, the burden of proving causation should also shift to the healthcare organisation, consistent with the approach already recognised in German law and warranting comparable development in US medical negligence law.

In conclusion, liability for negligent clinical risk management is a crucial aspect of medical error prevention because it can deter unsafe organisational behaviour, improve patient safety culture by abating individual providers' fears of being shamed, blamed, and sanctioned in the liability system, and curb the practice of defensive medicine by making liability a more reliable identifier of organisational injury-causing behaviour. However, courts adjudicating claims of negligent clinical risk management must use evidentiary and proof rules as tools to strike the delicate balance between providing confidentiality required to maintain a safety culture in healthcare organisations and transparency required to hold healthcare organisations accountable for negligent clinical risk management. While the medical liability system cannot, and is not expected to, be the driving force for medical error prevention, it should reinforce the accepted norms governing error prevention in modern healthcare and, at the very least, not hinder the industry's prevention efforts. A well-crafted legal theory of negligent clinical risk management will help better align the medical liability system in both the US and Germany with the healthcare industry's systems-based approach to medical error prevention.

Bibliography

Advisory Council for the Concerted Action in Health Care, 'Health Care Finance, User Orientation and Quality (Report 2003 Summary)' (2003).

Aktionsbündnis Patientensicherheit (APS), 'Requirements on Clinical Risk Management Systems in Hospitals' (February 2017).

Albrecht, M et al, 'Studie zu den Wirkungen des Patientenrechtegesetzes' (IGES Institut, 2016).

Barth, S, 'Aus Fehlern lernen – Schwachstellen im System rechtzeitig erkennen' (2009) I *Berliner Ärzte* 14.

Bates, WD et al, 'The Potential of Artificial Intelligence to Improve Patient Safety: A Scoping Review' (2021) 4 *NPJ Digital Medicine* 54.

Bergmann, KO and Kienzle, HF (eds), *Krankenhaushaftung: Organisation, Schadensverhütung und Versicherung – Leitfaden für die tägliche Praxis* (Düsseldorf, Kohlhammer Verlag, 2015).

Bergmann, KO et al, 'Krankenhaushaftung un Versicherung' in *Krankenhaushaftung: Organisation, Schadensverhütung und Versicherung – Leitfaden für die tägliche Praxis* (KO Bergmann and HF Kienzle (eds) (Düsseldorf, Kohlhammer Verlag, 2015) 337–80.

Blumenthal, D and Abrams, M, 'The Affordable Care Act at 10 Years – Payment and Delivery System Reforms' (2020) 382 *New England Journal of Medicine* 1057.

Bodnari, A and Travis, J, 'Scaling Enterprise AI in Healthcare: The Role of Governance in Risk Mitigation Frameworks' (2025) 8 *npj Digital Medicine* 272.

Briller, R et al, 'Are Neurology Residents in the United States Being Taught Defensive Medicine?' (2006) 108 *Clinical Neurology and Neurosurgery*.

Briner, M, 'Assessing Hospitals' Clinical Risk Management: Development of a Monitoring Instrument' (2010) 10 *BMC Health Services Research* article no 337.

Burkle, C, 'Medical Malpractice: Can We Rescue a Decaying System?' (2011) 86 *Mayo Clinic Proceedings* 326.

Chassin, MR and Loeb, JM, 'High-Reliability Health Care: Getting There from Here' (2013) 91 *The Milbank Quarterly* 459.

Chiozza, ML and Ponzetti, C, 'FMEA: A Model for Reducing Medical Errors' (2009) 404 *Clinica Chimica Acta* 75.

Classen, DC et al, 'Inpatient EHR User Experience and Hospital EHR Safety Performance' (2023) 6 *JAMA Network Open* e2333152.

Council of the European Union, 'Council Conclusions on Patient Safety and Quality of Care, including the Prevention and Control of Healthcare Associated Infections and Antimicrobial Resistance' (Employment, Social Policy, Health and Consumer Affairs Council Meeting, Brussels, 1 December 2014).

Danzon, P, 'The Frequency and Severity of Medical Malpractice Claims: New Evidence' (1986) 49 *Law and Contemporary Problems* 57.

Davenport, T and Kalakota, R, 'The Potential for Artificial Intelligence in Healthcare' (2019) 6 *Future Healthcare Journal* 94.

Daverio, M et al, 'Failure Mode and Effective Analysis Ameliorate Awareness of Medical Errors: A 4-Year Prospective Observational Study in Critically Ill Children' (2015) 25 *Paediatric Anaesthesia* 1227.

de Cruppé, W and Geraedts, M, 'Hospital Choice in Germany from the Patient's Perspective: A Cross-Sectional Study' (2017) 17 *BMC Health Services Research* 720.

de Hoop, T and Neumuth, T, 'Evaluating Electronic Health Record Limitations and Time Expenditure in a German Medical Center' (2021) 12 *Applied Clinical Informatics* 1082.

Debono, DS et al, 'Nurses' Workarounds in Acute Healthcare Settings: A Scoping Review' (2013) 13 *BMC Health Services Research* 175.

Deutscher Ärzte-Verlag, *The Healthcare System in Germany: A Short Introduction* (2012).

Dietz, JJP, 'Roentgendiagnosis in Miliary Tuberculosis' (1918) 1 *Nederlands Tijdschrift voor Geneeskunde* 50.

Dollar, CJ, 'Promoting Better Healthcare: Policy Arguments for Concurrent Quality Assurance and Attorney-Client Hospital Incident Report Privileges' (1993) 3 *Health Matrix* 259.

Duffourc, MN, 'Filling Voice Promotion Gaps in Healthcare Through A Comparative Analysis of Error Reporting and Learning Systems and Open Communication and Disclosure Policies in the United States and Germany' (2018) 44 *American Journal of Law and Medicine* 579.

— 'Malpractice by the Autonomous AI Physician' (2023) 2023 *Illinois Journal of Law, Technology & Policy* 1.

Duffourc, MN and Gerke, S, 'Decoding U.S. Tort Liability in Healthcare's Black-Box AI Era: Lessons from the European Union Black Box Era' (2024) 27 *Stanford Technology Law Review* 1.

Elhaddad, M and Hamam, S, 'AI-Driven Clinical Decision Support Systems: An Ongoing Pursuit of Potential' (2024) 16 *Cureus* e57728.

European Commission, Directorate-General for Health and Consumer Protection, 'Patient Safety – Making it Happen! Luxembourg Declaration on Patient Safety' (2005).

European Network for Patient Safety (EUNetPaS), 'Patient Safety Culture Report: Focusing on Indicators' (2010).

— 'Use of Patient Safety Culture: Instruments and Recommendations' (2010).

Fedtke, J, 'The Culture of German Tort Law' (2012) 3 *Journal of European Tort Law* 183.

Ferrara, M et al, 'Risk Management and Patient Safety in the Artificial Intelligence Era: A Systematic Review' (2024) 12 *Healthcare* 549.

Freidson, E, *Profession of Medicine: A Study of the Sociology of Applied Knowledge* (New York, Harper & Row, 1970).

Giesen, D, *International Medical Malpractice Law: A Comparative Law Study of Civil Liability Arising from Medical Care* (Tübingen, JCB Mohr (Paul Siebeck), 1988).

Goldbach, C, *Risikomanagementsysteme im Krankenhaus nach dem Patientenrechtegesetz: Sozialrechtliche Pflicht und haftungsrechtlicher Standard* (Kassel, Kassel University Press, 2014).

Hafemeister, TL and Porter, JH, 'The Health Care Reform Act of 2010 and Medical Malpractice Liability: Worlds in Collision or Ships Passing in the Night' (2011) 64 *Southern Methodist University Law Review* 735.

Halbesleben, JR et al, 'Rework and Workarounds in Nurse Medication Administration Process' (2010) 35 *Health Care Management Review* 124.

Hansis, ML and Hart, D, *Gesundheitsberichterstattung des Bundes, Medizinische Behandlungsfehler* (Robert Koch-Institut, Berlin, Paul Fieck KG, 2001).

Hart, D, 'Patientensicherheit, Fehlermanagement, Arzthaftungsrecht – zugleich ein Beitrag zur rechtlichen Bedeutung von Empfehlungen' (2012) 30 *Medizinrecht* 1.

— 'Patientensicherheit nach dem Patientenrechtegesetz' (2013) 31 *Medizinrecht* 159.

Heinrichs, H et al, 'Physicians' Attitudes Toward Artificial Intelligence in Medicine: Mixed Methods Survey and Interview Study' (2025) 27 *Journal of Medical Internet Research* e74187.

Heller, TA, 'An Overview of Medical Malpractice Law in the United States Including Legislative and the Health Care Industry's Responses to Increased Claims' (2017) 10 *Medicine Law & Society* 139.

Hodge, SD and Steinhaus, MZ, 'The Ever-Changing Landscape of Informed Consent and Whether the Obligation to Explain a Procedure to the Patient May Be Delegated' (2019) 71 *Arkansas Law Review* 727.

Infantino, M and Zervogianni, E, 'The European Ways to Causation' in Infantino, M and Zervogianni, E (eds), *Causation in European Tort Law* (Cambridge, Cambridge University Press, 2017).

Institute of Medicine (IOM) Committee on Quality of Health Care in America, 'To Err is Human: Building a Safer Health System' (Kohn, LT, Corrigan, JM and Donaldson, MS eds, Washington DC, National Academies Press, 2000).

Iper, HST et al, 'ST-PRA+FMEA Hybrid Risk Analysis Application for Catastrophic Events at Hospitals' (2022) 41 *European Journal of Science and Technology* 221.

Jochimsen, B, 'Elektronische Patientenakte: Meilenstein der Digitalisierung' (2025) 105 *Wirtschaftsdienst* 318.
Jonitz, G and Barth, S, 'Etablierung von Patientensicherheit – national und international' (2013) 15 *Trauma und Berufskrankheit* 154.
Katzfey, RP, 'JCAHO's Shared Visions–New Pathways: The New Hospital Survey and Accreditation Process for 2004' (2004) 61 *American Journal of Health-System Pharmacy* 1358.
Kearney, KA and McCord, EL, 'Hospital Management Faces New Liabilities' (1992) 6 *Health Law* 1.
Kerkmeester, H and Visscher, L, 'Learned Hand in Europe: A Study in the Comparative Law and Economics of Negligence' (2003) *German Working Papers in Law and Economics* Paper 6.
Kilgour, FG, 'Modern Medicine in Historical Perspective' (1962) 50 *Bulletin of the Medical Library Association* 42.
Kilpatrick, C et al, 'WHO First Global Patient Safety Challenge: Clean Care Is Safer Care, Contributing to the Training of Health-Care Workers Around the Globe' (2010) 7 *International Journal of Infection Control*.
Koch, BA (ed), *Medical Liability in Europe: A Comparison of Selected Jurisdictions* (Berlin, De Gruyter, 2011).
Kohlberg, KR, 'The Medical Peer Review Privilege: A Linchpin for Patient Safety Measures' (2002) 86 *Massachusetts Law Review* 157.
Koppel, R et al, 'Workarounds to Barcode Medication Administration Systems: Their Occurrences, Causes, and Threats to Patient Safety' (2008) 15 *Journal of the American Medical Informatics Association* 408.
Latin, H, 'Problem-Solving Behavior and Theories of Tort Liability' (1985) 73 *California Law Review* 677.
Laufs, A et al, *Arztrecht*, 8th edn (Munich, CH Beck, 2026).
Lauterberg, J, 'Abschlussbericht: Befragung zum Einführungsstand von klinischem Risiko-Management (kRM) in deutschen Krankenhäusern' (IfPS, 2012).
Lawton, T et al, 'Clinicians Risk Becoming "Liability Sinks" for Artificial Intelligence' (2024) 11 *Future Healthcare Journal* 100007.
Leape, LL, 'Error in Medicine' (1994) 272 *Journal of the American Medical Association* 1581.
Leroy, P, 'Medical Errors: The Importance of the Bullet's Blunt End' (2011) 170 *European Journal of Pediatrics* 251.
Liebermeister, H, 'How to Avoid Liability Litigation in Courts – Suggestions from a German Example' (2010) 8 *German Medical Science* 3.
Linden-Lahti, C et al, 'Facilitators and Barriers in Implementing Medication Safety Practices Across Hospitals Within 11 European Union Countries' (2019) 17 *Pharmacy Practice* 1583.
Lindsey, R et al, 'Deep Neural Network Improves Fracture Detection by Clinicians' (2018) 115 *Proceedings of the National Academy of Sciences* 11591.
Loewenbrück, K et al, 'Disclosure of Adverse Outcomes in Medicine: A Questionnaire Study on Voice Intention and Behaviour of Physicians in Germany, Japan and the USA' (2016) 30 *German Journal of Human Resource Management* 313.
Markesinis, B et al, *The German Law of Torts: A Comparative Treatise*, 5th edn (Oxford, Hart Publishing, 2021).
Martin, GA, 'The Privilege against Self-Incrimination under Foreign Law' (1960–61) 51 *Journal of Criminal Law, Criminology and Police Science* 161.
Marx, D and Slonim, A, 'Assessing Patient Safety Risk before the Injury Occurs: An Introduction to Sociotechnical Probabilistic Risk Modelling in Health Care' (2003) 12 (Suppl 2) *BMJ Quality & Safety* ii33.
McDermott, F et al, 'Deutschlandweite Befragung zum Einführungsstand des klinischen Risikomanagements' (IfPS, 2016).
Mehlman, MJ, 'Promoting Fairness in the Medical Malpractice System' in WM Sage and R Kersh (eds), *Medical Malpractice and the US Health Care System* (Cambridge, Cambridge University Press, 2006) 137–53.

Mello, MM and Studdert, DM, 'Deconstructing Negligence: The Role of Individual and System Factors in Causing Medical Injuries' (2008) 96 *Georgetown Law Journal* 599.

Mello, MM and Studdert, DM, 'The Medical Malpractice System: Structure and Performance' in Sage, WM and Kersh, R (eds), *Medical Malpractice and the US Health Care System* (Cambridge, Cambridge University Press, 2006) 11–29.

Nasef, D et al, 'Integrating Artificial Intelligence in Clinical Practice, Hospital Management, and Health Policy: Literature Review' (2025) 9 *Journal of Hospital Management and Health Policy* online.

Nightingale, F, *Notes on Nursing: What It Is, and What It Is Not* (Philadelphia, JB Lippincott Company, 1946).

Ofri, D, *When We Do Harm: A Doctor Confronts Medical Error* (Boston, Beacon Press, 2020).

Olsen, R, 'The Reform of Medical Malpractice Law: Historical Perspectives' (1996) 55 *American Journal of Economics and Sociology* 257.

Ott, C and Schäfer, HB, 'Negligence as Untaken Precaution, Limited Information, and Efficient Standard Formation in the Civil Liability System' (1997) 17 *International Review of Law and Economics* 15.

Pascarella, G et al, 'Risk Analysis in Healthcare Organizations: Methodological Framework and Critical Variables' (2021) 14 *Risk Management and Healthcare Policy* 2897.

Pauli, A, *Risikomanagement und CIRS als Gegenstand der Krankenhaushaftung* (Baden-Baden, Nomos, 2013).

Petry, FM, 'Medical Liability in Germany' in BA Koch (ed), *Medical Liability in Europe: A Comparison of Selected Jurisdictions* (Berlin, De Gruyter, 2011).

Phillips, RL et al, 'The AAFP Patient Safety Reporting System: Development and Legal Issues Pertinent to Medical Error Tracking and Analysis' in K Henriksen et al (eds), *Advances in Patient Safety: From Research to Implementation, Volume 3: Implementation Issues* (Agency for Healthcare Research and Quality, 2005).

Plesner, LL et al, 'Autonomous Chest Radiograph Reporting Using AI: Estimation of Clinical Impact' (2023) 307 *Radiology* e222268.

Pohl, D, 'Arzthaftpflicht: Der Markt schrumpft weiter' (2013) 110 *Deutsches Ärzteblatt* 18.

Popper, AF, 'In Defense of Deterrence' (2012) 75 *Albany Law Review* 101.

Porter, R, *The Greatest Benefit to Mankind: A Medical History of Humanity* (London, HarperCollins, 1997).

Posner, JR, 'Trends in Medical Malpractice Insurance, 1970–1985' (1986) 49 *Law and Contemporary Problems* 37.

Posner, RA, 'Guido Calabresi's "The Costs of Accidents": A Reassessment' (2005) 64 *Maryland Law Review* 12.

Posner, RA and Landes, WM, 'The Positive Economic Theory of Tort Law' (1980) 15 *Georgia Law Review* 851.

Priest, GL, 'Modern Tort Law and Its Reform' (1987) 22 *Valparaiso University Law Review* 1.

Prior, M, 'The Remedy Worse Than the Disease' (first published 1714) in A Dobson (ed), *Selected Poems of Matthew Prior* (London, Kegan Paul, Trench & Co, 1889).

Püster, D, *Entwicklungen der Arzthaftpflichtversicherung* (Berlin, Springer, 2013).

Raab, EL, 'The Parameters of Informed Consent' (2004) 102 *Transactions of the American Ophthalmological Society* 225.

Reason, J, 'Human Error: Models and Management' (2000) 320 *British Medical Journal* 768.

Reineck, LA and Kahn, JM, 'Quality Measurement in the Affordable Care Act: A Reaffirmed Commitment to Value in Health Care' (2013) 187 *American Journal of Respiratory and Critical Care Medicine* 1038.

Riotte, T, 'Medical Negligence in Nineteenth-Century Germany' in M Dickson, E Taylor-Brown and S Shuttleworth (eds), *Progress and Pathology: Medicine and Culture in the Nineteenth Century* (Manchester, Manchester University Press, 2020) 56–77.

Sage, WM, 'Malpractice Reform as a Health Policy Problem' in WM Sage and R Kersh (eds), *Medical Malpractice and the US Health Care System* (Cambridge, Cambridge University Press, 2006).

Schäfer, AT, 'Plädoyer für einen besseren Schutz der Patienten: 10 Forderungen zur Reform der Haftung bei Behandlungsfehlern' (2013).

Schwappach, DB, 'Nach dem Behandlungsfehler: Umgang mit Patienten, Angehörigen und dem involvierten Personal' (2015) 58 *Bundesgesundheitsblatt* 80.

Seroog, F, 'Torts: Bing v Thunig: The End of Hospital Immunity in New York' (1958) 41 *Marquette Law Review* 311.

Shi, Y et al, 'The Value of Machine Learning Approaches in the Diagnosis of Early Gastric Cancer: A Systematic Review and Meta-Analysis' (2024) 22 *World Journal of Surgical Oncology* article no 40.

Shuman, D, 'The Psychology of Deterrence in Tort Law' (1993) 42 *University of Kansas Law Review* 115.

Sinha, R, 'The Role and Impact of New Technologies on Healthcare Systems' (2024) 3 *Discover Health Systems* article no 96.

Slawomirski, L et al, 'The Economics of Patient Safety: Strengthening a Value-Based Approach to Reducing Patient Harm at National Level' (2017) *OECD Health Working Papers* No 96.

Sommer, SA et al, 'Medical Liability and Patient Law in Germany: Main Features with Particular Focus on Treatments in the Field of Interventional Radiology' (2016) 188 *RoFo: Fortschritte auf dem Gebiete der Röntgenstrahlen und der Nuklearmedizin* 353.

Spickhoff, A (ed), *Medizinrecht*, 4th edn (CH Beck, 2022).

Standing Committee of European Doctors (CPME), 'Patient Safety and Quality of Care Joint Action (PaSQ) 2012–2016'.

Stauch, M, *The Law of Medical Negligence in England and Germany: A Comparative Analysis* (Oxford, Hart Publishing, 2008).

Stelfox, HT et al, 'The "To Err Is Human" Report and the Patient Safety Literature' (2006) 15 *BMJ Quality & Safety* 174.

Streimelweger, B et al, 'Improving Patient Safety through Human-factor-based Risk Management' (2015) 64 *Procedia Computer Science* 69.

Studdert, DM et al, 'Claims, Errors and Compensation Payments in Medical Malpractice Litigation' (2006) 354 *New England Journal of Medicine* 2024.

Stukes, KT, 'The Medical Peer Review Privilege After Virmani' (2002) 80 *North Carolina Law Review* 1860.

Sugarman, SD, 'A Comparative Law Look at Pain and Suffering Awards' (2006) 55 *DePaul Law Review* 399.

Taekema, S, 'Private Law as an Open Legal Order: Understanding Contract and Tort as Interactional Law' (2014) 43 *Netherlands Journal of Legal Philosophy* 140.

Thüß, J, *Rechtsfragen des Critical Incident Reportings in der Medizin* (Heidelberg, Springer-Verlag Berlin, 2012).

Valentinuzzi, ME and Leder, R, 'The Modern Hospital in Historical Context' (2009) 2009 *Annual International Conference of the IEEE Engineering in Medicine and Biology Society* 1089–91.

Voigt, T in *BeckOGK BGB* (Beck online, 1 February 2026) BGB § 823.

Voit, W, 'Entsprechung und Abweichungen nach deutschem Arzthaftungsrecht' in P Jabornegg et al (eds), *Haftungsfragen im System der Leistungserbringung des Krankenversicherungsrechts: Beiträge zu den Deutsch-Österreichischen Sozialrechtsgesprächen 2006* (Essen, CW Haarfeld, 2006) 23–38.

Wah, JK, 'The Rise of Robotics and AI-Assisted Surgery in Modern Healthcare' (2025) 19 *Journal of Robotic Surgery* 311.

Waseem, HM et al, 'Data-Driven FMEA Approach for Hazard Identification and Risk Evaluation in Digital Health' (2025) 15 *Scientific Reports* 52856.

Watson-Dunham, B, *Medical Malpractice Law and Litigation* (Clifton Park, Delmar Cengage Learning, 2006).
Wiet, MJ, 'Darling v Charleston Community Memorial Hospital and Its Legacy' (2005) 14 *Annals of Health Law* 399.
Wienke, A, 'Errors and Pitfalls: Briefing and Accusation of Medical Malpractice – The Second Victim' (2013) 12 *GMS Current Topics in Otorhinolaryngology – Head and Neck Surgery* 1.
World Health Organization, 'Quality of Care: Patient Safety' (WHA55.18, 18 May 2002).
— 'World Alliance for Patient Safety: Forward Programme' (October 2004).
— 'WHO Draft Guidelines for Adverse Event Reporting and Learning Systems: From Information to Action' (2005).
— 'Patient Safety Curriculum Guide: Multi-Professional Edition' (2011).
— 'Patient Safety: Making Health Care Safer' (2017).

Index

www.ingramcontent.com/pod-product-compliance
Ingram Content Group UK Ltd.
Pitfield, Milton Keynes, MK11 3LW, UK
UKHW020809260926
475945UK00003B/36

9 781509 993277